W9-ADH-708

GEORG WILHELM FRIEDRICH HEGEL
LECTURES ON THE PHILOSOPHY OF WORLD HISTORY

INTRODUCTION: REASON IN HISTORY

Cambridge Studies in the History and Theory of Politics

EDITORS

MAURICE COWLING   E.KEDOURIE
G.R.ELTON   J.R.POLE
WALTER ULLMANN

GEORG WILHELM FRIEDRICH
HEGEL
LECTURES ON THE PHILOSOPHY OF
WORLD HISTORY

INTRODUCTION: REASON IN HISTORY

translated from the German edition of Johannes Hoffmeister by
H. B. NISBET
Professor of German, University of St Andrews

with an Introduction by
DUNCAN FORBES
Fellow of Clare College, Cambridge

WITHDRAWN

The right of the
University of Cambridge
to print and sell
all manner of books
was granted by
Henry VIII in 1534.
The University has printed
and published continuously
since 1584.

CAMBRIDGE UNIVERSITY PRESS
CAMBRIDGE
LONDON NEW YORK NEW ROCHELLE
MELBOURNE SYDNEY

MILSTEIN

D
16.8
. H46
1980p

Published by the Press Syndicate of the University of Cambridge
The Pitt Building, Trumpington Street, Cambridge CB2 IRP
32 East 57th Street, New York, NY 10022, USA
10 Stamford Road, Oakleigh, Melbourne 3166, Australia

© Cambridge University Press 1975

First published 1975
First paperback edition 1980
Reprinted 1982 1984

British Library Cataloguing in Publication Data
Hegel, Georg Wilhelm Friedrich
[Vorlesungen über die Philosophie der Geschichte. *English.*
Selections]. Lectures on the philosophy of world history,
introduction. – (Cambridge studies in the history and theory
of politics).
1. History – Philosophy
I. Title II. Lectures on the philosophy of world history
III. Nisbet, Hugh Barr IV. Series
901 D16.8 74-79137

ISBN 0 521 20566 2 hard covers
ISBN 0 521 28145 8 paperback

Transferred to digital printing 2002

CONTENTS

CONTENTS

INTRODUCTION

1. The Cloud of Unknowing and *die Sache selbst*[1]

The English reader is given here a translation not of the whole of Hegel's philosophy of history, but of Johannes Hoffmeister's edition of Hegel's own Introduction to his lectures on the philosophy of world history. Since for Hegel philosophy is the science without presuppositions, through and through self-critical, and thus a self-developing whole or circle whose end is its beginning, any introduction to any section of it can only be a preliminary sketch of what is to come in the light of the whole. Hegel's Introduction therefore contains his whole philosophy in epitome.

There is no danger in this for those who know the other main texts. But because the philosophy of history is by far the easiest of these – Hegel himself seems to have thought of these lectures as a popular introduction to his philosophy – it is liable to be used as a substitute rather than an introduction, especially as a substitute for the *Philosophy of Right*, and one suspects that much of the misunderstanding and misrepresentation of Hegel has been due to this.[2] It contains the notorious phrases about the state being the divine Idea on earth, reason ruling the world and so on, which have been made to mean precisely the opposite of what Hegel intended. Even those who have spent years of suffering as well as enjoyment on this mountain can slip badly at times, and this should be sufficient warning to those critics and quick-reading, quick-judging able men – from whom God defend the history of ideas – who, taking a quick look through the telescope, usually someone else's, feel competent to lecture the crowd, always ready to enjoy the deflating of large balloons,

---

[1] I am not using this term with Hegel's *Phenomenology of Spirit* in mind (*Das geistige Tierreich...oder die Sache selbst*) but in the hope that it can mean simply the heart of the matter or "the real Mackay". Another heading for this section could be "The philosophy of life and love and the dead critics".

[2] Cf. Walter Kaufmann, *Hegel*, p. 15. "The *Philosophy of History* is probably Hegel's best known book; but in the more demanding sense of that word, it is scarcely 'known' at all..."

on the iniquities of a system which they have not begun to understand properly. And there are the sly innuendoes of otherwise learned men, which are difficult to nail because the nature and depth of the ignorance involved cannot be properly established. It is not easy to gauge how much of the old Hegel legend still survives; judging by the remarks still liable to be made by highly placed academic persons it is by no means defunct, even in the most scholarly circles. But an Introduction of this sort cannot put this right; one must take a lot for granted and hope for the best.

Another difficulty is that Hegel's philosophy of history is nowadays generally regarded as the prime example of what philosophy of history is not, without being adequately understood. Those who do philosophy of history in the contemporary analytical style do not fully understand Hegel – why should they? Those who know Hegel do not as a rule care for his philosophy of history, and do not think it worthy of intensive study in the light of modern developments – to appreciate it properly, moreover, one would need to be something of a historian and a historian of history as well. The qualities demanded are not likely to be combined these days.

So Hegel's philosophy of history is largely unexplored, and indeed, in spite of the enormous literature, one is tempted to say the same for the whole of his mature philosophy. Nothing like the amount of detailed thorough scholarship which has been expended on his early writings, up to and including the *Phenomenology of Spirit*, has been used for most of this century to illuminate the texts of his maturity. This is brought home by the fact that it is precisely the philosophy of history that raises some of the most crucially difficult central questions – perhaps the most crucial and difficult of all – in connection with Hegel's mature philosophy, which in a sense transcends time and historical specificity and yet is tied down to its own age; the philosopher cannot "leap over Rhodes"; he can only describe what is given; indeed, "Science", that is Hegel's philosophy, is only possible at all, Spirit or *Geist* is only able to be fully self-conscious, as the result of the culmination of a process in time in the Europe of Hegel's day. Thus philosophy is limited and tied down, and yet unlimited and free-ranging; able to survey the whole of reality, it is final and closed in one sense, wholly open in another, in a way that is not easy to grasp. For the philosophy of history is not simply a temporal ladder to "Science" which can be dispensed with once one has arrived, if the result includes the process of getting there, both logical and historical – otherwise why should the philosopher bother with history at all, since that is not an eternal recurrence? There must be a philosophy of history for

Geist to be fully self-conscious, but this can only become explicit at a certain point in time. And in one sense this point is the fullness of time, but in another sense it is not, because it is not the end of history, and some commentators are fond of drawing attention to those passages which show Hegel pointing towards an unknown future and the possibility of further developments even in philosophy. To take refuge in the Logic alone and ignore the historical manifestations of Spirit; alternatively, to historicize the whole philosophy[1] is to shirk the issue in one way or another. Somehow Hegel's Absolute has to be comprehended as a unity of finite and infinite, in which the finite and contingent are necessary as such to the philosophy which "overcomes" them.

This can be gone into no further here.[2] Enough has been said to suggest that all the classical misunderstandings of Hegel are due to failure to get as far as the point where the difficulties begin; they all seem to have one root cause: viz., failure to really grasp the central idea of identity in difference, what Hegel calls the 'Notion' (which modern translators prefer to call the 'concept', because 'notion' gives a misleading impression of cloudiness or vagueness; on the other hand it must be always remembered that a very peculiar kind of 'concept' is involved). Every kind of seriously mistaken interpretation of Hegel seems to spring in one way or another from the belief that this philosophy of the Absolute involves the absorption of reality in the Idea: it is an "absolute idealism" which "resolves", meaning abolishes, the contradictions of existence, absorbs the other phases of reality into the Absolute in such a way that they are rendered meaningless and "unreal". But if this were so, there would be no reality left at all. The principle of negativity is given full play, and finally "overreached" in an affirmation that will therefore be total, but for that very reason "overreached" does not mean abolished.

What is required therefore is some understanding of what Hegel meant when he said that the basis of "Science" was pure self-recognition in absolute otherness, or that the true infinite was the unity of itself and the finite, or that identity was the union of identity and non-identity (an earlier form of this was that union was the union of union and non-union), and the clue to this is provided by his claim that the content of his philosophy is Christianity. This in fact is the most direct route to the heart of Hegel's philosophy (and its central difficulties); it has the advantage of

---

[1] See, for example, K. Löwith, *Meaning in History*, p. 58: "since he transposed the Christian expectation of a final consummation into the historical process as such, he saw the world's history as consummating itself".

[2] The reader is referred to Emil Fackenheim, *The Religious Dimension in Hegel's Thought*.

allowing one to dispense with labels like "romantic" or "child of the Enlightenment", which probably do more harm than good and are certainly in the initial stages of understanding wholly misleading; and, as is now well established and well known, it happened to be Hegel's own route to philosophy in so far as that emerged out of his double quest for the true and the historical Christianity and for a living religion. Christianity as false religion was a flight from the world, a pathological symptom of a society and a consciousness divided against itself; Christianity as true religion, the Christianity of Hegel's mature philosophy, was the union of divine and human, in which the divine remained wholly divine but for that needed and was dependent on the human, and the human remained fully human but for that needed and depended on the divine. Christianity was the perfection and completion of religion because in Christianity God fully reveals himself as the union of finite and infinite. Philosophy is the wholly rational expression of this truth. Spirit finds itself in its other, and is a perpetually re-enacted process of seeking and finding itself in its other which cannot mean abolishing the otherness of the other: the other must remain other for Spirit to be at all. As Hegel wrote in one of his early fragments, Reason is analogous to love; both go out and lose themselves but also find themselves in the other, in the Not-I.[1]

Whatever philosophers and theologians may think of this, it is clearly wrong to regard Hegel's philosophy as a variety of transcendental, reality-behind-appearance metaphysic, or optimistic pan-rationalism in the eighteenth-century mode ("reason rules the world") reflected in philosophy of history as a unilinear progress, or a kind of cosmic Toryism ("the real is the rational"), or a closed super-system of reasoning deducing the whole of reality from arbitrarily asserted *a priori* first principles by the use of the only too famous formula, never in fact used by Hegel, of thesis–anti-thesis–synthesis, shunning experience and rendering super-fluous the work of the natural scientist and historian. Views of this kind, commonly held, miss the whole point of Hegel's philosophy, which is precisely that it does *not* shun or in any way devalue the objective world, of fact and contingency and finitude, the historian's world and the natural scientist's world and the world of every-day experience; its whole object is to show how necessary all this is to the life of Spirit. If reality, which is not just substance but active subject as well, is a perpetually re-enacted process of self-realization, and the result includes the process, then Spirit's other, which is necessary to the process, must always remain

---

[1] See H. S. Harris, *Hegel's Development*, p. 143, and elsewhere.

other – its being "overreached" by Spirit means just that. This is a point which Emil Fackenheim insists on again and again: "...the entire Hegelian philosophy, far from denying the contingent, on the contrary seeks to demonstrate its inescapability"; "The system can *be* comprehensive of the world only by means of total self-exposure to it"; "Hegel asserts an Understanding which confronts, analyses and keeps separate facts, not merely *beside* a Reason which speculatively unites them but rather... *within* a Reason empty without it"; "Hegel's life-long endeavour was to find the Absolute not beyond, but present *in* the world, the world in which men suffer and labor..."; "The Absolute, if accessible to thought at all, is accessible only to a thought which remains with the world of sense, not to a thought which shuns it in 'monkish fashion'."[1]

Hegel's philosophy can be seen as an exhaustive working out, in ever-increasing fullness and complexity, of every possible variation, each growing out of its predecessor, on this theme of the unity of universal and particular. Any manifestation of the one contains and needs the other, which, if it is denied, will assert itself as alien, as, to give just two examples, the neglected universal stands over against the wholly selfish self of pure hedonism as an alien "fate" which is yet its own, and the neglected particular self reasserts itself in the wholly "self-less" man so that in reality, 'art for art's sake' means art for Jones' sake, the 'pure' scholar is wholly selfish, etc.; and this is the negativity which is the principle of dialectical progression.

Hölderlin, who was Hegel's close friend, wrote, towards the end of *Hyperion*, "Wie der Zwist der Liebenden, sind die Dissonanzen der Welt. Versöhnung ist mitten im Streit und alles Getrennte findet sich wieder",[2] and this has been regarded as a suitable motto for the dialectic. If so, it must not be taken to mean that love and reconciliation and harmony abolish pain, strife and separation, but only their meaninglessness. Spirit's "pathway of despair", of self-diremption and self-overcoming, is not solely a temporal process; if it were, either it would never be complete (and "Science" accordingly impossible) or else it would be completed once and for all (but Spirit is perpetually active, always alive – death for Hegel means the absence of opposition, the absorption of the particular in the universal).[3] Pain, suffering, conflict, the contingent

---

[1] *Op. cit.* pp. 4, 18, 19, 79, 80. Cf. p. 107. Spirit's conquest of the contingent and finite "requires the persistent reality of what is conquered by it. For this conquest is a 'result' which is nothing but the perpetually re-enacted 'process' of conquering it".

[2] "The dissonances of the world are like the quarrels of lovers. Reconciliation is in the midst of strife, and everything that is separated finds itself again".

[3] *Encyclopaedia of the Philosophical Sciences*, §§ 375–6.

and the particular in all its particularity remain; there is no love, harmony, reconciliation, true unity or true universality without them. This is the most profound meaning of the 'concrete universal', inspired by Christianity and inconceivable without it. Seen from this central point, Hegel's philosophy looks very different from the 'idealist system' scorned by Kierkegaard and Nietzsche, misunderstood by Feuerbach, Marx and countless others, and presented as 'Hegelian' by the British and American Idealists. It is one of Hegel's most constant themes from his earliest writings onwards, that all varieties of reality-behind-appearance metaphysic and religion are pathological, a symptom of alienation in man and society which must be *aufgehoben*. But that does not mean simply done away with: alienation is Spirit's self-alienation, the negation of Spirit is ever present. It is profoundly mistaken therefore to think that the serenity of Hegel's philosophy means the final resolution of conflict or that the "overcoming" of negation means the abolition of suffering and contingency and otherness. This would be precisely the sort of night in which all cows are black which Hegel said his philosophy was not, and which he himself presented in his lectures on the history of philosophy as marking more primitive phases of philosophical insight.

This, then, is the truth grasped by Reason; this is the 'rationality' of the universe; this is how 'reason' rules the world; this is the 'rationality' of the idea of the modern state: it contains the strains and tensions and conflicts of the world of self-seeking individuals which destroyed the simple, undifferentiated unity of the Greek polis, negates its negations. The state which such a Spirit creates for itself must be a pluralistic state, which allows the particular, the private quest for self-satisfaction, full play, but not to the extent and in such a way that it defeats or destroys itself; a state in which freedom is a concrete living reality, not an abstract 'right', or mere 'ought'; a state in which the universal and particular sides of the will are in harmony, an organic unity of differences, and the greater the differentiation, the greater the unity. Similarly the World-Spirit or *Weltgeist* would be neither "real" nor rational, if it were what it is so often taken to be: a wholly supra-empirical, supra-individual objective entity, or super puppet-master.

Clearly the Reason that rules the world is not the reason of the ordinary rationalist, for that is more properly called the 'Understanding', and the truths of Reason are opaque to the 'Understanding', the sort of thinking that is especially appropriate to natural science and history, that must analyse and separate: "everything is what it is and not another thing". What is rational and true or "adequate to its notion" is what has brought forth, developed and "overcome" its inherent contradictions, that is, contains them in "might" and "love"[1] and is mature, in an individual or truly civilized state. It is something that has objectified itself, brought itself forth; it cannot be true to itself otherwise – indeed the pith and marrow of Hegel might be said to be contained in the Gaelic proverb, "if it is in, it will out".[2] That is the truth in the description of Hegel as one of the most anti-metaphysical of philosophers.[3]

By the same token the philosophy of the Absolute is absolutely open to experience, "tough-minded" in William James' sense, as empirical as any empiricist should wish, which is why so much of its content is now closed to us. It is not a question of Feuerbach or Marx or anybody else "rescuing" sense experience from its "humble place" in Hegel, or standing his philosophy right way up, but sense experience, in itself and as such, the most immediate and therefore most abstract form of experience, cannot be the full truth about reality, and if one tries to make it so, the result is self-contradiction. The same holds good for every partial, more or less abstract form of experience. None of them by itself is able to make the world fully intelligible; they all negate themselves in the attempt to do so. But if we are thereby provided with one of the world's most fully stocked medicine chests of scepticism and mental and moral hygiene, nevertheless all the rungs on the ladder of experience which ends with philosophy are rungs *in* the ladder of philosophy, and that means that they are all in themselves perfectly valid, necessary aspects of truth.

It is wrong therefore to think of the dialectic as functioning as a process of logical demonstration or deduction in a closed system. This could be called 'vulgar Hegelianism'. The best example in English is the well-known and otherwise not unhelpful exposition by W. T. Stace. Stace is worried by what he regards as logical lapses or breaks in the chain of reasoning. But the dialectic is not like that at all. It was the result of Hegel's desire "to think life"; it is a way of thinking concretely and seeing things whole, whose conclusions cannot be proved or disproved, but which can be seen to be more or less true to life; its purpose is to provide insight. The only way to appreciate it or understand what it is is to watch it at work. And one must watch intelligently and without pedantry (which

[1] See Hegel's *Science of Logic* (trs. Johnston and Struthers), II, p. 237.
[2] "If it is in, it will out, as the Gaelic old-word says". Neil Munro, *The Lost Pibroch*.
[3] J. N. Findlay, *Hegel, a Re-Examination*, p. 348. "despite much opinion to the contrary, Hegel's philosophy is one of the most anti-metaphysical of philosophical systems, one that *remains* most within the pale of ordinary experience..." One should, however, read Fackenheim, *op. cit.*, in order not to oversimplify the issue.

is not possible to anyone in a hostile, fault-finding mood), because although Hegel insisted that "Science" was wholly public and a discipline of thinking, and talked of "the seriousness, the pain and labour of the negative", nevertheless his philosophy is best approached in the spirit of Plato's, as something that is in danger of being destroyed or distorted if it is written down. Hegel in fact was extremely reluctant to publish; he only published two *books*, because the *Encyclopaedia* and the *Philosophy of Right* are compendia for courses of lectures. The present edition of the introductory lectures on the philosophy of history has the advantage of bringing home the fact that so much of Hegel's philosophy was talked, not without humour and anecdote and personalities and contemporary reference – Haldane's "dry man" is quite wrong – and also constant tacking and changes of course.

Croce has good things to say about the "Bacchic delirium" which for Hegel is the movement of reality. "Reality seems mad, because it is life: philosophy seems mad, because it breaks up abstractions and lives that life in thought. It is a madness which is the highest wisdom, and the true and not metaphorical madmen are they who become mad with the empty words of semi-philosophy, who take formulas for reality, who never succeed in raising themselves to that clear sky whence they can see their work as it really is..."[1] More recent exponents of the dialectic have insisted that it must not be approached with unintelligent rigidity.[2] Kaufmann makes much of the influence on Hegel of Schiller's *Letters on the Aesthetic Education of Man*,[3] and the theory of freedom as 'play', and Müller quotes Hegel's description of the Reichenbach Falls, written about the same time as the publication of Schiller's Letters, as an anticipation of the dialectic of the mature philosophy, in which Hegel delights in the spectacle of "free play" (*das Bild eines freien Spieles*).[4] Indeed Hegel's description of the Falls is as good a *Vorstellung* or pictorial representation of his philosophy as one is likely to find, though he does not seem to have used it himself as such. The artist, he says, cannot

---

[1] *What is Living and What is Dead of the Philosophy of Hegel* (trs. Douglas Ainslie), p. 29.

[2] G. R. G. Mure, *The Philosophy of Hegel*, p. 38. The reader "must not be tempted by the display of triadic notation to ask if dialectic has the cogency of mathematical deduction. It certainly has not, but the comparison is inept...In deduction one false step ruins the argument. If dialectic errs it is because its freedom degenerates to a capricious and arbitrary movement...There is no possible external test of dialectic, no applicable rule of formal logic...What matters is whether Hegel's general conception of spirit is justified, and whether he shows a deeper insight than other thinkers into man's nature and destiny."

[3] *Op. cit.* pp. 46–58.

[4] G. E. Müller, *Hegel, Denkgeschichte eines Lebendigen*, p. 79.

capture the essential thing: *das ewige Leben, die gewaltige Regsamkeit*; the fact that what one sees is always the same and yet always different... Those who profess to see in Hegel's philosophy only a lifeless mechanical system or intellectual gymnastic had better first make sure that they are not themselves   the hollow men
                                    the stuffed men.

2. Hegel and the historians

The *Philosophy of History* is where professional historians have made contact with Hegel's philosophy, if they can be said to have come into contact with it in any real sense at all. From Ranke onwards, they and their philosophical allies have denounced and criticized it with an enviable self-confidence not shared by those who really have "fought at Arques", and the result of what can in most cases only be described, to borrow a phrase of Tovey's, as "encyclopaedic inattention" to the texts.[1] Ranke had only the most rudimentary notion of what he made such a show of rejecting, and the professional historians, as one might expect, tend to range themselves behind him without further ado.[2] Acton, in his famous essay on German Schools of History, is magisterially staccato, cryptic and quite wrong; Geyl fulminated against Hegel's "abuse of history with a vengeance" and his "presumptuous, egocentric system";[3] one could heap up an imposing pile of such misrepresentations. They have their main source in the unquestioned, and mistaken, belief that Hegel's philosophy of history is a ready-made scheme, not drawn from observation of the facts but imposed on them, thus making a mockery of the conscientious spade work about which historians are, rightly, so sensitive; that it shows no respect for or grasp of the individual fact as such, because the Idea is prior to the facts, so that the historian is turned into the merest under-labourer at best, even if he is not rendered altogether superfluous.

But if Logic (the Idea)–Nature–Spirit is, like everything 'rational', a threefold union or syllogism, in which each of the members takes the place both of one of the extremes and of the mediating middle, if "truth

---

[1] *Essays in Musical Analysis*, IV, p. 74. "The impregnable fortress of Berlioz's encyclo- paedic inattention" to Byron's poem.

[2] E.g. H. Butterfield, *Man on his Past*, p. 104. Von Laue, *Leopold Ranke*, p. 123. A. D. Momigliano, *Studies in Historiography*, p. 105. P. Geyl, *Debates with Historians*, p. 7. F. Engel-Janosi, *The Growth of German Historicism*, p. 47. F. Meinecke, *Machiavellism* (trs. D. Scott), p. 383.

[3] P. Geyl, *Use and Abuse of History*, pp. 35–9.

is its own self-movement" and "the true is the whole" and "its own becoming", and philosophy a circle, so that nothing 'comes first', except for purposes of exposition, and there is no *a priori*, and the Idea has no existence apart from the world of experience, any *a priori* scheme of history would be a non-entity and inconceivable. And as has been seen, in the full circle of experience, the 'Understanding' in natural science and history as well as the 'common sense' view of the world, the "vulgar consciousness" in the light of which we daily live, have their vital roles to play and are in no way rendered superfluous or disvalued by Reason or philosophy, that "Science" which views the whole in the light of the whole. The historian's world in all its phases and modes and varieties of historical explanation is, as such, absolutely intact, philosophy of history presupposes it, as philosophy of nature presupposes natural science. But did not Hegel attack Niebuhr, one of the fathers of modern scientific historiography? He did so because he was so anxious to champion the historians on their own ground that he failed to appreciate the value of Niebuhr's reconstruction of early Roman history; he thought that Niebuhr was sacrificing the documentary evidence to *a priori* subjective intuition, thus illegitimately interpreting the past in the light of the present. And not only did Hegel have a respect for and appreciation of fact, an insatiable appetite for sheer information in every subject, that is almost unique in the history of philosophy, but, as has been seen, his philosophy is such that sheer fact and contingency are given a unique philosophical status; 'Reason' is such that 'Reason in history', properly understood, must, among other things, mean precisely that grasp of the particular fact and appreciation of the uniqueness of historical indivi- duality which Hegel has been accused of lacking, regarding them only as steps to a pre-ordained goal.

Croce however would have none of this. He was so anxious to take up the cudgels on behalf of "actual history" and the professional historian, that the insight shown earlier in his book, when he explains why it is grossly misleading to describe Hegel's philosophy as "optimistic",[1] fades when he comes to the application of the dialectic in history. He sees Hegel's idea of history as operating on two mutually exclusive planes – the plane of empirical fact and that of *a priori* speculation – and therefore as self-contradictory. Hegel himself, he says, divides history into "reflective"

---

[1] *Op. cit.* pp. 58–9. "Hegel cancels neither the evil nor the ugly, nor the false, nor the vain: *nothing could be more alien to his conception of reality, so dramatic, and in a certain sense so tragic.* What he sets himself to do is to understand the function of evil and of error; and to understand it as evil and as error is surely not to deny it as such, but rather to strengthen it."

and "philosophical" history, but you cannot have two different methods for the same set of facts; one of them must be rendered nugatory and meaningless, so that Hegel's "various declarations of the great respect due to actual fact" are a fraud, although "Hegel never dared to declare the empirical and positive method altogether erroneous so that it could be wholly replaced by the speculative method" (p. 169). In effect "he had to negate, as he did negate, the history of the historians" (p. 138).

But Croce, like the professional historians, thought that "philosophical" history in Hegel means *a priori* history, "history of a second degree", having "the character of an *a priori* construction", "a *history already complete* which needs only to be clothed in names and dates", or "nothing but a rough anticipation of what is given by actual history" (see Chapter 7). The wine of historical fact is poured into previously existing bottles, and if most of it spills over, as Croce thinks it does, then it is not 'real and rational' and doesn't matter (p. 145). The historian in fact is being asked to hand over his work to the philosopher to be revised and completed, and he rightly rebels. "It is just as if a painter or musician were told to consign to the philosophers his picture or his score when he had completed it, so that they might raise it to the second power..." (p. 138). Croce's powerful criticism has obviously been very influential, but what it amounts to is a failure to sustain and deepen his understanding and appreciation of the dialectic when he comes to Hegel's philosophy of history. He writes as though there were a hard and fast line in Hegel between the realm of actual historical fact and that of *a priori* philosophical deduction, and in the final analysis this misunderstanding may be traced to his belief that Hegel's philosophy "resolves religion into itself and substitutes itself for it" (p. 71). Thus he supported the instinctive reaction of the professional historians with a more sophisticated version of the fundamental error previously noted.

Hegel's account of the three kinds of history at the beginning of his lectures on the philosophy of history is well known. What is not perhaps so well known is that it is an interesting example of the dialectic in action, as anyone familiar with Hegel's treatment of any other subject would expect, though the dialectical movement is not so obvious here as elsewhere, perhaps because it has been rather blurred in the processes of editing (and translating). To ignore it is to miss the point of much of what Hegel says, but it can be roughly reconstructed, and a free and abridged version would run somewhat as follows.

The first, most primitive (that is logically primitive) kind of history, "original" history, is barely history at all in so far as it represents an immediate unity between the historian's consciousness or *Geist* and the *Geist* of what he is describing; this sort of contemporary history is necessarily limited. When this sort of chronicle, seen at its most sophisticated in Thucydides, is extended to meet the need for a view of the whole history of a people or even for a history of the world, we get the first primitive phase of what Hegel calls "reflective" history, "reflective" in so far as now the historian's consciousness and what he is describing have fallen apart; the past is now outside and different from the historian's consciousness, past and present are separate spheres and the past has to be consciously retrieved and made present in a way that doesn't happen in "original" history. This is therefore the phase of "mediacy", the special province of the 'Understanding'. At the first, most unsophisticated stage of "reflective" history, which is still very close to "original" history, when a historian like Livy, for example, aims to present an account as circumstantial as that, it is the *Geist* of the historian's present that prevails and the result is no more than a one-dimensional extension of "original" history backwards in time. But "reflective" history proper means abridgement; here we have another meaning of 'reflection', when one reflects and tries to understand, and the 'Understanding' is the great epitomiser (*der Verstand ist der mächtigste Epitomator*). In its most primitive and immediate form this sort of "reflective" history, which one can also see in Livy, is so abridged as to be wholly lifeless, a dry and abstract record of events, qualitatively undifferentiated. But at the other extreme, the effort to immerse the reader wholly in the past by heaping up antiquarian detail is lifeless in so far as it is wholly particular: there is nothing universal, no unifying principle in such mere catalogues. Antiquarian detail as an end in itself, the study of the past for its own sake, ceases to be history and comes into its own in the historical novel. Sheer antiquarianism, and its nemesis, for the attempt to 'live' and make the reader 'live' in a past regarded as wholly alien by putting lots of pieces of it together in a manner that is necessarily wholly external and mechanical ends in a dead pedantry,[1] can be taken as providing the dialectical transition to the next stage of "reflective" history, viz., "pragmatic" history. All historical writing is pragmatic in so far as a past is present in a mind which gives the events a unity which they do not possess in themselves, so that the past is *aufgehoben*: taking it up into the present means that it is abolished as sheer past, whatever antiquarians may try

---

[1] Presumably the *Geist* of the historical novel, what is alive in it, is not truly historical, and what is historically accurate in the historical novel is not truly alive. What belongs to the present and what belongs to the past never cohere in a living unity.

to think. But nemesis follows the attempt to make it wholly present and of general import: the pulsing life of the present spurns the pale, power-less generalizations that are the 'lessons' of a past that can never be exactly similar or truly relevant, and the reader, bored by these general reflections alleged to be of universal validity but which must in fact differ from writer to writer and from age to age, turns back with relief to sheer chronicle, which has no particular point of view. "Critical" history, the next logical step and a reaction against utilitarian history or pragmatic history as such, is not so much history as a preliminary history of history; it prides itself especially on extracting more from the records of the past than is apparently contained in them, but carried to the point where subjective fancies are substituted for historical data, it is simply another way of importing the present into the past; the so-called "higher criticism" ceases to be properly historical or critical. *Spezialgeschichte*, the final phase of "reflective" history, is an abstraction from the living whole of a culture or cultures of a single topic for historical study, as in constitutional history or legal history or the history of art, or science or religion, etc. In so far as this apparently 'external' approach, when properly pursued, however, yields the inner connection or *leitmotiv* of events (*die innere leitende Seele der Begebenheiten*), and in so far as its point of view is general, it forms the transition to the third stage; philo-sophy of history, the realm no longer of the 'Understanding', but of Reason. The point of view here is no longer abstract and special, as in the highest stage of "reflective" history, but truly concrete and universal; in philosophy of history past and present are re-united, but no longer as in the immediate, unreflective unity of "original" history. *Geist* is ever present and has no past, yet it comes to full self-consciousness in history; it is ever the same, but, as manifested in each unique *Volksgeist* or culture, ever different.

Critics however like Croce cannot see why the dialectic has to proceed beyond "reflective" history, for what does philosophical history do which cannot be done by "reflective" history? The answer is nothing, *qua* history. The situation is much the same here as in the *Philosophy of Right*, where critics like M. B. Foster[1] can see no need for the transition from "civil society", the dialectic of which, like that of "reflective" history, moves from a world of fragmentation and particularism to a kind of unity, which is not, however, that of philosophy, to the "state". This transition, argues Foster, Hegel only brings about in the sinister interests of the ruling class. In "civil society" everything necessary for the realiza-

[1] *The Political Philosophies of Plato and Hegel.*

tion of *Sittlichkeit* (objective ethical life), and in "reflective" history everything necessary for true history are said to be already present; the progress of the dialectic means the superseding and destruction by philosophy of the possibility of democracy and the historian's history respectively.

And the answer to the objection applies in both cases: neither at the level of "reflective" history, nor in "civil society", both of which are fragmented worlds of the 'Understanding', is the universal "seen in the light of the universal". The administration of justice in "civil society", for example, can only be an end in itself from a pragmatic point of view; however well administered it cannot be always or truly just: it is, however, necessary to the proper functioning of the whole, and in time of war, for example, many aspects of it may have to be dispensed with; however, what appears arbitrary, external and unjust at the level of "civil society" will not be so when seen in the light of the whole. When I view the administration of justice, which as such is the universal (the law) applied in my particular case, in the light of the whole, I can see that it cannot be an end in itself, that in time of crisis, for instance, it may have to be suspended in the interests of the state and therefore in the final analysis in the interest of the freedom maintained by the state. "Civil society" is therefore "the state as envisaged by the 'Understanding'." Its freedom cannot be the last word about freedom in the state.

Similarly, in "reflective" history every historian has more or less consciously and adequately a 'philosophy of history', some preconceived ideas without which he cannot function as a historian at all. They are necessary hypotheses, and there may be as many of them as there are historians, and one cannot be said to be any more true than another at this level. Which is the point made by modern analytical philosophers of history. Mandelbaum, for example, in *The Problem of Historical Knowledge*, is anxious to show that an empirical philosophy of history is impossible and a contradiction in terms. This is Hegel's point, and it brings out the sceptical and analytical side of the dialectic which the critics are prone to overlook. The dialectic shows that history as such cannot be 'useful'; the past as studied by the historian has no 'lessons' – Hegel's saying to this effect is well known.

In the realm of "reflective" history the history of *Geist* as the realization of freedom is just one more hypothesis among many. As such it is purely formal and abstract and its content is purely arbitrary. There is nothing to decide which particular version of the history of freedom or which particular 'philosophy of history' is true – any criterion of truth will appear to be a universal imposed arbitrarily from without, with no

generally recognized or public claim to be in any way superior or qualitatively different from any other. This is the true historian's attitude, *qua*
historian, to the philosophy of history, but the historian's experience, as
such, is not the last word about the whole of experience (in art, religion
and philosophy, the sphere of Absolute *Geist*, history and historical
development as such cease to have importance or meaning), and historians
who act as though they were claiming that it is simply fall to quarrelling
among themselves: the assertion is self-negating; what was a useful
working hypothesis becomes a menace to the discovery of the (historian's) truth. And this is the negation which philosophy negates. 'Com-
pleting' "reflective" history does not mean negating it, but negating its
negations; in the same way, the state negates the negations of "civil
society", a world of self-interest which in itself, regarded as an absolute,
is self-destructive. The true historical content of the philosophy of history
is not therefore solely a matter for "reflective" history as such.

Only philosophy can provide the true 'notion' of freedom which
'reflective' history as such cannot comprehend, that is, it provides the
content of the idea of freedom (and therefore the content of the philosophy
of history), because to think freedom philosophically, that is concretely,
not abstractly, is to think the organized life described in the *Philosophy of
Right*, viz. the 'Idea' of the modern democratic state in which alone
freedom can be fully realized and the claim of modern man to self-
realization and self-satisfaction made any sort of reality. (And it is already
some sort of historical reality because otherwise it could not be thought
by philosophy, where merely describes the given, and cannot describe
something which does not exist.) This gives one the criterion of truth
lacking in history as such and the content without which the philosophy
of history as such is purely formal and abstract. A history of freedom at
the level of "reflective" history might be a history of 'totalitarian
freedom', or of anarchism; it is open to all the manipulated interpretations
and newspeak of the men of 1984 or anybody: its content is wholly
arbitrary. A true history of freedom presupposes the philosophy of *Recht*,
and philosophy of history is the logical conclusion of that. The history of
freedom cannot be divorced from the political organization and law and
the idea of law without which freedom is a mere abstraction and unreal.
(To say that for Hegel, true freedom "in typical idealist fashion, is
possible only through discipline"[1] is just silly, either a pale relic of the

---

[1] W. H. Dray, *Philosophy of History*, p. 70. A remark which spoils one of the better
attempts by a modern philosopher of history to give a brief account of Hegel's
philosophy of history.

old nonsense about Hegel being "anti-liberal", or a timid half-conscious professorial bow in the direction of some noisy but mindless 'permissiveness'. Only if one is an anarchist can one reject Hegel's philosophy of the state, and Hegel himself in the *Phenomenology of Spirit* shows what logical and moral absurdities the anarchist gets into if he thinks his beliefs right through.)

This means that the philosophy of history will *not* be universal history or world-history as that is conceived by the 'Understanding': viz., everything in the bag, but highly selective, and it is badly off target to criticize Hegel's philosophy of history for being selective,[1] or for treating the whole of history as though it were 'political', which was Collingwood's main criticism.[2] "The moral", wrote Collingwood, "is that political developments should be conceived by the historian as integrated with economic, artistic, religious and philosophical developments, and that the historian should not be content with anything short of a history of man in his concrete actuality." Although Hegel was not doing history *qua* historian, this in principle is what his philosophy of history is, even if his lectures on the history of art, religion and philosophy formed separate courses. But in the lectures that are called "the philosophy of world history", Hegel is dealing with the ground of these activities, without which they are impossible, hence the "central position of the state", which Collingwood objected to and called an "anachronism". But Hegel's idea of the state is comprehensive, like Aristotle's, and a philosophy of history in which it is central, or rather fundamental, is not "political" in the sense criticized by Collingwood, but a history of civilization. (To be more precise, a history of civilization, from one point of view, of civilizations, from another – a synthesis, as some would describe it, of 'rationalist' and 'romantic' historiography.) And since Hegel's philosophy is not the 'idealist' photographic negative, which Marx thought he was developing into a true picture, and since "civil society", which incorporates what Hegel called the "system of needs", is an essential aspect of the 'Idea' of the modern state, and therefore of freedom properly conceived, Hegel's philosophy of history, in principle at any rate, incapsulates and postulates a materialist or economic interpretation of history.

And if the task of the philosopher is to think experience concretely

---

[1] It is also fashionable to display one's broadmindedness by criticizing Hegel for being arrogantly Europo-centric or Western-orientated. The latest example is W. H. Walsh in *Hegel's Political Philosophy, Problems and Perspectives* (ed. Z. A. Pelczynski). But isn't Hegel's perspective broadly the right one? Or at least should one not wait until world history has shown its hand a bit more clearly?

[2] R. G. Collingwood, *The Idea of History*, p. 122.

and to describe the given, the philosophy of history cannot be an *a priori* scheme, thought out prior to observation of the facts and the work of the historian as such. The *Geist* of modern man, his claim to freedom, is real enough, and must have come about in history. Hegel does not say that this was ineluctably necessary, but that it can be seen to have happened. This is the "outline" or "skeleton plot" which W. H. Walsh says must be an *a priori* deduction.[1] But this "outline", surely, is precisely what is most obviously and palpably given to observation? Men know and have and want freedom as they once did not, just as they know and have and want electricity as they once did not. This fact or event or process *is* the meaning of history: the fact is the meaning. One could object to the way in which Hegel presents the details of this development, though one should always remember that it is wrong to think of the dialectic as a rigid pattern of ultimate and unchangeable truth.

Hegel was concerned in the *Philosophy of Right* and in the philosophy of history with the inherent 'rationality' of the modern state and of world-history respectively; in neither case was he, so to speak, simply photographing the facts. The *Philosophy of Right* is not a description of any one actual state, although it is full of empirical detail, but of the inherent rationality of the modern state as such. In both cases one has a rational 'deduction', or logical core, with a great deal of empirical content. The difficulty therefore does not concern the 'outline' or 'skeleton plot' or sheer logic of freedom but, since the dialectic is neither wholly deductive nor wholly inductive, how far into empirical detail must the philosopher venture? How does one draw the line, and where, between what is an object for philosophy (like the state, which clearly is) and what is not (like Jones' red hair, which clearly is not)? The jury, for example, is part of the rational state; but philosophy is not concerned with its size or composition. The decision seems arbitrary. But if the 'truth' of philosophy is the 'truth' of a portrait, not of a photograph, then to some extent what goes in, the empirical content, cannot be guided by any rigid, mechanical rule. The dialectic is essentially flexible, though there is a hard core: the logic of freedom.

Obviously there has been a development as a historical fact in man's consciousness of freedom, though to regard this as akin to a rationalistic idea of progress does scant justice to the depth of Hegel's insight and subtlety of his analysis. In describing it in detail, the philosopher is wholly dependent on the historian, and the state of contemporary historical knowledge, which will grow and alter and also reflect changing social

An Introduction to Philosophy of History (1951), p. 151.

conditions etc., as Hegel was very much aware. The empirical detail therefore of the philosophy of history must be regarded as tentative and subject to change. Detailed criticism of the content of Hegel's philosophy of history seems for this reason somewhat otiose. It is based on a misconception of what a "unitary view of history" means in Hegel. There can, of course, be only one philosophy of history, as there can be only one philosophy of the state, because there cannot be alternatives to reality, but the detailed pattern is subject to change in conformity with the basis of fact provided by the professional historians or political scientists (or for that matter the philosopher himself *qua* professional historian or political scientist in so far as that is practicable). There is more than one pattern of the philosophy of history in Hegel's own work, especially if one takes into account the *Phenomenology of Spirit* and the writings prior to that. Hegel with his insatiable appetite for information was apt to delve deeply into the empirical realm of observed fact, thereby dangerously extending his lines, in so far as he was dependent on the state of knowledge in his day, though for thus showing his appreciation of what Croce calls historian's history he has had nothing but abuse from the historians themselves, because they have regarded as a menace to their profession what is really a compliment. The more genuinely concrete a philosophy is, the more dead wood it is presumably fated to carry as time and research proceed, and the more purely antiquarian knowledge is required to properly appreciate and understand it. One of the difficulties in understanding Hegel, especially the philosophy of nature, is precisely that he was so deeply immersed and well informed in all the sciences of his time. Critics of the philosophy of history do not, as a rule, possess enough knowledge of the history of history and other sciences, or the historical imagination, to be able to make the necessary allowances; e.g., if anthropologists had discovered the 'state' among primitive peoples, still a somewhat controversial matter, Hegel would presumably have had to begin with them. As it is he begins with the East, and the development of freedom is given a geographical East–West movement. This sort of thing, emphasis, for instance, on the role of world-historical individuals, natural to someone who had lived under the shadow of Napoleon and admired him, for reasons usually misunderstood, belongs to the flexible, adjustable sector of the philosophy of history. And this belongs to the body of the lectures, so that anyone wanting to judge how far the dialectic applied to history did lead to new insights must go to them (and the full, critical edition has not been translated from the German). As in the *Philosophy of Right* so here, one must go behind the empirical description to the inherent rationality, or see the latter in the former, to distinguish what is living and what is dead in Hegel's account.

And if freedom and the idea of the modern state are in some sense objective realities of the modern world – they could not be thought by philosophy otherwise – then to this extent and in this sense the process of world-history relevant to the philosopher is complete, and the argument that a philosophy of history is impossible because history is open-ended, and therefore no human being can survey the whole scene, does not apply. The philosopher can survey the whole scene of the development of freedom; though this does not mean anything so absurd as that history comes to an end with Hegel.

Nearly all modern writers who discuss the nature of historical thinking feel obliged to take issue with Hegel, and some are more adequately equipped to do so than others. Thus W. H. Dray, for example, is aware of the difficulties involved in Hegel's alleged *a priorism*, but he ends up subscribing to a version of the "two level" interpretation.[1] Hegel does not show *in general*, he complains, that the passions of individuals are such as to bring about a situation in which there can be a dialectical development of Spirit. But what Hegel does is what numerous thinkers in the previous century had done, that is, point to two 'facts': on the one hand the progress of civilization; on the other the prevailingly selfish passions of men, so that something like what Hegel called the "cunning of reason" has to be posited as an explanation. Dray's short account is fairly full; more often the references to Hegel in recent writers are too brief and cryptic to be worth attempting to answer. Thus Danto in his *Analytical Philosophy of History* says that Hegel never asked what was the significance of the Absolute's final self-awareness, or if he had, he would doubtless have moved to a quite different sense of 'significant' than that applied to the ordinary events of history.[2] W. B. Gallie accuses Hegel of monstrously distorting the ideal of generous-mindedness which he glimpsed to meet the needs of his system.[3] After a survey of the literature one is left wondering why modern philosophers of history bother with Hegel at all. Mostly they only muddy the waters of interpretation without advancing the cause of the philosophy of history.

[1] *Philosophy of History*, p. 81. "The Hegelian account of history recognizes two levels at which the course of events can be described, each with its own kind of mechanism. The two levels, however, never really mesh."
[2] A. C. Danto, *Analytical Philosophy of History*, p. 14.
[3] *Philosophy and the Historical Understanding*, pp. 225–6.

3. Hegel and the political theorists

An adequate grasp of Hegel's idea of the state as the realization of the concept of freedom has until quite recently been an esoteric rarity. It was suggested earlier that the most fundamental cause of all the misunderstanding is the failure to appreciate properly the "religious dimension" of Hegel's philosophy, its heart and centre in his idea of Christianity. If one knows what Hegel means by "divine" one can see that his "deification" of the state means just the opposite of what it is usually taken to mean, and that MacIver's view of Hegel's state as "a sort of God whose thoughts are not our thoughts and whose ways are not our ways",[1] for example, is for Hegel quite literally a kind of blasphemy. It is blasphemy for a Christian to think of God as in any way unknown, a concealed object acting on mankind from without in a manner humanly unknown and unknowable. This constitutes the unholy alliance of rationalist agnostics and pietists (like Ranke, one might say): both think of God as an unknowable object. The 'totalitarian' interpretation of Hegel's political philosophy, according to which the state is said to be all-in-all and the individual nothing, has not as a rule gone deep enough nor realized that such a view is made totally impossible by the religious ground of his whole philosophy so that his rejection of it could not possibly be more sincere or deep-seated.

And the 'Idea' of the state, its 'rationality' properly understood, quickly disposes of the many varied accusations that Hegel's theory of the state endorses nationalism, relativism, and *Machtpolitik*. The state is the "overreaching" universal, which both needs and makes possible the particularity of the *Volk*, the unique culture of the 'nation' (which is an unfortunate word in this context, unless one realizes that it applies to the Greek *polis*, for example: 'culture-state' would be less apt to mislead than 'nation-state'), as it needs and makes possible the private satisfactions of the individual of "civil society", at the same time curbing the self-destructive excesses of self-seeking particularity in the light of principles of universal validity. Any 'nationalism' which is wholly particular is thus one-sided and self-destructive, like the self-seeking particularism of "civil society" in itself and as such.

It was because Meinecke failed to understand what he called Hegel's "philosophy of identity", in which he thought "the irrationality and uncleanness of historical reality as a whole" was "mere dissonance, which

---

[1] R. M. MacIver, *The Modern State*, p. 450.

is resolved in the (ultimate) harmony", and "all the rich and variegated activity of history re-interpreted as being merely the play of marionettes... guided by a higher hand", that he could see Hegel as an unholy compound of Machiavellian *raison d'état* and *Historismus*, the "doctrine of individuality", for whom national power was the supreme aim of the "deified" "supra-individual entity" of the state, whose right was all-in-all.[1] Meinecke historicized Hegel's philosophy: Hegel "reinterpreted the concept of reason, from being the static force it was before, into the fluid developmental process of historical humanity"; he equated the actually existing with the rational, so that "everything, absolutely everything", served to promote the progressive self-realization of divine reason.[2] Meinecke's complete failure to see the universal, natural law side of Hegel's philosophy vitiates his whole powerful-seeming denunciation of it as the evil culmination of Machiavellism.

But history is only the temporal and objective dimension of Spirit's self-realization; the philosophy of history is itself a stage in the dialectic. *The Philosophy of Right* does not in fact end with the state. The achievement of freedom in the rational state is not an end in itself; the political/moral freedom possible in the state is only a relative freedom: the sort of "manly, moral freedom" which Burke said must be limited in order to be possessed. It is a one-sided freedom, the freedom of *Geist qua* objective, not the absolute freedom of Absolute *Geist*, that is, the realization of truth in art, religion and finally and fully in philosophy. There must, therefore, be a transition from Objective *Geist* to Absolute *Geist*, and this is provided by world-history, the arena in which states achieve their self-hood as individuals and the recognition by others which individuality implies. Accordingly we move from the "Idea" of the rational state to the arena of world-history, in which states meet their doom, where their finitude *qua* particular nation-states is made manifest, a finitude and particularity brought home to man's consciousness by the fact of war. The "earthly God" is seen to suffer the fate of everything mortal and finite in what appears at first glance to be a realm wholly given over to the play of the contingent and the unforeseen. International law between sovereign states is no more than an "ought"; there is no higher court of judgment than history – the world's court.

It has been argued that Hegel finds himself in a logical dilemma at this point because any mere "ought" represents a retrogression after the

---

[1] F. Meinecke, *Machiavellism* (trs. by Douglas Scott of *Die Idee der Staatsräson*), pp. 355, 363, 367. But see the whole chapter on Hegel.
[2] *Op. cit.* pp. 363, 349. Carlo Antoni followed Meinecke. See *L'Historisme* (French trs. by A. Dufour), pp. 64–75.

ethical synthesis achieved by the rational state,[1] but this is to forget that the synthesis is not final: the unity of universal and particular achieved in the state is logically and empirically precarious in so far as the state belongs to the world of contingency and empirical fact. History as the world's court is not called in to mend a break in the progress of the dialectic: it is an essential and typical aspect of it; a typical example of the "labour of the negative", leading to a truer unity, a higher spirituality. The state's finitude in history forms the dialectical transition to Absolute *Geist* as the death of the animal organism is the transition from Nature to Subjective *Geist*. The onward march of the dialectic demands not, as Russell thought, a World-State, because such a thing does not exist and cannot be an object for philosophy, but a falling apart once again of universal and particular, subject and object, and this happens in world-history, where on the one hand we have the actions of states and individual historical persons promoting an end which was no part of their intention, and on the other, that end itself. It is fully in accord with the dialectic that Spirit, on its way to the absolute freedom of full self-consciousness, should plunge into another phase of self-diremption; "let itself go" into the world of contingency and particularity and externality and unfreedom; and find itself again in this world, the world of Volney and Gibbon, of *Les Ruines* and the dissolution of states and empires, of Shelley's *Ozymandias* and the chorus in *Hellas*, which is seen to be not just that but a transition to another, truer, phase of freedom and life more abundant. Universal and particular fallen apart, we have a world of particular states, each with its own unique *Geist* and culture, externally related, with no principle of unity, apparently, other than the purely formal universality of the "*Sollen*" of international law. And in war the particular individual is wholly absorbed in and by the universal (the state) and sacrifices his private satisfactions and self in whole or in part. In this self-sacrifice, as in the death of the physical organism, the universal triumphs over the particular, only death is now filled with a meaning lacking at that purely natural level of experience.

And when all the variety and individuality of the world of *Historismus* is seen to be also the working out of a single process, the universal (the *Weltgeist*) appears to stand above the ethos of particular nations and the particular passions of world-historical individuals, and direct them, through the "cunning of reason", to its own end, unknown to them, as though it were separate and apart, a transcendental object. And that is how it must appear to the 'Understanding', but since the diremption of

[1] H. A. Reyburn, *Hegel's Ethical Theory*, chapter XIII.

Spirit is a self-diremption, this cannot be the truth of the matter. If the Absolute is wrongly conceived as supra-individual object, *a fortiori* the *Weltgeist* is no such thing. It is *Geist*, the human spirit, in history, in its process of self-realization in time; the temporal dimension of Spirit's coming-to-be and being; it is the critics, using the one-dimensional 'Understanding', who are guilty of 'reification', seeing the *Weltgeist* as an external object.

The *Philosophy of Right* ends, not with the state, but with the higher right, the higher justice of world-history, and this does not mean the justification of the historical process as such and with it the sanctification of state power as such, the criterion of judgement being the mere survival or success of the state, but what is "rational and real" in that process, viz., the development of freedom. It is in this sense that world-history is a 'court' delivering 'judgement' according to a 'law', which is not the law of self-preservation and *Machtpolitik*, but belongs to *Recht*, as world-history is a section of the philosophy of *Recht*. Everything else is not *wirklich*, not 'real', not alive in the world, but so much lifeless husk deprived of Spirit. This applies to anything that stands in the way of the *Geist* of modern man, which is the 'reality' which the philosopher describes and cannot overleap, and would apply therefore to the Restoration, in so far as it did so. That is why it is inept to describe Hegel as a conservative or even conservative,[1] let alone as a kind of official apologist of the Restoration, unless one means to assert that everyone who is not an anarchist is 'conservative'.

Marx, at least, knew what he was doing when he undertook the criticism of Hegel's philosophy of the state, and curiously enough it was Marx who first refuted or anticipated later refutations of the 'totalitarian' interpretation of Hegel's idea of the *Rechtsstaat*. This was because in his critique of the state in Hegel's *Philosophy of Right* he was attacking the idea of the *Rechtsstaat* as such, and trying to show that the modern democratic state is a contradiction in terms: "true democracy" and the state are incompatible.

---

[1] As a great many have done and do. G. A. Kelly's account of Hegel in *Idealism, Politics and History* is vitiated by the notion of Hegel as "a conservative". As a corrective one could read Jacques d'Hondt, *Hegel en son temps*.

Coda: Marx's critique of Hegel's "Philosophy of Right" and the emergence of a new legend

With Marx's critique of Hegel's *Philosophy of Right*[1] another Hegel legend emerged, according to which not the state but "civil society" is all in all, the state being a mystical idea of unity veiling the empirical reality of the divisions of bourgeois society, and Hegel's philosophy is the owl of Minerva which appears at dusk to survey and sum up a civilization that has had its day. This interpretation has been endorsed by some modern scholars and is seen for instance in Shlomo Avineri's *Hegel's Theory of the State*.[2]

Marx's object was to demolish the idea of the modern democratic state as such by showing how it is illogical and inconsistent, as any true account, and Hegel's account was true in an important sense, even if "upside down", was bound to be, because it was the product of an alienated society. That is, Marx thought that if he could destroy the logic of the connection between the logic and the empirical content of the *Philosophy of Right*, he would have destroyed the logic of the modern state. And the commentators, Hippolyte, Rubel, Avineri, Kamenka and O'Malley, for example,[3] seem all more or less agreed that Marx succeeded in showing that Hegel does not manage to deduce his empirical content satisfactorily from his logical premises: his own logic breaks down. In fact this happens less frequently than the commentators appear to suppose.[4] That however is not the important thing. The important thing is that to suppose that there should be strict logical links in the movement of the dialectic is to miss its real meaning and significance and value as a device to enable one to think concretely about the state, freedom, etc. As has been seen, the whole point about Hegel's dialectic as a device of philosophical explanation is that it is *not* a process of rigid logical deduction: it moves freely, it is to be used flexibly, its purpose is to provide insight and understanding of the human condition. Free interpretation

---

[1] An English translation of the complete text was published by the Cambridge University Press in 1970: *Critique of Hegel's 'Philosophy of Right'* by Karl Marx (ed. Joseph O'Malley).

[2] See my review of Avineri in *Cambridge Review* (March 1973).

[3] J. Hippolyte, *Etudes sur Marx et Hegel*, p. 128. M. Rubel, *Karl Marx, essai de biographie intellectuel*, ch. III. S. Avineri, *The Social and Political thought of Karl Marx*, pp. 28–30. E. Kamenka, *The Ethical Foundations of Marxism*, ch. 4. J. O'Malley, *op. cit.*, Introduction.

[4] For example, Hegel's deduction of hereditary monarchy is usually misunderstood.

of the *Philosophy of Right* is in the spirit of the dialectic; rigidly strict interpretation violates it. And a strict interpretation, looking for logical lapses, being a misunderstanding of the dialectic, will not be powerful criticism either of Hegel's method or of what he is describing, in this case the modern state as such. It is Marx's great mistake to treat the logic of Hegel's account of the state as something brittle, broken up by formal contradictions; so that even if some of Marx's shells do fall on Hegel's rather exposed front-line, they are liable to miss the rational reality which on a more free, but perfectly legitimate interpretation, i.e. legitimate according to the spirit of the dialectic, constitutes Hegel's reserve line. There is a rationale of the modern state behind the front line onto which Marx directs all his artillery. And Marx's whole purpose is to criticize the modern *Rechtsstaat*; in criticizing Hegel he thinks he is doing this, but his critique is such that even when he has apparently played havoc with Hegel's alleged contradictions, the deeper rational meaning of the modern state suggested by Hegel's dialectic still stands. And therefore Marx's own alternative of "true democracy" is not established by a genuine critique of the modern state.

The fact is that Hegel's front-line is more advanced than it need be, beyond the sheer logic of freedom and into the region of actual empirical fact. This is the fascination of the *Philosophy of Right*, but there was the risk of incorporating institutions which, though they were a norm of civilized society in Hegel's day, might be difficult to defend in a rationale of the modern state as such. In his search for empirical content, Hegel's linking of logic and actuality was liable to feel the gravitational pull of contemporary European norms too strongly, and the more empirical actuality is incorporated, the greater the risk of rationalizing the merely contingent and laying oneself open to the charge of political conservatism. Obviously the philosopher has to be guided by the actually existing, if he cannot "leap over Rhodes"; equally obviously he cannot surrender to it wholesale, as he would if he were to be a political gazetteer or almanack, photographing the political institutions of any one particular state, unless of course that state was an exact representation of the rational state. And no actual state was.[1] And since Hegel was describing the inherent rationality or essential logic of the existing situation of modern post French-revolutionary civilization it is misleading to talk of his subservient attitude to existing political institutions unless one is very clear what one means by that. "He is committed *a priori* to the principle that the empirical

[1] Those who think that Prussia was have only to compare the *Philosophy of Right* with Prussian institutions at that time – or lack of them.

order is in the last analysis rational", says O'Malley.[1] Quite so, provided one leaves out the *a priori*; but neither Marx nor O'Malley manages to penetrate to the last analysis.

For example, in Hegel's account of the idea of the modern state there is (*a*) what seems the archaic institution of primogeniture and entailed landed estates guaranteeing the existence of what Hegel called the "agricultural class", rooted in landed property and family tradition, and (*b*) a rationale of which (*a*) was the contemporary expression: that is, the need to *ensure* that there are some people in the state, apart from the "universal class" or bureaucracy, who are under some sort of obligation to devote themselves to public service, because otherwise there is nothing to *guarantee* it, who are free from the pressures and temptations that lead to political corruption etc. Burke had put forward powerful reasons for the political existence of such a class; and at that time such a class actually existed. In our time (*a*) might take the form of payment to M.P.'s, Life-Peers, etc., institutions equivalent to the old hereditary aristocracy and necessary to the realization of freedom in the modern state. But even if one removed the "agricultural class" bodily from Hegel's state it would not make much difference to the rationale of the modern state as such. It takes up three paragraphs in the *Philosophy of Right*.

Marx however regarded it as crucial because he saw in it the political expression of alienated private property: the fact that landed property could not be alienated, in the legal sense, was the ultimate expression of alienation in the economic and social sense: these men are dominated by what they own. (One sees here the germ of what later became the theme of 'reification' and 'fetishism of commodities'.) A critique of primogeniture was a critique of private property as such, and hence of the modern state based on it. And Marx tries to show that this is in violent contradiction with Hegel's own definition of private property as such, as something essentially alienable at the will of its owner, which belongs to the private person to do what he likes with. Whereas landed property as a pillar of the state is essentially inalienable, and is as independent of the state as of the will of its owner, taking on a life of its own, with its "social nerves" cut, severed from civil society as well as from the family, whose principle of love it violates. "What kind of philosophy of right is this in which the independence of private property has diverse meanings in the spheres of private and state rights?", asks Marx. And primogeniture contradicts the principle of the family which Hegel says is the substantial basis of this class, because the family is a 'substantial unity' based on

[1] O'Malley, *op. cit.* p. xxxv.

love and here one of the children has to inherit the whole estate. Avineri endorses Marx's success in this critique of Hegel's account of primogeniture: Marx shows how property has become man's master and "this radical conclusion exposes the whole Hegelian political structure".[1]

But the whole point of Hegel's logic of the state is that any of its "moments" by themselves are abstract; they cannot be ends in themselves. Private property as such, as an abstract right of the individual, is socially divisive; the rational state controls it and modifies it to ensure that it is not. Indeed in so far as Marx does not want the abolition of property *per se*, but the *Aufhebung* of private property, i.e. negation of its negations or social control and modification of property in the interest of the truly human life, one could say that Hegel's state is doing precisely what Marx wants communism to do. "Derivation from the concept" means that private property is the creature of the state, apart from which it is a mere abstraction. As to the family, one could point out that it is not only primogeniture that encroaches on or breaks up the family unity as such, but also, for example, compulsory public education, or for that matter, divorce, which is only 'ethical' in so far as the family is not an end in itself but a member of the state. Primogeniture and the law of entail are an invasion of private property and the family in the interest of the state as a whole, and in the light of the whole will not appear as an assault on property or the family because it is only in the state that these institutions have any reality at all. Marx admits that for Hegel primogeniture is not an end in itself; the reason for it is political; but then goes on to say that this "decency" of Hegel's makes no difference. But it makes all the difference, because it brings out the fact that there is no logical inconsistency between Hegel's account of primogeniture and his account of property, and to see one is a grievous misunderstanding of the dialectic and the idea of the state as prior to its abstract "moments".

If it is to the advantage of the state to have a class of people whose position in the state is determined by inalienable landed property and birth, this does not mean that the state or any particular individual is subservient to property. On the contrary. The deepest level of meaning behind the apparent anachronism of primogeniture is that private property as such is *not* an absolute; it is the state that makes it a reality, but this involves whatever modification of the abstract right of property may be necessary in the interests of the whole.

If Marx's critique of primogeniture is the crux of his critique of Hegel's

---

[1] S. Avineri, *The Social and Political Thought of Karl Marx*, pp. 28–30. O'Malley follows Avineri, *op. cit.* p. xxxvii.

Idea of the state, as some commentators think, that critique fails. If it is not, what has just been said about it applies in principle to Marx's critique of the other agents which mediate between "civil society" and the state: the corporations, the bureaucracy, the Estates. The logic of the modern state demands something like them, as it demands some head of state like Hegel's hereditary monarch, if not as exactly described by Hegel. This mediation may be difficult to realize in practice: to say that it is impossible, which in effect is what Marx says, is dogmatic: viz. that the bureaucracy must necessarily be a self-interested, closed corporation; the Estates cannot represent the interests of society as a whole and cannot have any real effect on the bureaucracy and so on. In so far as Marx deduces these impossibilities logically as inherent contradictions in the modern state, his logic is more rigid then Hegel's. There is only one solution: what Marx calls "true democracy". Hegel's philosophy of the state allows for practical flexibility, though empirical adjustment is not the concern of the philosopher as such. Marx wants the empirical realization of perfection, which means the abolition of the state and achievement of communist society or "true democracy".

In fact this critique of Hegel, which reads superficially like a devastating blow-by-blow destruction of the Hegelian philosophy of the state, is in fact a deadly boomerang. No text of Marx or Engels brings into relief so sharply the fundamental weakness in their whole system as this one – which they did not publish. It spotlights the notorious weakness of their theory, or rather non-theory, of the state: that they recognize the need for political authority without having to call it 'political' or the 'state'. (As the Communist manifesto has it: "The public power will lose its political character.") In other words we are back to Hegel's base-line: the problem of freedom and control. One could in fact argue that Hegel's philosophy of the state is the truth of Marx's "true democracy", not vice-versa, in so far as Hegel is concerned with the eternal problem of liberty and authority: wherever two or three are gathered together it is there, as Marx and Engels had to more or less admit. Only Hegel did not shirk the issue, but tried, risky venture as it is, to work it out in concrete detail in the complex messy world of actual society and politics, which is what one would expect, provided one understands his philosophy properly. Marx couldn't, because having recently been mystified by Feuerbach's alleged de-mystification of Hegel's philosophy, he committed the classical mistake of thinking that the Absolute abolishes the tensions and conflicts of the real world in a world of thought, alleged to be the reality behind appearance. But the tensions and conflicts are of the essence of the human situation, and the democratic state *is* a standing contradiction in terms, and a perpetual tension and never-ending dialogue between freedom and order. But Marx too seems to have thought that struggle was the essence of the human situation; what ends is class-struggle, not conflict and tension as such. If this is so, and in so far as Marx admits the need for some authority and control, then the difference becomes a matter of degree. Hegel wants as much liberty as possible, and so does Marx. Hegel wants as little authority as is absolutely necessary, and so does Marx. And both want the maximum development of the individual. Marx's tragedy, and the tragedy of not only Marx, was his failure to realize this.

DUNCAN FORBES

TRANSLATOR'S PREFACE

In the following translation, I have attempted to follow the style and substance of the original text as closely as possible. For example, on those occasions when Hegel's own manuscript of the lectures lapses into note form, I have preserved its disjointed character as far as this could be done without prejudice to the sense. Johannes Hoffmeister, on whose edition the present translation is based, enclosed in square brackets all words and phrases which he had himself supplied in order to complete Hegel's sense or syntax, and, wherever possible, I have reproduced these brackets at the appropriate points in the English translation. On a few occasions, I was compelled to omit some of Hoffmeister's notes on minor linguistic details – such as German word endings and prepositional usage – which Hoffmeister thought necessary to correct or alter; I have done so, however, only in cases where a translation of Hegel's original word or words would have made no sense in relation to my rendering of Hoffmeister's corrected version.

At relevant points in the text, I have supplied footnotes on some of the main terms on which translators of Hegel have tended to disagree in the past. (These translator's notes, keyed by superior symbols, appear at the foot of the appropriate pages, whereas Hoffmeister's editorial notes, and notes by Hegel himself, are keyed by superior numerals and are printed at the end of the appropriate sections of the text.) I need only add here that, in the case of Hegel's well-known distinction between *Moral* and *Sittlichkeit*, I have followed the practice of several earlier translators of Hegel, such as T. M. Knox (in his edition of the *Philosophy of Right*, Oxford, 1942), in rendering *Moral* as 'morality' and *Sittlichkeit* as 'ethical life' whenever Hegel appears to be differentiating between the two. Similarly, I have translated the adjective *sittlich* as 'ethical' in all such contexts. But on those few occasions where it seemed that a distinction of this kind was unnecessary, I have translated both *Moral* and *Sittlichkeit* as 'morality'.

In translating those passages from Hoffmeister's (greatly enlarged) edition which overlapped with the earlier (and much shorter) edition by Karl Hegel from which J. Sibree translated the *Lectures on the Philosophy of History* in 1857, I was grateful for the opportunity to compare my renderings with those of my predecessor, and at times to borrow individual turns of phrase. But Sibree's now archaic style precluded any wholesale imitation. I was not able to consult the more recent translation of Hegel's Introduction to his lectures by Robert S. Hartman, entitled *Reason in History* (New York, 1953; Library of Liberal Arts, 35). Like Sibree's translation, it antedates Hoffmeister's edition, and is much shorter, being only 95 pages in length.

Since Hoffmeister's edition first appeared (in 1955), a new German edition of Hegel's lectures, by Eva Moldenhauer and Karl Markus Michel, has been published as Volume XII of the Suhrkamp edition of *Hegels Werke* (Frankfurt a. M., 1970). Although it incorporates a few of Hoffmeister's additions, the text of this latest version is essentially that of Karl Hegel as published in 1840. It accordingly lacks a great deal of the material subsequently included by Hoffmeister, whose edition remains easily the most comprehensive to date.

Finally, I wish to acknowledge my great debt of gratitude to Professor Hans Reiss of the University of Bristol for his immense care and patience in checking my translation against the original; his many valuable suggestions repeatedly enabled me to improve the accuracy of my formulations. I am alone responsible for all remaining inadequacies.

DECEMBER 1974   H. B. NISBET

GEORG WILHELM FRIEDRICH
HEGEL
LECTURES ON THE PHILOSOPHY OF
WORLD HISTORY

INTRODUCTION: REASON IN HISTORY

EDITED BY
JOHANNES HOFFMEISTER

Contents

Preface

The present editor is the fourth to edit Hegel's lectures on the philosophy of world history. They were originally edited by Eduard Gans in 1837 as part of the 'Complete Edition' ['Vollständige Ausgabe'] of Hegel's works produced 'by an association of friends of the deceased'; they were re-edited in 1840 by Karl Hegel; and the last edition, which underwent three impressions (1917, 1920, and 1930), was prepared by Georg Lasson as part of the 'Critical Edition' ['Kritische Ausgabe'] of Hegel's works in the 'Philosophical Library' ['Philosophische Bibliothek'] series. The text was modified by each of these editors in turn, and although the last of them, Georg Lasson, reproduced his version of the text unaltered in the second and third impressions of the 'Philosophical Library' edition, he expanded it to such an extent in the light of subsequently discovered manuscripts and lecture notes, from which he incorporated several important sections, that the manner in which he presented the work as a whole could no longer be justified and yet another revised edition became necessary.

Hegel held this course of lectures at two-yearly intervals, with four hours of lectures per week, from the winter semester of 1822–3 onwards; he delivered them for the last time during the winter semester of 1830–1; so that the course was given five times in all. But over the years, Hegel accumulated so much new empirical historical material of so varied a kind that, by the winter semester of 1830–1, he was no longer able to cope with it in its entirety and accordingly announced only 'The Philosophy of World History: *Part One*' as the title of his course for that year. The first editors, however, failed to do justice to this wealth of historical material; in both the first and the second edition, this lecture course, as compared with those of Hegel's other courses which, as in the present case, were not laid out in book form or in paragraph sections, occupies only a slim volume. One of the main achievements of my predecessor was that he remedied this deficiency and was the first to give Hegel's 'Philosophy

5

of World History' a shape in some measure commensurate with its weighty substance, its formal organisation, and above all, with its empirical breadth.

In his postscript 'On the Composition of the Text', Lasson himself gives an adequate account of how he achieved these ends by returning to the sources, i.e. to Hegel's own manuscripts and the rough lecture notes and fair copies made by his students. Those sections of the postscript which are still relevant and which show the ways in which both Lasson's text and the present version deviate from those of Eduard Gans and Karl Hegel are reproduced at the end of this volume; Lasson's other remarks, however, have been deleted or abridged.

Lasson's edition first appeared at a time of general lack of interest in Hegel, and it accordingly placed pedagogic and didactic considerations uppermost. Since then, however, the demands on editors of Hegel's works have become considerably more exacting. Nowadays, we expect a more rigorous philological approach in matters of detail, especially where students' lecture notes and fair copies are concerned, for much of what was taken down or subsequently enlarged upon by Hegel's pupils is demonstrably inaccurate or beside the point. In particular, we expect exact information on the provenance of individual expressions, sentences, and paragraphs, which certainly cannot always be pieced together like a mosaic, but at times vary considerably over the different years in which the course was delivered. And finally, we expect a closer overall insight into the thought structure of each set of lectures on which the complete text is based.

In my foreword to the introductory volume of Hegel's 'History of Philosophy' (Philosophische Bibliothek vol. xva, 1940, second impression 1944), I have discussed at length the philological and methodological consequences which the peculiar character of Hegel's thought has for any edition of his lectures. These consequences are such that they ought really to have transformed the shape of the present volume. But since I have not yet had a chance to evaluate the original or newly discovered source material with a view to producing a more authentic version of the text as a whole, the existing version, which Lasson constructed from the lecture notes he had at his disposal, had to be retained in essence. I have not been able to determine the exact manuscript sources and years of origin of these portions of the text. This meant that I also had to dispense with checking or altering the order in which they may have occurred in Hegel's original version. And it was not possible either to integrate the additions which Lasson took from two sets of lecture notes of the winter semester of 1826–7 after he had completed his text, and which he published as an appendix to his edition (although the material on which his main text was based had included another set of notes of the same year). These additions had once more to be placed at the end of the volume.

It was nevertheless possible to set out the volume in a more *uniform* manner, *firstly*, by restoring Hegel's own subdivisions. For closer inspection showed that the section numbers in the margins of Hegel's main manuscript (that of the 'Second Draft' in this edition), which Lasson had taken for nothing more than marks made by Hegel to aid his memory during lectures, correspond very closely to the methodological progression of the treatise as a whole, whereas Lasson's subdivisions are largely derived from the material he collected from students' lecture notes. I have accordingly restored Hegel's own divisions – at times supplying appropriate section headings in square brackets – and have left spaces and inserted asterisks* at points where Lasson considered further subtitles necessary to bring greater order into the mass of material. In addition, I have omitted Lasson's note on variants 'On the Text of Hegel's Manuscript' (i.e. of the 'Second Draft'); everything of value in it concerning Hegel's own subdivisions, remarks, and textual idiosyncrasies has been included in this edition in the form of notes to the appropriate parts of the text. And finally, the *second* respect in which the present edition is better integrated than its predecessor is that the chapter on 'The Varieties of Historical Writing' has been brought back into the main text, from which Lasson had excluded it.

When Lasson set about reconstructing the text of Hegel's Introduction in 1917, the only evidence he could find that Hegel had ever begun his lectures with this chapter was that of the old edition and some sets of students' notes. This did not seem conclusive enough, especially since the one original manuscript of Hegel's at his disposal – the 'Second Draft' of the winter semester of 1830–1 – quite clearly indicated a different beginning; he therefore simply relegated this chapter to the end of the volume as the first part of a 'Separate Introduction'. But soon afterwards, two different sheets of manuscript from this chapter, in Hegel's own handwriting, were discovered (one in private ownership in Zurich, the other in the Schiller Museum in Marbach), and from entries by Hegel on the first of these, it emerged that the lectures had begun with this section on at least two occasions, in 1822 and 1828. Admittedly, there was still every justification for continuing to use Hegel's second, fuller and more definitive draft of the Introduction as the main basis of the text and for leaving the lecture notes 'On the Varieties of Historical Writing' – along

---

* No asterisks appear in the German edition of this volume, and it would appear that Hoffmeister omitted to add them.

7

with the reflections on 'The Natural Context or the Geographical Basis of World History' – at the end of the volume. But it would nevertheless have been worth using these notes, along with the other material, to prepare a new critical text of this particular chapter. Instead, Lasson retained them unaltered as part of his 'Separate Introduction' in the form in which he had taken them from his original sources and from the old edition, and printed Hegel's manuscript observations separately as 'Addenda'. The same material therefore appeared twice, at two different places in his edition. A further complication was that the editor succeeded only partially in overcoming the difficulties with which the second (Marbach) sheet confronted him in his efforts to decipher it.

The real reason why it was imperative to prepare a new critical text of this chapter was, of course, that Lasson had failed to notice that the two newly discovered sheets were not merely, as he thought, 'originally fairly closely connected, probably separated by half a sheet at most', but in fact followed on *in unbroken sequence* from one word ('its') to the next ('consciousness'). I have marked the point at which the two manuscripts meet in a note to the text. Given the intimate connection between these sections, of which Lasson's predecessors were likewise ignorant, along with the missing concluding paragraphs, which had to be supplied once again from students' notes or from earlier editions, it is possible to piece together a self-contained treatise based almost entirely on Hegel's own manuscripts. This can legitimately be called the 'First Draft', since, on the evidence of Hegel's entries on the Zurich sheet, it really does contain the ideas with which he began his first lecture course on the philosophy of world history; and for the same reason, it deserves to be restored to the position the earlier editors accorded it in their editions. And finally, as can be seen even from the present table of contents, the content of the 'Second Draft' also follows on immediately from that of the first; but I did not consider it either necessary or justifiable to make any kind of alteration to the source material as it occurred in the original documents (as, for instance, Karl Hegel did on pp. 11f. of his edition) in order to make the direct connection between the ideas expressed in the two drafts clearer still.

The third newly discovered sheet of manuscript which Lasson published had to be excluded from the present volume; it belongs in content to the chapter on 'The Oriental World', and hence to the second half-volume in this edition of the lecture course.*

---

* Hoffmeister refers, of course, to his own German edition of Hegel's lectures. The present volume contains, in English translation, only the Introduction to the Philosophy of History, not the detailed survey of world history which followed it.

Hegel's original text is printed in italics, whereas the passages which Lasson added from students' notes appear in Roman type. Finally, I am greatly indebted to Dr Rolf Bachem for helping me to read the proofs and for preparing new indexes to the text.

Bonn   JOHANNES HOFFMEISTER
15 January 1955

First Draft (1822 and 1828)

The Varieties of Historical Writing

[begun] 31. x. 1822;
[repeated] 30. x. 1828

Gentlemen,

The subject of these lectures is the philosophical history of the world. We shall not occupy ourselves with general reflections abstracted from world history and illustrated by concrete historical examples, but rather with universal world history itself.

I have no text book[1] on which to base my lectures; but in my 'Elements of the Philosophy of Right' ['Grundlinien der Philosophie des Rechts'], §§341– 360 (i.e. the conclusion), I have already defined the concept of world history proper, as well as the principles or periods into which its study can be divided. This work should enable you to gain at least an abstract knowledge of those moments of world history with which we shall be concerned here.

By way of an Introduction, I shall begin these lectures with a (general, determinate*) representation† of what constitutes a philosophical history of the world; with this provisional object in mind, [I shall] first of all enumerate and describe the other methods of dealing with history and compare them with the philosophical method.

---

* *bestimmte.* Here and on most other occasions, I have followed the usual practice of writers on Hegel in the English-speaking world in rendering *bestimmt* as 'determinate', *Bestimmtheit* as 'determinateness', and *Bestimmung* as 'determination', except in those few cases where the more common senses of 'definite', 'definition', etc., seem intended. The noun *Bestimmung*, it should also be remembered, often carries with it the associations of the English word 'destiny'.

† *Vorstellung.* On the meaning of this term for Hegel, cf. J. N. Findlay, *Hegel, a Re-Examination*, second impression, London, 1964, p. 343: 'It [*Vorstellung*] is not exactly the same as an image or mental picture...but is an image "raised to the form of universality, of thinking". What Hegel means is that Representations are thoughts which, despite their essential differences from mental pictures, none the less have some of the properties of the latter.' It can also denote the faculty or mode of representational thinking. The term, except when Hegel uses it in the more general sense of 'idea' or 'impression', is translated throughout this volume as 'representation', 'representational thinking', or 'faculty of representation'.

I distinguish three different modes of historical writing:[2]
  a. original history
  β. reflective history
  γ. philosophical history

a. *As to the first mode, the mention of a few names should give a definite picture of what I mean. Herodotus, Thucydides and their like belong to this class – that is, to the class of historians who have themselves witnessed, experienced and lived through the deeds, events and situations they describe, who have themselves participated in these events and in the spirit which informed them. They have compiled a written record of these deeds and events, thereby transferring what were previously mere extraneous happenings into the realm of intellectual representation. What was originally mere existence thereby takes on an intellectual aspect and becomes a representation of the internal and external faculties of mind. In the same way, the poet works on the material supplied by his emotions, creating from it an object which can be represented to the senses. Admittedly, such historians also make use of the narratives and reports of others;*[3] *but these are simply the more scattered, fortuitous and subjective of their raw materials, of less significance than the rest. The poet has a ready-made mother tongue [as an ingredient of his work and] owes much to the knowledge he has gained through education, but the greater part of his achievement is nevertheless his own; in the same way, the historian in question fashions a whole out of material from the past, of material scattered here and there in subjective and fortuitous reminiscences, or indeed preserved [only] in the shape of fleeting recollections, and sets it up in the Temple of Mnemosyne, thereby investing it with immortal life.*[4] *Such historians transplant [the past] into a better and more exalted soil than the soil of transience in which it grew, into the realm of the departed but now immortal spirits (as the Ancients describe their Elysium), so that their heroes now perform for ever the deeds they performed but once while they lived.*

From this category of original history I would exclude all legends, folk-songs, traditions, and poems;[5] *for legends and traditions are but obscure records [of actual events], and are accordingly the product of nations – or parts of them – whose consciousness is still obscure. But I shall return later to the relationship between nations and their history. Nations whose consciousness is obscure, or the obscure history of such nations, are at any rate not the object of the philosophical history of the world, whose end is to attain knowledge of the Idea in history – the spirits of those nations which [have] become conscious of their inherent principle, and have become aware of what they are and of what their actions signify,*[6] *are its object.*

[*We shall*] *later examine* [*the relationship between*] *historia* [*and*] *res gestae; the real objective history of a nation cannot be said to have begun until it possesses*[7] *a written historical record. A culture which does not yet have a history has made no real cultural progress* [*, and this applies to the pretended history*] *of India over three and a half thousand years.*

*Such original historians, then, transmute the events, deeds and situations they have witnessed into a work of representational thinking for the representational faculty.**

[*Several*] *conclusions* [*follow directly*] *from this:*

αα. *The content of such historical narratives cannot therefore be very comprehensive in scope.*[8] *Their proper subject matter includes all that is of living and immediate interest in the personal experiences and external environment of men.*

The author[9] *describes events in which he has himself played some part, or which he has at least witnessed as a contemporary. He covers short periods of time, and depicts individual human beings and events. He works from the immediate intuitions†* *of his experience, assembling a series of separate, unreflected elements into a composite picture, in order to give to posterity a representation as determinate as that which he experienced through his own intuition or through the intuitive‡ narrative of someone else.*

ββ. *With historians of this kind, the author's personal development and the events on which his work is based, or the spirit of the writer and the spirit of the actions he relates, are one and the same. His first concern, therefore, will not be to reflect upon his subject; for he is immersed in the spirit of the events he describes, and does not rise above it to reflect upon it. This unity of author and events also means* [*that, if*] *the historian lives in an age in which the social classes have become more clearly differentiated* [*and in which*] *the culture and maxims of each individual are related to his social class, he will himself have to belong to the class of statesmen, generals, and the like, whose aims, intentions, and deeds are part of the political world he describes.*[10] *When the spirit of events is fully developed, it becomes aware of itself; one of the main characteristics of its life and activity is its*[11] *consciousness of its own ends and interests and of the principles which underlie them – and another is the way in which it interprets itself to others and acts on their powers of representation§ in order to manipulate their will.*

---

* *ein Werk der Vorstellung für die Vorstellung.*
† *Anschauungen.* The usual English translation of the term *Anschauung* as used in German philosophy is 'intuition', although the word *Anschauung* also carries with it the idea of direct *visual* perception of external reality.
‡ *anschaulich.*
§ *auf ihre Vorstellung.*

Speeches are actions among human beings; indeed, they are extremely important and momentous actions[12]. Admittedly, one often hears those whose utterances have been badly received protesting that what they said was 'only words'. If they are right in this judgement, [they] must certainly be pronounced not guilty; for words which are no more than words are merely empty chatter, which at least has the advantage of being innocuous. But speeches on a national or international plane, issuing from nations themselves or from their sovereigns, are actions, and, as such, are an essential object of history (and particularly of earlier history).[13]

The writer, then, does not depict and interpret this consciousness by means of personal reflections; on the contrary, he must allow the individuals and nations themselves to express their aspirations and their awareness of what their aspirations are. He has no need to explain their motives (and emotions) on his own initiative, or to assimilate them into his personal consciousness.[14] He does not put his words or those of others into their mouths; and even if he does enlarge on what they originally said, the substance of his narrative and his own culture and consciousness are in equal measure the substance and consciousness of those whose words he renders. In the work of Thucydides, we read the speeches of Pericles, the truest, noblest, and most profoundly cultured of statesmen, and those of other orators, national ambassadors, etc.[15] In their speeches, these men express the maxims of their nation and of their own personality, their consciousness of their political position and of their moral and spiritual nature, and the principles which underlie their designs and conduct. The historian has left himself little or no room for personal reflections, and what he makes his characters say is not the expression of an alien consciousness projected into them, but of their own culture and consciousness. Anyone who seeks to study the substance of history, the spirit of nations, to live in it and with it, must immerse himself in such original historians and spend much time on them; indeed, it is impossible to spend too long on them. For the history of a nation or government as they relate it comes to us fresh, alive, and at first hand. Anyone whose aim is simply to enjoy history and not to become a learned historian can afford to limit himself almost entirely to the works of these writers.[16]

[17]And besides, such historians are not as common as one might suppose. I have already mentioned Herodotus, the father (i.e. the originator) of history – and at the same time the greatest historian – and Thucydides. [They are both] to be admired for their naivety. Xenophon's 'Anabasis' is an equally original work – Polybius; Caesar's 'Commentaries' are also a masterpiece of great simplicity – the product of a mighty spirit. But

such works are not the exclusive prerogative of antiquity. For a nation to possess such historians, it must not only enjoy a high level of culture;[18] *it must also have a culture which is not just the isolated privilege of clerics, scholars, and the like, but which is shared by the leaders of the state and of the armed forces. In the Middle Ages, for example, there were plenty of naive chroniclers, but they were monks rather than statesmen. Admittedly, there were learned bishops among them who had been at the centre of affairs and were familiar with the business of state, and who [were therefore] themselves statesmen; but in other respects, [there was] no fully developed political consciousness.*[19] *In modern times, all this has changed. Our culture is such that all events are at once recorded and transformed directly into historical representations.* We have excellent modern accounts of military and other events which are simple, lively, and clear, and which can stand comparison with those of Caesar; and indeed, the richness of their content – i.e. the detailed information they supply on methods employed and other attendant circumstances – makes then even more informative.*

Works of this kind include numerous French memoirs. Many of them are lively enough, but full of trivialities and anecdotes – their content and sphere of reference are petty; many others, however, are not only lively but also written by men of great ability and set in a grander and more interesting context; the memoirs of Cardinal de Retz [are a] masterpiece [of this kind]. In Germany, such masterpieces by writers who themselves took part in the events they describe are rare, although Frederick the Great's 'Histoire de mon temps' is in some ways a notable exception. It is not enough for the writer to have been a contemporary of such events, or [to have] witnessed them at first hand and had the opportunity to obtain reliable information about them; the writer must himself be of the same rank, circle, attitudes, mentality, and culture as those whose actions he describes. Only from an elevated position can one view the subject properly and see everything in its correct place – but not if one squints up at it from the narrow confines of some moral dogma or other restrictive system. In the present age, [it is] even more imperative [for us to free ourselves] from the restrictive attitudes of our social class [and] to let those on whom the authority of the state and the power of government rests speak for themselves. For those classes which are more or less excluded from political activity console themselves with moral principles which they use to compensate for their position and to set themselves up as superior to the higher classes: in short, they do not leave their own circumscribed province.[20]

---

* *Berichte für die Vorstellung* (literally, 'reports for the faculty of representation').

β. *The second mode of history may be called reflective. It covers more than just those events which were actually present to the writer; it depicts not only what was present and alive in this or that age, but that which is present in spirit, so that its object is in fact the past as a whole.*[21] *It is practised by a wide variety of writers – indeed by all those whom we generally call historians. The most important thing about it is the way in which it treats the historical material, for the writer approaches it in his own spirit, which is different from the spirit of the object itself; everything therefore depends on the maxims, ideas, and principles which the author applies both to the content of his work (i.e. to the motives behind the actions and events he describes) and to the form of his narrative. Here in Germany, this reflective history – and the skill with which it is practised – varies greatly; each historian has his own peculiar aims and idiosyncrasies. The English and French, as a rule, know how history should be written; much more than the Germans, they share the attitudes of a common culture, whereas with us, each writer laboriously works out his individual point of view. For this reason, the English and French have excellent historians; but here in Germany, if one looks at reviews of historical works over the last ten or twenty years, one finds that nearly every review begins with an individual theory of how history should be written, a theory which the reviewer sets up against that of the historian he is discussing. We are still in the position of continually struggling to find out how to write history.*

αα. *There is always a demand for complete surveys of the history of a nation or country, or indeed of the world in general;*[22] *and to satisfy this demand, history books must be written. These are necessarily compilations from the works of original historians proper, from other written reports, and from scattered items of information. They are not based on intuition* and the language of intuition*; [they do not possess the character] of eye-witness accounts. This first variety of reflective history approaches closest to the preceding kind when its exclusive aim is to present the entire history of a country or of the world. The character of any such compilation will depend primarily on how exhaustive the history is intended to be.*[23] *It often happens that such historians try to write in a manner so directly expressive of personal experience† that the reader has the impression of listening to contemporaries and eye witnesses recounting the events. But such attempts must always be more or less unsuccessful. – The whole work should and indeed must be uniform in tone; for the author is a single individual with a definite culture of his own;*

---

* *Anschauung.*
† The last five words are a free translation of Hegel's adverb *anschaulich.*

16

but the various ages covered by a history of this kind have widely differing cultures, as do the historians on whose work the writer draws, and the spirit which speaks through them in the words of the author is different from the spirit of the ages he describes. When the historian tries to depict the spirit of bygone times, it is usually his own spirit which makes itself heard.* Thus Livy puts into the mouths of the old kings of Rome, the consuls and generals of ancient times, speeches which only an accomplished advocate (or factious orator) of Livy's own times could have delivered, and which contrast glaringly with genuine traditions passed down from antiquity (such as Menenius Agrippa's fable of the belly and the members). He likewise gives us extremely thorough and detailed descriptions of battles and other events in such a tone and with such distinct perception of detail that he appears to have witnessed them himself; clearly, such narratives cannot have their roots in the ages in which they are set. They have features which could well be used to describe the battles of any age, yet on the other hand, their distinctness contrasts with their lack of coherence and the inconsistency which often prevails elsewhere in the main sequence of events. The difference between compilers of this kind and original historians can best be appreciated by comparing the narrative of Polybius with the way in which Livy uses, selects from and abridges his accounts of the period covered by the surviving portions of Polybius' work – Johannes von Müller, in an attempt to give a faithful portrait of the times he describes, has given his history[24] a stilted, pompous and pedantic air. The old chronicle of Tschudy[25] related the same events in a much more endearing, naive and natural way than Müller's contrived and affected archaisms.

[marginal addition in MS]

This is an attempt to transport us completely into the past as something immediate and alive, – [which] we [can] no more achieve than can the writer himself; the writer is one of us, he is part of his own world with all its needs and interests, and he honours the same things which it esteems. For example, whatever [the age] we live in, we can [immerse ourselves] as fully as we like in the life of Ancient Greece – which is congenial to us in so many important respects – yet we will never be able to sympathise with the Greeks and to share their feelings in the most important issues of all. For instance, however much the city of Athens captures our interest,

---

* Hegel is here quoting freely the lines of Faust to Wagner in Goethe's *Faust*:
　　'The spirit of the times, I've long suspected,
　　Is but the spirit of the men – that's all –
　　In which the times they prate of are reflected.'
(*Goethe's Faust*, translated by Sir Theodore Martin, revised, with an introduction and notes, by W. H. Bruford, London, 1954, p. 20.)

and however much we may sympathise [with] the actions and perils [of its citizens] – and it is undoubtedly the worthy fatherland of a cultured people – [we nevertheless can]not share their feelings when they prostrate themselves before Zeus, Minerva, etc., [or when they] toil over their sacrifices on the anniversary of the battle of Plataea – slavery. The deficiency – tone, atmosphere – Just as [we] cannot share the sensations of a dog, [even if we] have a clear impression of a particular dog, know it well, and can predict its mannerisms, attachments, and idiosyncrasies.

But there are other ways in which historians have tried to bring the past closer to us, not by writing in a tone designed to enlist our sympathy, but at least by eliciting intuitive and lively emotional responses, responses as lively as those of immediate experience, entering into all the details of the events, – location – mode of perception – distinct presentation.

[continuation of the main text]

This kind of thing inevitably happens with any historical work which tries to cover long periods or indeed the whole of world history; it is compelled to dispense more or less with individual accounts of reality and to make do with abstractions, summaries, and abridgements. This [means] not only that many events and actions must be omitted, but also that thought or understanding, the most effective means of abridgement, must intervene. For example, a battle was fought, a great victory was won, a town was unsuccessfully besieged, and so on. – A battle, a great victory, a siege – these are all general representations which condense a complex individual whole into a simple specification for the faculty of representation. If we are told that, at the beginning of the Peloponnesian War, Plataea was besieged over a long period by the Spartans, and that, after some of the inhabitants had fled, the town was taken and the remaining citizens executed, this is a short summary of what Thucydides describes in full with so much interest and in so much detail – and the same applies if we are told that an Athenian expedition to Sicily came to an unfortunate end. But as I have already observed, we have to make do with such reflect[ive] representations if we wish to obtain an overall view; and an overall view is also necessary.[26] But it inevitably makes for a correspondingly drier narrative. How can it possibly interest us when Livy, after describing a hundred wars with the Volscians, repeats for the hundredth time such phrases as: 'In this year, war was successfully waged against the Volscians, Fidenates, etc.'. – Such historical writing is lifeless; such formulas and abstract representations make the content of the work dry.

To counteract this mode of writing, [certain historians attempt to attain] at least an intuitive or representational liveliness, if not an emotional liveliness, by depicting each individual trait in a faithful and lifelike manner:

in short, they do not seek to reproduce past ages by means of a personal interpretation of them, but to create a faithful and accurate portrait of them. [They] gather the materials for this from every conceivable source (Ranke).[27] A motley assortment of details, petty interests, actions of soldiers, private affairs, which have no influence on political interests, – they are incapable [of recognising] a whole, a general design. [A] series of individual characteristics – as in one of Walter Scott's novels – collected from every quarter, painstakingly and laboriously assembled, – characteristics drawn from historical writings, correspondence and chronicles, – such a procedure involves us in numerous fortuitous details, [which are] historically no doubt authentic; yet the main interest [is] in no way clarified [by them], but rather confused, – and thus [it is] immaterial whether such and such a soldier called – –, precisely the same effect. [They ought to] leave this sort of thing to Walter Scott's novels, this detailed portraiture incorporating all the minutiae of the age, in which the deeds and fortunes of a single individual constitute the work's sole futile interest and wholly particular matters are all put forward as equally important; but in works which portray the central interests of states, such particulars of individual lives disappear altogether. Each single trait should be characteristic, and of significance for the spirit of the age, – the work should be executed in a grander and worthier manner, [so that] the political deeds, actions and sit[uations] themselves [come to the forefront, and] matters of universal interest [are depicted] in a determinate form.

ββ. *The first variety of reflective history leads directly to the second,[28] i.e. to pragmatic history. [This second variety actually has] no specific name; nevertheless, it is the end to which historians in general aspire: [namely to provide] a fully developed [impression] of a past age and its life. [For if we[29]] have no such totality before us and have no living experience of it, but are dealing instead with a reflective world, i.e. with a past stage in the spirit, interests, and culture of the society in question, [we at once feel[30]] the need for a present. This present [is] not [to be found] in history; [it arises out of] the insights of the understanding, the subjective activity and efforts of the mind itself. The external aspect of [the events[31]] is pale and wan; their end – the state, the fatherland – their meaning, their inner continuity, the universal aspect of their inner relationships is what endures, for it is as valid and present now as it was in the past and always will be. Every state is an end in itself, – external self-preservation; – its internal development and evolution follow a necessary progression whereby the rational, i.e. justice and the consolidation of freedom, gradually emerges.[32] [It is a] system of institutions, a) as a system the* *constitution, β) its content likewise,* through which the true interests of the state become conscious and fight their way to reality. In every advance which the object makes, [there is] not only an external coherence and necessary continuity; there is also a necessity at work within the object itself, within the concept.† This [is] the true substance of history. For example, [a] modern state, [the history of the] Holy Roman Empire, great individuals[33] or great individual events – the French Revolution, – any great necessity, – this [is] the object and end of the historian, but also the end pursued by the nation, by the age itself. Everything [is] related to this.*

Such pragmatic reflections, although highly abstract, thus indeed belong to the present, and should animate the records of the past and fill them with the life of today.[34] Whether such reflections are in fact interesting and enlivening depends on the spirit of the writer himself.

The worst kind of pragm[atic historian is the] petty psychologist who looks for subjective motives, deriving these not from a concept [but] from particular inclinations and passions, [and who] does not regard the object itself as the effective motive force; then there is the moralising pragm[atist, who] is also a compiler [but] one who sporadically awakens from his weary ramblings to utter edifying Christian reflections, attacking events and individuals in the flank with his moral onslaughts, and throwing in an edifying thought, a word of exhortation, a moral doctrine, or the like.

The second variety of reflective[35] history, then, is the pragmatic one. When we study the past and occupy ourselves with a remote world, a present opens up before the mind, a present created out of the mind's own activity and bestowed upon it as a reward for its exertions. The events are various, but their general significance, their inner quality and coherence, are one. This circumstance cancels out‡ the past and raises the event into the present. (The general relationships, the concatenation of circumstances, are no longer, as before, bound up with a series of separate, individual events; they themselves become the event, so that the

---

* The preceding portion of this sentence is translated literally; its sense is no clearer in Hegel's cryptic and fragmentary notes than in the English translation.

† *Begriff*: cf. *Hegel's Philosophy of Right*, translated with notes by T. M. Knox, Oxford, 1952, p. viii: 'The concept is the thought in so far as the thought determines itself and gives itself a content; it is the thought in its vivacity and activity. Again, the concept is the universal which particularises *itself*, the thought which actively creates and engenders itself.' (The words are those of Knox, not of Hegel.)

‡ The verb Hegel uses here is *aufheben*, which has several meanings – e.g. to raise up, to preserve, and to cancel or overcome. Hegel frequently uses the word to describe the workings of the dialectical process, to which it can apply in several or indeed all of its main senses: cf. Findlay, *op. cit.*, p. 47.

general, not the particular, is presented. If purely individual occurrences are interpreted in as general a fashion as this, the undertaking is fruitless and ineffectual; but if the event is expounded in its wider context, the writer's own spirit is revealed.)[36]

A word must be said at this point about moral reflections in particular, and the moral lessons we can supposedly learn from history – indeed histories are often written for this very purpose. It must be conceded that examples of virtue elevate the soul, especially with young people, and that they can be used for the moral instruction of children as concrete representations of general truths, in order to impress excellence upon their minds. But the destinies of nations, the convulsions of states and their interests, predicaments, and involvements are of a different order from that of morality. (Moral methods are very unsophisticated; Biblical history is adequate for this kind of instruction. But the moral abstractions of historians are completely useless.)

Rulers, statesmen and nations are often advised to learn the lesson of historical experience. But what experience and history teach is this – that nations and governments have never learned anything from history or acted upon any lessons they might have drawn from it. Each age and each nation finds itself in such peculiar circumstances, in such a unique situation, that it can and must make decisions with reference to itself alone (and only the great individual can decide what the right course is). Amid the pressure of great events, a general principle is of no help, and it is not enough to look back on similar situations [in the past]; for pale recollections are powerless before the stress of the moment, and impotent before the life and freedom of the present. (The instruction to be gained from history is not to be found in any reflections we may base on it. No two instances are exactly alike; they are never sufficiently identical for us to say that what was best on one occasion will also be best on another. Each nation has its own problems, and there is no need to look to history to discover the correct course.) In this respect, there is nothing so insipid as the constant appeals to Greek and Roman precedents we hear so often, as for example during the French Revolution. Nothing could be more different than the character of those nations and that of our times. Johannes von Müller, in his *General History*[37] and his *History of the Swiss Confederation*, had moral aims of this sort in mind, and laid down appropriate doctrines for the instruction of princes, governments, and nations, particularly for the Swiss. He compiled his own collection of maxims and reflections, and he frequently mentions in his correspondence[38] the exact number of reflections he has managed to put together in a given week. (He then proceeded to pepper his narrative at will with his sayings; but they can only come to life when they are applied to a concrete instance. His thoughts are very superficial; he thus becomes tedious, and) this portion of his work certainly cannot be classed as his greatest achievement. (Reflections must be concrete.) Only a thorough, open-minded, comprehensive view of historical situations and a profound sense for the Idea* and its realisation in history can endow such reflections with truth and interest. This is the case with Montesquieu's *Spirit of Laws*,³⁹ which is both thorough and profound.

Accordingly, **one** reflective history gives way to **another**; each writer has the same materials before him, each believes himself capable of arranging them and of fashioning a work out of them, and each will infuse his own spirit into them in the guise of the spirit of the age he depicts. This has produced a general reaction against such reflective histories, and readers have often turned back to precise descriptions which look at an event from every possible angle. These are certainly not without value, but they usually consist only of raw materials. We Germans are content with this; but the French show particular ingenuity in creating an imaginary present and in relating the past to the present situation.

γγ. The third kind of reflective history is critical history; it deserves to be mentioned since it is the principal method employed at present by historians in Germany. It does not constitute history as such, but rather the history of history; it evaluates historical narratives and examines their authenticity and credibility. (Niebuhr's *Roman History*⁴⁰ is written in this manner.) Its distinguishing characteristic and intention are to be found not so much in the subjects it deals with, but rather in the acuteness with which the writer wrests new information from the narratives he examines. (He scrutinises every circumstance to test the credibility of the whole.) The French have done much thorough and discriminating work in this field. They have not claimed, however, that this critical procedure is itself a form of history, but have presented their judgements in the form of critical treatises. Here in Germany, the so-called 'higher criticism' has invaded not only the whole realm of literary studies, but also that of historical writing (in which, by abandoning the basic task of history, i.e. judicious historical studies, writers have left the way open for the most arbitrary ideas and combinations). This higher criticism has been the pretext for introducing all the un-historical monstrosities a vain

---

* The word *Idee* is translated with a capital on all occasions when it denotes that ultimate, ideal principle which, according to Hegel, progressively realises itself in history.

imagination could suggest. It too is a method of bringing a present into the past,[41] namely by substituting subjective fancies for historical data – fancies which are considered the more excellent the bolder they are, that is, the less they have to substantiate them, the scantier the details on which they are based, and the more widely they diverge from the best established facts of history.

δδ. The last kind of reflective history is specialised history. It can readily be recognised by its fragmentary and particular character, for it selects a single general perspective (for instance, the history of art, of law, or of religion) from the wider context, i.e. from the whole of national life. It is admittedly abstract, but since its perspectives are general, it also provides a point of transition to the philosophical history of the world.

(When we form a picture of a nation, our faculty of representation* commands a wider range of perspectives than the Ancients could encompass, for we realise that spiritual determinants must also be taken into consideration. Such general perspectives include the history of art, of religion, of learning, constitutions, law, property relations, and navigation. The culture of today is such that this variety of history has received more attention and become more highly developed than before.[42] Legal and constitutional history have been particularly conspicuous in our times. Constitutional history is already more closely related to universal history, for it has no sense or significance unless it is based on a survey of the state as a whole. If it is conducted in a thorough and interesting manner, and does not confine itself merely to externals or insignificant superficialities – as does Hugo's *History of Roman Law*[43] – it can be really excellent. Eichhorn's *History of German Law*[44] is a more substantial work in this respect.)

Such branches of national activity are directly related to the history of the nation as a whole, and everything depends on whether this wider context is brought fully to light, or merely glossed over in favour of external relationships. In the latter event, the activities in question appear as purely contingent national peculiarities. But it must be emphasised that, if reflective history has reached the stage of adopting general perspectives, and if these perspectives are valid ones, such activities appear not just as an external thread, a superficial sequence, but as the inward guiding spirit of the events and deeds themselves.

γ. The third kind of history, the **philosophical history of the world**, is related to this last variety of reflective history in that it also adopts a

* *Vorstellung.*

general perspective, but without focussing on a single aspect abstracted from national life to the exclusion of the rest. The general perspective of philosophical world history is not abstractly general, but concrete and absolutely present; for it is the spirit which is eternally present to itself and for which there is no past. [Or it is the Idea.] Just like Mercury, the guide of departed souls, the Idea is truly the leader of nations and of the world; and it is the spirit, with its rational and necessary will, which has directed and continues to direct the events of world history. To gain an understanding of it and its guiding influence is the aim of the present investigation.

Second Draft (1830)

The Philosophical History of the World

[*begun*] *8. xi. 1830*

Gentlemen,
The subject of these lectures is the philosophy of world history.

As to what is meant by history or world history, I need say nothing; the common conception of it is adequate, and we are more or less agreed on what it is. But what may strike you about the title of these lectures and call for a word of elucidation, or rather of justification, is that we are here concerned with a philosophy of world history, and are about to consider history from a philosophical point of view.

But the philosophy of history is nothing more than the application of thought to history; and thinking is something we cannot stop doing. For man is a thinking being, and it is this which distinguishes him from the animals. All that is truly human, as distinct from animal – feeling, knowledge, and cognition – contains an element of thought, and this applies to all historical studies. But to appeal in this way to the participation of thought in all human activities may seem inadequate, for it could be argued that thought is subordinate to being, to the data of reality, and is based upon and determined by the latter. Philosophy, on the other hand, is credited with independent thoughts produced by pure speculation, without reference to actuality; speculation, it might further be contended, approaches history as something to be manipulated, and does not leave it as it is, but forces it to conform to its preconceived notions and constructs a history a priori.

History, however, is concerned with what actually happened. Its methods would therefore seem completely at variance with the essentially self-determining activity of conceptual thought. It is, of course, possible to present events in such a way that we can imagine they are taking place directly before our eyes. Even then, however, the links between the events must be taken into account; in other words, our procedure must be pragmatic, for we have to discover the causes and reasons behind the events. But as one can imagine, this will require the assistance of concepts, which does not, however, imply that the conceptual thought involved will be at odds with its own nature. Nevertheless, in a procedure of this kind, the events will always remain basic, and the activity of the concept will be limited to the formal and general aspects of the factual material, i.e. to rules, fundamentals, and principles. It is generally accepted that logical thinking is required for all such deductions from history; their justification, however, must come from the world of experience. But what philosophy understands by conceptual thinking is something quite different; in this case, comprehension is the activity of the concept itself, and not a conflict between a material and a form of separate origin. An alliance of disparates such as is found in pragmatic history is not sufficient for the purposes of conceptual thinking as practised in philosophy; for the latter derives its content and material essentially from within itself. In this respect, therefore, despite the alleged links between the two, the original dichotomy remains: the historical event stands opposed to the independent concept.

But [even if we disregard philosophy,] the same relationship emerges in the study of history itself as soon as we look at it from a higher vantage point. For on the one hand, we have in history ingredients and higher determinants which are remote from the conceptual world – i.e. all kinds of human arbitrariness and external necessity. On the other hand, we set up against this the idea of a higher necessity, an eternal justice and love, the absolute and ultimate end which is truth in and for itself. In contrast to natural being, this second, opposite pole is based on abstract elements, on the freedom and necessity of the concept. This opposition contains many interesting features; it comes to our notice once again in the Idea of world history. Our present aim is to show how it is resolved in and for itself in the world-historical process.

The sole end of history is to comprehend clearly what is and what has been, the events and deeds of the past. It gains in veracity the more strictly it confines itself to what is given, and – although this is not so immediately evident, but in fact requires many kinds of investigations in which thought also plays a part – the more exclusively it seeks to discover what actually happened. This aim seems to contradict the function of philosophy; and it is this contradiction, and the accusation that philosophy imports its own ideas into history and manipulates it accordingly, that I wish to discuss in the Introduction to these lectures. In other words, we must first obtain a general definition of the philosophy of world history and then consider its immediate implications. As a result, the relationship between thought and the events should automatically appear in the correct light.[1] For this reason, and

26

since I do not wish the introduction to become too long-winded (for the material of world history itself is so abundant), there is no need for me to spend time refuting and correcting the endless individual misconceptions and mistaken reflections – some of which are current now, others of which are periodically resuscitated – regarding perspectives, principles, and opinions on the aim and interests of historical studies, and in particular on the relationship of conceptual thought and philosophy to historical fact.[2] I can omit all this entirely, or merely touch on it in passing.

A[3]

[Its general concept]

The first thing I wish to say concerning our provisional concept of world history is this. As already remarked, the main objection levelled at philosophy is that it imports its own thoughts into history and considers the latter in the light of the former. But the only thought which philosophy brings with it is the simple idea of reason – the idea that reason governs the world, and that world history is therefore a rational process.[4] From the point of view of history as such, this conviction and insight is a presupposition. Within philosophy itself, however, it is not a presupposition; for it is proved in philosophy by speculative cognition that reason – and we can adopt this expression for the moment without a detailed discussion of its relationship to God – is substance and infinite power; it is itself the infinite material of all natural and spiritual life, and the infinite form which activates this material content. It is substance, i.e. that through which and in which all reality has its being and subsistence; it is infinite power, for reason is sufficiently powerful to be able to create something more than just an ideal, an obligation which supposedly exists in some unknown region beyond reality (or, as is more likely, only as a particular idea in the heads of a few individuals); and it is the infinite content, the essence and truth of everything, itself constituting the material on which it operates through its own activity. Unlike finite actions, it does not require an external material as a condition of its operation, or outside resources from which to derive its sustenance and the objects of its activity; it is self-supporting, and is itself the material of its own operations. On the one hand, it is its own sole precondition, and its end is the absolute and ultimate end of everything; and on the other, it is itself the agent which implements and realises this end, translating it from potentiality into actuality both in the natural universe and in the spiritual world –

27

that is, in world history. That this Idea is true, eternal, and omnipotent, that it reveals itself in the world, and that nothing is revealed except the Idea in all its honour and majesty – this, as I have said, is what philosophy has proved, and we can therefore posit it as demonstrated for our present purposes.

The sole aim of philosophical enquiry is to eliminate the contingent. Contingency is the same as external necessity, that is, a necessity which originates in causes which are themselves no more than external circumstances. In history, we must look for a general design, the ultimate end of the world, and not a particular end of the subjective spirit or mind; and we must comprehend it by means of reason, which cannot concern itself with particular and finite ends, but only with the absolute. This absolute end is a content which speaks for itself and in which everything of interest to man has its foundation. The rational is that which has being in and for itself, and from which everything else derives its value. It assumes varying shapes; but in none of them is it more obviously an end than in that whereby the spirit explicates and manifests itself in the endlessly varying forms which we call nations. We must bring to history the belief and conviction that the realm of the will is not at the mercy of contingency. That world history is governed by an ultimate design, that it is a rational process – whose rationality is not that of a particular subject, but a divine and absolute reason – this is a proposition whose truth we must assume; its proof lies in the study of world history itself, which is the image and enactment of reason. The real proof, however, comes from a knowledge of reason itself; for reason appears in world history only in a mediate form. World history is merely a manifestation of this one original reason; it is one of the particular forms in which reason reveals itself, a reflection of the archetype in a particular element, in the life of nations.

Reason is self-sufficient and contains its end within itself; it brings itself into existence and carries itself into effect. Thought must become conscious of this end of reason. The philosophical method may at first strike us as odd; bad habits of thinking may even lead us to imagine that it is itself contingent or no more than an arbitrary whim. But anyone who does not accept that thought is the sole truth and the highest factor in existence is not in a position to pass any judgement whatsoever on the philosophical method.

Some of you gentlemen, may not yet be acquainted with philosophy. I could easily appeal to all such persons to approach these lectures on world history with a faith in reason and a thirst for knowledge of it; – and we must surely assume that a desire for rational insight, for knowledge, and not just for a collection of assorted information, is the subjective motive which inspires those who seek to study the learned disciplines. But I need not, in fact, make any such claims upon your faith.[5] These provisional remarks and the observations I shall subsequently add to them are not, even within our own discipline, to be regarded simply as prior assumptions, but as a preliminary survey of the whole, as the result of the ensuing enquiry; for the result is already known to me, as I have covered the whole field in advance. It has already been shown and will again emerge in the course of this enquiry that the history of the world is a rational process, the rational and necessary evolution of the world spirit. This spirit [is] the substance of history; its nature is always one and the same; and it discloses this nature in the existence of the world. (The world spirit is the absolute spirit.)[6] This, as I have said, must be the result of our study of history. But we must be sure to take history as it is; in other words, we must proceed historically and empirically. For example, we must not allow ourselves to be misled by the professional historians; for certain of them, at least in Germany (and they even include some leading authorities who pride themselves on what they call their study of the sources), are guilty of precisely what they accuse the philosophers of doing – of introducing a priori fictions into history. Thus it is a widely accepted fiction (to quote one example) that there was an original primeval people, directly instructed by God, living in perfect understanding and wisdom, and possessing a thorough knowledge of all natural laws and spiritual truth; or again, that various nations of priests at one time existed; or (to take a more specific example) that the Roman historians based their accounts of ancient history on a lost Roman epic, etc. Let us leave such a priori inventions to those ingenious professional historians, among whom (at any rate in Germany) they are not uncommon.

We can therefore lay it down as our first condition[7] that history must be apprehended accurately. But general expressions such as apprehend and accurately are not without ambiguity. Even the ordinary, run-of-the-mill historian who believes and professes that his attitude is entirely receptive, that he is dedicated to the facts, is by no means passive in his thinking; he brings[8] his categories with him, and they influence his vision of the data he has before him. The truth is not to be found on the superficial plane of the senses; for, especially in subjects which claim a scientific status, reason must always remain alert, and conscious deliberation is indispensable. Whoever looks at the world rationally will find that it in turn assumes a rational aspect; the two exist in a reciprocal relationship.

It is perfectly correct to say that the design of the world should be distinguishable by observation. But to recognise the universal and the rational, it is necessary to use reason too. The objects are stimuli to thought; otherwise, we find that the world takes on an aspect corresponding to the way in which we look at it. Anyone who views the world purely subjectively will see it in terms of his own nature; he will know everything better than everyone else, and see how things ought to have been done and what course events ought to have taken. But the overall content of world history is rational, and indeed has to be rational; a divine will rules supreme and is strong enough to determine the overall content. Our aim must be to discern this substance, and to do so, we must bring with us a rational consciousness. Physical perception and a finite understanding are not enough; we must see with the eye of the concept, the eye of reason, which penetrates the surface and finds its way through the complex and confusing turmoil of events. Yet people say that this approach to history is an a priori procedure, and intrinsically wrong. Whether they do so or not is a matter of indifference to philosophy. In order to perceive the substance, we must apply our own reason to it. This does not mean, however, that one-sided reflections are admissible; for they distort history and arise out of mistaken subjective opinions. But philosophy is not concerned with these. Sure in the knowledge that reason governs history, philosophy is convinced that the events will match the concept; it does not pervert the truth after the fashion which is now prevalent – especially among the philologists, who employ their so-called acumen to introduce wholly a priori ideas into history.[9] Admittedly, philosophy does follow an a priori method in so far as it presupposes the Idea. But the Idea is undoubtedly there, and reason is fully convinced of its presence.

The perspective adopted by the philosophical history of the world is accordingly not just one among many general perspectives, an isolated abstraction singled out at the expense of the rest. Its spiritual principle is the sum total of all possible perspectives. It concentrates its attention on the concrete spiritual principle in the life of nations, and deals not with individual situations but with a universal thought which runs throughout the whole. This universal element is not to be found in the world of contingent phenomena; it is the unity behind the multitude of particulars. The object of history is the most concrete of all, for it comprehends every aspect of existence; the world spirit is its individuality. What philosophy is therefore concerned with in its treatment of history is the concrete object in its concrete form, and it traces the necessary development of this object. Thus the destinies, passions, and energies of nations are not its prime consideration, with the events following on in second place. On the contrary, its chief concern is the spirit of the events themselves, the moving spirit within them, for this is the true Mercury, the leader of nations. We must therefore not imagine that the universal object of the philosophical history of the world is only one aspect of history (no matter how important this aspect might be), with other alternative determinants existing independently of it. On the contrary, the universal object is infinitely concrete, all-comprehending and omnipresent, for the spirit is eternally present to itself; it has no past, and remains for ever the same in all its vigour and strength.

The understanding must always be brought to bear on history in order that we may comprehend the causes and effects at work in it. In this way, we try to discover what is essential in world history and to disregard what is inessential. The understanding brings out everything that is important and inherently significant. Its criteria of the essential and the inessential will vary according to the end it is pursuing in its examination of history, and the ends it sets itself can also vary enormously. Whenever a particular aim is chosen, further considerations at once present themselves, and we are compelled to distinguish between principal and secondary aims. Accordingly, when we are comparing the facts of history with the ends of the spirit, we will ignore everything which might otherwise be of interest and stick to essentials. Thus the historical content which presents itself to reason is not simply equivalent to the entire events of the past. Some ends are of essential interest to the intellect, and others to the emotions, so that we can be moved to sorrow, admiration, or joy when we read about them.

But it is not our business to discuss the various types of reflection, attitudes, and judgements, not even the ways of distinguishing the important from the unimportant (and these are the most obvious categories), or [of deciding what to emphasize most] in the unlimited material at our disposal.

[Nevertheless, we ought to give a brief account of the categories under which the historical process generally presents itself to thought.] The first category comes from our observation of the changing individuals, nations, and states which flourish for a while, capture our interest, and then disappear. This is the category of change.

We witness a vast spectacle of events and actions, of infinitely varied constellations of nations, states, and individuals, in restless succession. Everything that can occupy and interest the human mind, every sensation of the good, the beautiful and the great, comes into play; everywhere we see others pursuing aims which we ourselves affirm and whose fulfilment we desire, and we share their hopes and fears. In all these events and contingencies, our first concern is with the deeds and sufferings of men; we see elements of ourselves in everything, so that our sympathies constantly oscillate from one side to the other. Sometimes we are captivated by beauty, freedom, and riches, sometimes we are impressed by human energy, which can invest even vice with greatness. Sometimes we see the accumulated weight of a popular cause lose its impetus and finally disintegrate, to be sacrificed to an infinite complex of minor exigencies. Sometimes we see how a huge expenditure of effort can produce only a trifling result, or conversely, how an apparently insignificant thing can have momentous consequences. Everywhere we see a motley confusion which draws us into its interests, and when one thing disappears, another at once takes its place.

The negative aspect of the idea of change moves us to sadness. It oppresses us to think that the richest forms and the finest manifestations of life must perish in history, and that we walk amidst the ruins of excellence. History cuts us off from the finest and noblest of our interests: the passions have destroyed them, for they are transient. It seems that all must perish and that nothing endures. Every traveller has experienced this melancholy. Who has stood among the ruins of Carthage, Palmyra, Persepolis or Rome without being moved to reflect on the transience of empires and men, to mourn the loss of the rich and vigorous life of bygone ages? It is not a sorrow like that which we experience at the graves of those dear to us, when we lament our personal losses and the transience of our own aspirations; it is rather a disinterested sorrow at the downfall of the brilliant cultures of the past.

But the category of change has another, positive side to it. For out of death, new life arises. The Orientals have understood this idea; it is perhaps the greatest idea they have ever produced, and it is certainly the most sublime of their metaphysical doctrines. It is implicit, but with individual reference, in their notion of metempsychosis: but an even more celebrated example is the image of the Phoenix, of natural life, which for ever constructs its own funeral pyre and is for ever consumed upon it, only to rise again from the ashes as fresh and rejuvenated life. This, however, is only an image of the East; it applies to the body, but not to the spirit. Its Western counterpart is the realisation that the spirit too rises up again, not only rejuvenated but also enhanced and transfigured. Admittedly, it becomes divided against itself and destroys the form it earlier occupied, but in so doing, it rises up to a new stage of development. But when it abandons the shell of its former existence, it does not merely migrate into a new shell; it emerges as a purified spirit from the ashes of its earlier form. This is the second category of the spirit, the category of rejuvenation. The rejuvenation of the spirit is not just a return to an earlier shape; it is a purification or further elaboration of itself. The solution of its problem creates new problems for it to solve, so that it multiplies the materials on which it operates. Thus we see how the spirit in history issues forth in innumerable directions, indulging and satisfying itself in them all. But the only result of its labour is that its activity is once more increased, and it is again consumed. Each of the creations in which it found temporary satisfaction presents itself in turn as a new material, challenging the spirit to develop it further still. The forms it produced become the material on which it labours to raise itself up to new forms. It manifests all its powers in every possible way. We learn what powers it possesses from the very wealth of forms it produces. In this sheer delight in activity, it is entirely absorbed in itself. Nature admittedly imposes internal and external limitations on it, and these not only resist it and place obstacles in its path but can even cause it to fail completely in its endeavours. But even when it is frustrated, it remains true to its character as a spiritual being, a being whose end is not the finished product but the activity of production, so that it still affords the spectacle of having exhibited its active nature.

But the immediate result of these intriguing speculations is that we grow weary of particulars and ask ourselves to what end they all contribute. We cannot accept that their significance is exhausted in their own particular ends; everything must be part of a **single** enterprise. Surely some ultimate end must be promoted by this enormous expenditure of spiritual resources. We are compelled to ask whether, beneath the superficial din and clamour of history, there is not perhaps a silent and mysterious inner process at work, whereby the energy of all phenomena is conserved. What may well perplex us, however, is the great variety and even inconsistency of the content of history. We see complete opposites venerated as equally sacred, capturing the attention of different ages and nations. We feel the need to find a justification in the realm of ideas for all this destruction. This reflection leads us to the third category, to the question of whether there is such a thing as an ultimate end in and for itself. This is the category of reason proper; it is present in our consciousness as a belief that the world is governed by reason. Its proof is to be found in the study of world history itself, which is the image and enactment of reason.

I only wish to mention two points concerning[10] *the general conviction that reason has ruled and continues to rule the world*[11] *and hence also world history; for these should give us an opportunity to examine more closely the main difficulty which confronts us, and to touch provisionally on matters which will have to be discussed later.*

The first point is as follows. As history tells us, the Greek Anaxagoras was the first to declare that the world is governed by a 'nous', i.e. by reason or understanding in general. This does not signify an intelligence in the sense of a self-conscious reason or a spirit as such, and the two must not be confused. The movement of the solar system is governed by unalterable laws; these laws are its inherent reason. But neither the sun nor the planets which revolve around it in accordance with these laws are conscious of them. It is man who abstracts the laws from empirical reality and acquires knowledge of them. An idea of this kind, that there is reason in nature or that it is governed by unalterable general laws, does not strike us as in any way strange, and Anaxagoras had as yet applied it only to nature. We are accustomed to such ideas, and do not find them at all extraordinary. One of the reasons why I mentioned this historical fact at all was to show how we can learn from history that what may now seem trivial was once unknown to the world, and that such ideas were in fact of epoch-making significance in the history of the human spirit. Aristotle says of Anaxagoras, as the originator of this idea, that he stood out like a sober man in a company of drunkards.

This idea was taken over from Anaxagoras by Socrates, and it then became the ruling principle in philosophy – except in the case of Epicurus, who attributed everything to chance. We shall see in due course what other religions and nations came to accept it. Plato (Phaedo, Stephanus edition pp. 97–8) makes Socrates say of this discovery that thought (not conscious thought but thought of a nature as yet undefined, equivalent to neither conscious nor unconscious reason) governs the world: 'I was delighted with it and hoped I had at last discovered a teacher who would explain nature to me rationally, who would reveal the particular end of each particular phenomenon and also the ultimate end, the good, in nature as a whole. It was a hope which I was not at all eager to relinquish. But how very disappointed I was', Socrates continues, 'when I turned, full of anticipation, to the writings of Anaxagoras himself! I discovered that, instead of reason, he dealt only with external causes such as air, ether, water, and the like.' It is evident from this that what Socrates took exception to was not Anaxagoras' principle as such, but his failure to apply it adequately to concrete nature, and to interpret nature in the light of the principle; for this principle was never anything more than an abstraction, or more precisely, nature was not presented as a development of the principle, as an organisation produced by it, with reason as its cause.

34

I wish, from the outset, to emphasise this distinction between a definition, principle, or truth which remains abstract, and one whose specific determination and concrete development are also explained. This distinction is to be found throughout our subject, and one of the principal occasions on which we shall encounter it will be at the end of our survey of world history when we come to examine the political situation in recent times.

Another of the main reasons why I have cited this earliest[12] instance of the idea that reason rules the world and discussed its inadequacy[13] is because it has also been applied more fully to another subject with which we are all familiar[14] and of whose truth we are personally convinced – I refer, of course, to the religious truth that the world is not a prey to chance and external, contingent causes, but is governed by providence. I declared earlier that I did not wish to make any demands on your faith in the above-mentioned principle. I might, however, have appealed to your faith in it in this religious form, if it were not that the peculiar nature of philosophy forbids us to attach authority to prior assumptions; or, to put it differently, I cannot do so, because the discipline we are studying must itself furnish the proof of the principle's correctness (if not of its actual truth), and display its concrete reality. The truth, then, that the world's events are controlled by a providence, indeed by divine providence, is consistent with the principle in question. For divine providence is wisdom, coupled with infinite power, which realises its ends, i.e. the absolute and rational design of the world; and reason is freely self-determining thought, or what the Greeks called 'nous'.

But[15] there is also a difference, indeed a contradiction, between this faith in providence and our original principle, a difference akin to that between the principle of Anaxagoras and the expectations with which Socrates approached it. For this general faith in providence is likewise indeterminate, and lacks a determinate application to the whole, to the entire course of world events. [Instead of giving it this] application [men are content] to explain history [by natural causes. They confine themselves to] human passions, the relative strengths of armies, the abilities and genius of this or that individual, or the lack of such an individual in a given state – in short, to so-called natural causes of a purely contingent nature, such as Socrates [criticised in the work of Anaxagoras. They conceive of providence as an] abstraction [and] make do with a general idea of it [without discussing its determinate application]. The determinate aspects of providence, the specific actions it performs, constitute the providential plan (i.e. the end and means of its destiny and aims). But this plan is supposed to be hidden from our view, and we are told that it is presumptuous to try to comprehend it. The ignorance of Anaxagoras

35

as to how understanding manifests itself in reality was unfeigned; the development of thought, and man's awareness of its development, had not progressed beyond this point either in him or in Greece as a whole. He was as yet unable to apply his general principle to concrete reality, or to interpret reality in terms of the principle. It was Socrates who took the first step towards finding a means of combining the concrete with the universal, if only in a subjective and one-sided way; thus his polemics were not directed against concrete applications of the principle. But those who believe in providence are hostile to all attempts to apply the idea on a large scale, i.e. to any attempts to comprehend the providential plan. No-one objects to it being applied in isolated cases, and pious souls discern in numerous particular occurrences, where others see only the agency of chance, not just dispensations of God himself, but of divine providence – i.e. the ends which providence pursues by means of such dispensations. But this usually happens only in isolated instances; and when, for example, an individual in great perplexity and distress receives unexpected help, we must not hold it against him if his gratitude at once leads him to see the hand of God at work. But the design of providence in such cases is of a limited nature; its content is merely the particular end of the individual in question. In world history, however, the individuals we are concerned with are nations, totalities, states. We cannot, therefore, be content with this (if the word be permitted) trivial faith in providence, nor indeed with a merely abstract and indeterminate faith which conceives in general terms of a ruling providence but refuses to apply it to determinate reality; on the contrary, we must tackle the problem seriously. The concrete events are the ways of providence, the means it uses, the phenomena in which it manifests itself in history; they are open to our inspection, and we only have to relate them to the general principle referred to above.

But in mentioning the possibility of comprehending the plan of divine providence, I have touched on a question which is of central importance today: I mean the question of whether it is possible to obtain knowledge of God – or rather, since it has ceased to be a question – the doctrine, now hardened into a prejudice, that it is impossible to know God, notwithstanding the teaching of the Scriptures that it is our highest duty not only to love God but also to know him. This prejudice goes against the Scriptural saying that the spirit leads into truth, searches all things, and penetrates even into the deep things of God.*

Simple faith can well dispense with a fuller understanding of history and make do with the general notion of a divine world order; and we

---

* Cf. 1 Corinthians 2, 10.

ought not to condemn those who take this course, so long as their faith does not become a polemical one. But it is also possible to defend such views in a spirit of prejudice, and the general proposition, by virtue of its very generality, can also be given a specifically negative application, so as to suggest that the divine being is remote from all human things and transcends human knowledge. Those who adopt this attitude reserve the right to dismiss the claims of truth and rationality, with the added advantage of being able to indulge their own fancies at will. Seen from this point of view, all ideas of God are reduced to empty talk. If God is placed beyond the reach of our rational consciousness, we are no longer obliged to trouble ourselves about his nature, or indeed to look for reason in world history; the way is then open for any arbitrary hypotheses. Pious humility knows very well what it stands to gain from its sacrifices.

I could have refrained from mentioning that our principle (i.e. that reason governs the world and always has done so) has a religious equivalent in the doctrine of a ruling providence; this would have allowed me to avoid the question of whether it is possible to obtain knowledge of God. But I did not wish to do so, partly in order to bring out some further implications of these questions, and partly also to allay any suspicions that philosophy has or should have any cause to fear discussing religious truths, or that it circumvents them because it does not, so to speak, have an easy conscience about them. On the contrary, we have recently reached the point where philosophy has had to defend the content of religion against certain kinds of theology.

As I have said, we are often told that it is presumptuous to try to fathom the plan of providence. This is a direct consequence of the idea (which has now become an almost universally accepted axiom) that it is impossible to obtain knowledge of God. And when theology itself is in so desperate a position, we must take refuge in philosophy if we wish to learn anything about God. Certainly, reason is often accused of arrogance in presuming to attain such knowledge. But it would be more accurate to say that true humility consists precisely in recognising and revering God in everything, especially in the theatre of world history. Furthermore, the traditional view that God's wisdom is manifest in nature has not yet been altogether abandoned. It was indeed fashionable at one time to admire the wisdom of God as manifested in animals and plants. But to marvel at human destinies or products of nature is already an indication that we have some knowledge of God. If we admit that providence reveals itself in such objects and materials, why should we not do the same in world history? Is it because history seems too vast a subject? It is certainly customary to conceive of providence as taking a hand only in minor matters, to picture it as a wealthy benefactor who distributes alms among men and furthers their ends. But it is a mistake to think that the material of world history is too vast for providence to cope with; for the divine wisdom is one and the same in great things and in small. It is the same in plants and insects as in the destinies of entire nations and empires, and we must not imagine that God is not powerful enough to apply his wisdom to things of great moment. To believe that God's wisdom is not active in everything is to show humility towards the material rather than towards the divine wisdom itself. Besides, nature is a theatre of secondary importance compared with that of world history. Nature is a field in which the divine Idea operates in a non-conceptual medium; the spiritual sphere is its proper province, and it is here above all that it ought to be visible. Armed with the concept of reason, we need not fear coming to grips with any subject whatsoever.

The contention that we should not attempt to know God in fact requires closer examination than is possible within the scope of these lectures. But since this matter has so close a bearing upon our present aim, it is essential that we should consider at least the general perspectives involved. Thus if knowledge of God is impossible, the only thing left for the mind to occupy itself with is the non-divine, the limited, the finite. Of course it is necessary for man to occupy himself with finite things; but there is also a higher necessity which requires that there should be a sabbath in his existence, a time when he can rise above his daily labours to occupy his mind consciously with truth.

If the name of God is to be more than an empty word, we must consider God as benevolent, or at least as in some way communicative. In the earlier phases of Greek thought, God was seen as subject to envy, and there was much talk of the envy of the gods; it was said that the divinity is hostile to greatness, and that it is the mission of the gods to humble the great. Aristotle says, however, that poets are much given to lying, for envy cannot be an attribute of God. And if we were to maintain in turn that God does not reveal himself at all, this would amount to an allegation that he is envious. But God cannot lose anything by communication any more than a light can be diminished when a second one is lit from it.

It is often said that God does reveal himself, but only in nature on the one hand, and in the heart, in the feelings of men, on the other. We are usually told nowadays that this is the point at which we must draw a halt, for God is present only to our immediate consciousness or intuition. Intuition and emotion, however, are both unreflecting forms of consciousness, and we must insist in reply to such arguments that man is a thinking being, for it is thought which distinguishes him from the animals. He behaves as a thinking being even when he is himself unaware of it. When God reveals himself to man, he reveals himself essentially through man's rational faculties; if he revealed himself essentially through the emotions, this would imply that he regarded man as no better than the animals, who do not possess the power of reflection – yet we do not attribute religion to the animals. In fact, man only possesses religion because he is not an animal but a thinking being. It is a trivial commonplace that man is distinguished from the animals by his ability to think, yet this is something which is often forgotten.

God is the eternal being in and for himself; and the universal in and for itself is an object of thought, not of feeling. It is true that all spiritual things, all data of the consciousness, all products and objects of thought – and above all religion and morality – must also come to us through the medium of feeling, and indeed primarily through this medium. Feeling, however, is not the source from which they are derived, but only the form which they assume in man; and it is the basest form they can assume, a form which man shares in common with the animals. All substantial things must be able to assume the form of emotion, yet they can also assume a higher and worthier form. But to insist on translating all morality and truth and every spiritual substance into feeling, and to endeavour to preserve them in this form is tantamount to saying that their proper form is the animal one – although the latter is in fact incapable of comprehending their spiritual content. Feeling is the lowest form which any such content can assume, for its presence in feeling can only be minimal. So long as it retains this form, it remains inchoate and completely indeterminate. The content of our feelings remains entirely subjective, and is only subjectively present to us. To say 'I feel such and such' is to shut oneself up within oneself. Everyone else is equally entitled to say 'But I feel differently', and then all common ground is lost. In purely particular matters, feelings are perfectly justified. But to maintain that a given content is present in the feelings of everyone is to contradict the emotional point of view one has adopted, the point of view of personal subjectivity. As soon as the emotions have a content, everyone is placed in a position of subjectivity. And if one person should choose to say unpleasant things about another who has acted only on his feelings, the second is entitled to say the same of the first, and both would be equally justified – from their own point of view – in taking offence. If one man says that he has religious emotions, and another says that he cannot feel God, they are both right. If the divine content – i.e. the revelation of God, the relationship between man and God, and the being of God for mankind – is reduced in this way to mere emotion, it is thereby confined to the level of individual subjectivity, of arbitrariness, of random inclinations. In fact, this has been a convenient way of getting round the problem of the truth which exists in and for itself. If I rely only on my emotions, which are indeterminate, and have no knowledge of God and his nature, I have nothing to guide me except random inclinations; the finite alone has validity and is the dominant power. And if I know nothing whatsoever of God, there can be no serious talk about the limits of such knowledge either.

The truth is inherently universal, essential, and substantial; and as such, it exists solely in thought and for thought. But that spiritual principle which we call God is none other than the truly substantial, inherently and essentially individual and subjective truth. It is the source of all thought, and its thought is inherently creative; we encounter it as such in world history. Whatever else we describe as true is merely a particular form of this eternal truth, which is its sole foundation; it is but a single ray of the universal light. If we know nothing of this truth, we must remain ignorant of all truth, rightness, and morality.

But what, we may ask, is the plan of providence in world history? Has the time come for us to understand it? [*I shall confine myself for the present to*] *the following general remarks.*

God has revealed himself through the Christian religion; that is, he has granted mankind the possibility of recognising his nature, so that he is no longer an impenetrable mystery. The fact that knowledge of God is possible also makes it our duty to know him, and that development of the thinking spirit which the Christian revelation of God initiated must eventually produce a situation where all that was at first present only to the emotional and representational faculties can also be comprehended by thought. Whether the time has yet come for such knowledge will depend on whether the ultimate end of the world has yet been realised in a universally valid and conscious manner.[16]

Now the distinctive feature of Christianity is that, with its advent, this time has indeed come. Its significance for the history of the world is therefore absolutely epoch-making, for the nature of God has at last been made manifest. If we say that we know nothing of God, Christianity becomes something superfluous, a belated arrival, or even a symptom of decay. But this is not the case, for Christianity does give us knowledge of God. Its content, admittedly, appeals to our emotions too. But since the feeling it evokes is a spiritual one, it at least brings into play the faculty of representation – and not just sensory representation either, but also representational thought, the true medium through which man perceives God. Christianity is the religion which has revealed the nature and being of God to man. Thus we know as Christians what God is; God is no longer an unknown quantity: and if we continue to say that he is, we are not Christians. Christianity demands that humility to which we have already referred, a humility which makes us seek to know God not through our own unaided efforts but with the help of divine knowledge and wisdom. Christians, then, are initiated into the mysteries of God, and this also supplies us with the key to world history. For we have here a definite knowledge of providence and its plan. It is one of the central doctrines of Christianity that providence has ruled and continues to rule the world, and that everything which happens in the world is determined by and commensurate with the divine government. This doctrine is opposed both to the idea of chance and to that of limited ends (such as the preservation of the Jewish people). Its end is the ultimate and absolutely universal end which exists in and for itself. Religion does not go beyond this general representation; it remains on the level of generality. But we must proceed from this general faith firstly to philosophy and then to the philosophy of world history – from the faith that world history is a product of eternal reason, and that it is reason which has determined all its great revolutions.

We can therefore conclude that, even in the absolute sense, the time has come in which this conviction and inner certainty need no longer remain a mere representation, but can also be thought, developed, and recognised as a definite piece of knowledge. The original faith makes no attempt to elaborate its content further or to gain any insight into historical necessity – for only knowledge can do that. The fact that the spirit never stands still guarantees that such a time must eventually come; the culminating phase of the spirit – thought or the concept – insists on its rights, and it alone, in its most general and essential being, constitutes the true nature of the spirit.

A distinction is often made between faith and knowledge, and the two have come to be commonly accepted as opposites. It is taken for granted that they are different, and that we therefore have no knowledge of God. People are affronted if we tell them that we seek to know and understand God, and to impart such knowledge to others. But if it is defined correctly, the distinction between faith and knowledge is in fact an empty one. For if I have faith in something, I also know it and am convinced of it. In religion, we have faith in God and in the doctrines which explain his nature more fully; but this is something we know and of which we are certain. To know means to have something as an object of one's consciousness and to be certain of it; and it is exactly the same with faith. Cognition, however, perceives that the content of knowledge – and indeed of faith – is necessary, and discerns the reasons behind it; it does so without reference to the authority of the Church or of feeling, which is something immediate, and goes on to analyse this content into its various determinate elements. These determinate elements must first become objects of thought before we can obtain a true cognition of them and perceive them in their concrete unity within the concept. And if there is any further suggestion that it is presumptuous to seek such cognition, we might then reply that all this fuss is unnecessary, since cognition merely takes note of necessity and watches the inner development of the content unfold before its eyes. As a further reason why such cognition cannot be branded as presumptuous, one might also maintain that it differs from faith only in its greater knowledge of particulars. But this argument would be misplaced, and indeed inherently false. For the spiritual is not by nature abstract, but a living thing, a universal individual, a subjective, self-determining, decision-making being. We cannot therefore truly know the nature of God unless we recognise its determinate elements. Christianity too speaks of God in this way, for it recognises him as a spirit, and this spirit is not an abstraction, but the process in itself; and this in turn presupposes the existence of absolute distinctions – in fact, the very distinctions which Christianity has made known to mankind.

God does not wish to have narrow-minded and empty-headed children. On the contrary, he demands that we should know him; he wishes his children to be poor in spirit but rich in knowledge of him, and to set the highest value on acquiring knowledge of God. History is the unfolding of God's nature in a particular, determinate element, so that only a determinate form of knowledge is possible and appropriate to it.

The time has now surely come for us to comprehend even so rich a product of creative reason as world history. The aim of human cognition is to understand that the intentions of eternal wisdom are accomplished not only in the natural world, but also in the realm of the [spirit] which is actively present in the world. From this point of view, our investigation can be seen as a theodicy, a justification of the ways of God (such as Leibniz attempted in his own metaphysical manner, but using categories which were as yet abstract and indeterminate). It should enable us to comprehend all the ills of the world, including the existence of evil, so that the thinking spirit may be reconciled with the negative aspects of existence; and it is in world history that we encounter the sum total of concrete evil. (Indeed, there is no department of knowledge in which such a reconciliation is more urgently required than in world history, and we shall accordingly pause for a moment to consider this question further.)

A reconciliation of the kind just described can only be achieved through a knowledge of the affirmative side of history, in which the negative is reduced to a subordinate position and transcended altogether. In other words, we must first of all know what the ultimate design of the world really is, and secondly, we must see that this design has been realised and that evil has not been able to maintain a position of equality beside it.

In order to justify the course of history, we must try to understand the role of evil in the light of the absolute sovereignty of reason. We are dealing here with the category of the negative, as already mentioned, and we cannot fail to notice how all that is finest and noblest in the history of the world is immolated upon its altar.[17] Reason cannot stop to consider the injuries sustained by single individuals, for particular ends are submerged in the universal end. In the rise and fall of all things it discerns an enterprise at which the entire human race has laboured, an enterprise which has a real existence in the world to which we belong. Phenomena have become real independently of our efforts, and all that we need to understand them is consciousness, or more precisely, a thinking consciousness. For the affirmative element is not to be found merely in emotional enjoyment or in the imagination, but is something which belongs to reality and to us, or to which we ourselves belong.

Reason, it has been said, rules the world. But 'reason' is just as indefinite a word as 'providence'. People continually speak of reason, without being able to define it correctly, to specify its content, or to supply a criterion by which we might judge whether something is rational or irrational. Reason in its determinate form is the true substance; and the rest – if we confine ourselves to reason in general – is mere words. With this information* before us, we may proceed to the second point which, as earlier remarked, has to be considered in this introduction.

* The text reads *Ausgabe* ('edition', 'emission' or 'expense'). It seems much more likely that the word Hegel intended was either *Aufgabe* ('task', 'problem') or *Angabe* ('indication', 'information'). Lasson's edition of the text (third edition, Philosophische Bibliothek, 1930) in fact gives the reading *Angabe*, which Hoffmeister appears to have altered in favour of the unintelligible *Ausgabe*.

B

[The realisation of spirit in history]

To try to define reason in itself – if we consider reason[18] in relation to the world – amounts to asking what the ultimate end of the world is; and we cannot speak of an ultimate end without implying that this end is destined to be accomplished or realised. We therefore have two points to consider: firstly, the content of the ultimate end itself – i.e. its definition as such – and secondly, its realisation.

We must first of all note that the object we have before us, i.e. world history, belongs to the realm of the spirit. The world as a whole comprehends both physical and spiritual nature. Physical nature also plays a part in world history, and we shall certainly include some initial remarks on the basic outlines of this natural influence. But the spirit and the course of its development are the true substance of history. We do not have to consider nature here as a rational system in its own right – although it is indeed a rational system, operating in its own distinct element – but only in relation to spirit.[19]

After the creation of the natural universe, man appears on the scene as the antithesis of nature; he is the being who raises himself up into a second world. The general consciousness of man includes two distinct provinces, that of nature and that of the spirit. The province of the spirit is created by man himself; and whatever ideas we may form of the kingdom of God, it must always remain a spiritual kingdom which is realised in man and which man is expected to translate into actuality.

The spiritual sphere is all-embracing; it encompasses everything that has concerned mankind down to the present day. Man is active within it; and whatever he does, the spirit is also active within him. Thus it may be of interest to examine spiritual nature in its real existence – that is, spirit in combination with nature, or human nature itself. The expression 'human nature' is usually taken to represent something fixed and constant. Descriptions of human nature are meant to apply to all men, past and present. The general pattern is capable of infinite modifications, but, however much it may vary, it nevertheless remains essentially the same. Reflective thought must disregard the differences and isolate the common factor which can be expected to behave in the same way and to show itself in the same light under all circumstances. It is possible to detect the general type even in those examples which seem to diverge most widely from it, and we can recognise human nature even in the most distorted of forms.

44

We can derive a kind of comfort and reassurance from the knowledge that such forms still retain a vestige of humanity. Those who look at history from this point of view will tend to emphasise that men are still the same as they always were, and that vices and virtues have remained constant despite changing circumstances. One might fittingly add with Solomon that there is nothing new under the sun.*

For example, if we see someone kneeling in prayer before an idol, and the content of his prayer is contemptible in the eyes of reason, we can still respect the feelings which animate it and acknowledge that they are just as valuable as those of the Christian who worships truth in symbolic form, or of the philosopher who immerses himself in eternal truth through rational thought. Only the objects of such feelings are different; but the feelings themselves are one and the same. If we call to mind the history of the Assassins, and their relationship with their ruler, the Old Man of the Mountains, we find that they sacrificed themselves for him in order to perpetrate his crimes. In a subjective sense, this sacrifice is no different from that of Curtius, who leaped into the abyss to save his fatherland. Once we have accepted this, we might even say that there is no need to refer to the great theatre of world history at all. According to the well known anecdote, Caesar found in a small municipality the same ambitions and activities he had encountered in the wider context of Rome. The same motives and aspirations can be found in a small town as in the great theatre of world events. It is obvious that this way of looking at history abstracts from the content and aims of human activity. Such sovereign disregard of the objective situation is particularly common among French and English writers, who describe their works as 'philosophical history'. Nevertheless, no fully formed intellect can fail to distinguish between impulses and inclinations which operate in a restricted sphere and those which are active in the conflict of interests of world history. This objective interest, which affects us both through the general design and through the individual who implements it, is what makes history attractive. Such designs and individuals are the ones whose downfall and destruction we most lament. When we contemplate the struggle of the Greeks against the Persians, or the momentous reign of Alexander, we are fully aware of where our interests lie: we wish to see the Greeks liberated from the barbarians, and feel concern for the preservation of the Greek state and for the ruler who subjugated Asia at the head of a Greek army. Let us imagine for a moment how we would feel if Alexander had failed in his

* Cf. Ecclesiastes 1, 9.

45

enterprise. We would certainly have no sense of loss if we were interested only in human passions, for we would still not have been denied the spectacle of passions in action. But this would not have satisfied us: for we are interested in the material itself, in the objective situation.

But what, we may ask, is the nature of the substantial end in which the spirit acquires its essential content? Our interest is of a substantial and determinate kind, and its object is some determinate religion, knowledge, or art. But how does the spirit acquire such a content, and where does this content come from? The empirical answer is simple. Each individual, at any given moment, finds himself committed to some essential interest of this kind; he exists in a particular country with a particular religion, and in a particular constellation of knowledge and attitudes concerning what is right and ethically acceptable. All that is left for him to do is to select particular aspects of it with which he wishes to identify himself. But when we realise that whole nations are occupied with such objects and immersed in such interests, we are once again faced with the problem of world history, whose content we are trying to define. The empirical approach is not adequate for our purposes, and we must pass on to the more specific question of how the spirit – i.e. the spirit as such, whether it is present in ourselves, in other individuals, or in nations as a whole – acquires such a content. We must define the content solely in terms of specific concepts. What has been discussed hitherto is part of our ordinary consciousness. But the concept to which we now turn is of a completely different order (although this is not the place for us to analyse it systematically). Philosophy is by no means ignorant of the popular conception, but has its own reasons for departing from it.

Our business here is to consider world history in relation to its ultimate end; this ultimate end is the intention which underlies the world. We know that God is the most perfect being; he is therefore able to will only himself and that which is of the same nature as himself. God and the nature of the divine will are one and the same thing; it is what we call in philosophy the Idea. Thus it is the Idea in general which we have to consider, and particularly its operation within the medium of the human spirit; in more specific terms, it is the Idea of human freedom. The Idea reveals itself in its purest form in thought, and it is from this angle that logic approaches it. It expresses itself in another form in physical nature, and the third form which it assumes is that of spirit in the absolute sense.

But in the theatre in which we are about to witness its operations – i.e. the theatre of world history – the spirit attains its most concrete reality.

46

Despite this – or rather precisely so that we may comprehend the general characteristics of the spirit in its concrete reality – we must begin with a few abstract definitions of its nature. I must also point out that these remarks cannot claim to be anything more than simple assertions, for this is not the time or place for a speculative exposition of the Idea of the spirit. It is more important that these deliberations should be presented in such a way as to suit the level of education and outlook which can be expected among the present audience. For anything that is said in an introduction should, as already remarked, be seen as purely historical, as a provisional assumption which has either been explained and demonstrated elsewhere, or which will at least be confirmed at a later stage in the course of the treatise itself.

a. [The determination* of spirit]

The first thing we must do is to define the abstract determination of spirit.[20] *It must, however, be pointed out* that the spirit is not in itself abstract, for it is not an abstraction invented by man; on the contrary, it is entirely individual, active, and absolutely alive: it is consciousness, but it is also the object of consciousness – for it is in the nature of the spirit to have itself as its object. The spirit, then, is capable of thought, and its thought is that of a being which itself exists, and which thinks that it exists and how it exists. It possesses knowledge: but knowledge is consciousness of a rational object. Besides, the spirit only has consciousness in so far as it is conscious of itself; in other words, I only know an object in so far as I know myself and my own determination through it, for whatever I am is also an object of my consciousness, and I am not just this, that or the other, but only what I know myself to be. I know my object, and I know myself; the two are inseparable. Thus the spirit forms a definite conception of itself and of its essential nature. It can only have a spiritual content; and its sole content and interest are spiritual. This, then, is how the spirit acquires a content: it does not find its content outside itself, but makes itself its own object and its own content. Knowledge is its form and function, but its content is the spiritual itself. Thus the spirit is by nature self-sufficient or free.

The nature of spirit can best be understood if we contrast it with its direct opposite, which is matter. Just as gravity is the substance of matter, so also can it be said that freedom is the substance of spirit. It is immediately obvious to everyone that freedom is one of the various attributes of spirit; but philosophy teaches us that all the attributes of spirit exist

---

* *Bestimmung.* As already remarked, this word also has associations akin to those of the English term 'destiny'. Cf. note to p. 11 above.

only by virtue of freedom, that all are merely means of attaining freedom, and that the sole object which they all seek and to whose realisation they all contribute is freedom. Speculative philosophy has shown that freedom is the one authentic property of spirit. Matter possesses gravity in so far as it is impelled to move towards a central point; it is essentially composite, and consists entirely of discrete parts which all tend towards a centre; thus matter has no unity. It is made up of separate elements and aspires to a condition of unity; it thus endeavours to overcome itself and seeks its own opposite. If it were to succeed, it would no longer be matter, but would have ceased to exist as such; it strives towards ideality, for unity is its ideal existence. Spirit, on the other hand, is such that its centre is within itself; it too strives towards its centre, but it has its centre within itself. Its unity is not something external; it always finds it within itself, and exists in itself and with itself. Matter has its substance outside itself; spirit, on the other hand, is self-sufficient being,* which is the same thing as freedom. For if I am dependent, I am beholden to something other than myself, and cannot exist without this external point of reference. If, however, I am self-sufficient, I am also free.

When the spirit strives towards its centre, it strives to perfect its own freedom; and this striving is fundamental to its nature. To say that spirit exists would at first seem to imply that it is a completed entity. On the contrary, it is by nature active, and activity is its essence; it is its own product, and is therefore its own beginning and its own end. Its freedom does not consist in static being, but in a constant negation of all that threatens to destroy† freedom. The business of spirit is to produce itself, to make itself its own object, and to gain knowledge of itself; in this way, it exists for itself. Natural objects do not exist for themselves; for this reason, they are not free. The spirit produces and realises itself in the light of its knowledge of itself; it acts in such a way that all its knowledge of itself is also realised. Thus everything depends on the spirit's self-awareness; if the spirit knows that it is free, it is altogether different from what it would be without this knowledge. For if it does not know that it is free, it is in the position of a slave who is content with his slavery and does not know that his condition is an improper one. It is the sensation of freedom alone which makes the spirit free, although it is in fact always free in and for itself.

The most immediate knowledge spirit can have of itself when it assumes the shape of a human individual is that it is capable of feeling. It does

---

* *Beisichselbstein*, which can also mean 'the state of being conscious'.
† *aufheben.*

not as yet have an object, and the individual simply feels himself determined in some particular way. He then tries to distinguish between
himself and this determinate quality, and sets about creating an internal
division within himself. Thus, my feelings are split up into an external
and an internal world. My determinate nature thereby enters a new phase,
in that I have a feeling of deficiency or negativity; I encounter a contradiction within myself which threatens to destroy me. But I nevertheless
exist; this much I know, and I balance this knowledge against my
feeling of negation or deficiency. I survive and seek to overcome* the
deficiency, so that I am at the same time an **impulse**. The object towards
which my impulse is directed is accordingly the means by which I can
attain satisfaction and the restoration of my unity. All living things are
endowed with impulses. We are therefore natural beings, and all our
impulses are of a sensuous character. Objects, in so far as I am drawn to
them by impulse, are means of integration, and this is the entire basis of
theory and practice alike. But in our intuitions† of the objects to which
our impulses are drawn, we are dealing directly with externals and
are ourselves external. Our intuitions are discrete units of a sensuous
nature, and so also are our impulses, irrespective of their content. By
this definition, man would be no different from the animals; for impulses
are not conscious of themselves. But man has knowledge of himself, and
this distinguishes him from the animals. He is a **thinking** being. Thought,
however, is knowledge of universals, and it simplifies the content of
experience, so that man too is simplified by it so as to become something
inward and ideal. Or, to be more precise, this inwardness and simplicity
is inherent in man, and the content of our experience only becomes
universal and ideal if we proceed to simplify it.

What man is in reality, he must also be in ideality. Since he possesses
ideal knowledge of reality, he ceases to be merely a natural being at the
mercy of immediate intuitions and impulses which he must satisfy and
perpetuate. This knowledge leads him to control his impulses; he places the
ideal, the realm of thought, between the demands of the impulse and their
satisfaction. In the animal, the two coincide; it cannot sever their
connection by its own efforts – only pain or fear can do so. In man, the
impulse is present before it is satisfied and independently of its satisfaction; in controlling or giving rein to his impulses, man acts in accordance with ends and determines himself in the light of a general principle.
It is up to him to decide what end to follow; he can even make his end a
completely universal one. In so doing, he is determined by whatever

* *aufzuheben.*   † *Anschauungen.*

49

conceptions he has formed of his own nature and volitions. It is this which constitutes man's independence: for he knows what it is that determines him. Thus he can take a simple concept as his end – for example, that of his own positive freedom. The conceptions of the animal are not ideal and have no true reality; it therefore lacks this inner independence. As a living creature, the animal too has its source of movement within itself. But it can only respond to those external stimuli to which it is already inwardly susceptible; anything that does not match its inner being simply does not exist for it. The animal is divided from itself and within itself. It cannot interpose anything between its impulse and the satisfaction of its impulse; it has no will, and cannot even attempt to control itself. Its activating impulses come from within itself, and their operation presupposes that they contain the means of their own fulfilment. Man, however, is not independent because he is the initiator of his own movement, but because he can restrain this movement and thereby master his spontaneity and natural constitution.

The fundamental characteristic of human nature is that man can think of himself as an ego. As a spirit, man does not have an immediate existence but is essentially turned in upon himself. This function of mediation is an essential moment of the spirit. Its activity consists in transcending and negating its immediate existence so as to turn in again upon itself; it has therefore made itself what it is by means of its own activity. Only if it is turned in upon itself can a subject have true reality. Spirit exists only as its own product. The example of the seed may help to illustrate this point. The plant begins with the seed, but the seed is also the product of the plant's entire life, for it develops only in order to produce the seed. We can see from this how impotent life is, for the seed is both the origin and the product of the individual; as the starting point and the end result, it is different and yet the same, the product of one individual and the beginning of another. Its two sides fall asunder like the simple form within the grain and the whole course of the plant's development.

Every individual has an example even closer to hand in the shape of his own person. Man can only fulfil himself through education and discipline; his immediate existence contains merely the possibility of self-realisation (i.e. of becoming rational and free) and simply imposes on him a vocation and obligation which he must himself fulfil. The animal's education is soon complete; but this should not be seen as a blessing bestowed on the animal by nature. Its growth is merely a quantitative increase in strength. Man, on the other hand, must realise his potential through his own efforts, and must first acquire everything for himself, precisely because he is a spiritual being; in short, he must throw off all that is natural in him. Spirit, therefore, is the product of itself.

The most sublime example is to be found in the nature of God himself; strictly speaking, this is not a genuine example in the sense of one casual instance* among others, but rather the universal truth itself, of which all other things are examples. It is true that the older religions also referred to God as a spirit; but this was no more than a name which could as yet contribute nothing towards explaining the nature of spirit. In the Jewish religion too, the spirit was at first conceived only in general terms. Christianity, however, contains a revelation of God's spiritual nature. In the first place, he is the Father, a power which is universal but as yet enclosed within itself. Secondly, he is his own object, another version of himself, dividing himself into two so as to produce the Son. But this other version is just as immediate an expression of him as he is himself; he knows himself and contemplates himself in it – and it is this self-knowledge and self-contemplation which constitutes the third element, the Spirit as such. In other words, the Spirit is the whole, and not just one or other of the elements in isolation. Or, to put it in terms of feeling, God is eternal love, whose nature is to treat the other as its own. It is this doctrine of the Trinity which raises Christianity above the other religions. If it did not have this doctrine, the other religions might well provide more material for thought than it does. The Trinity is the speculative part of Christianity, and it is through it that philosophy can discover the Idea of reason in the Christian religion too.

The essence of spirit, then, is self-consciousness. Let us now proceed to examine it more closely, and not just as it expresses itself in the individual human being. The spirit is essentially individual, but in the field of world history, we are not concerned with particulars and need not confine ourselves to individual instances or attempt to trace everything back to them. The spirit in history is an individual which is both universal in nature and at the same time determinate: in short, it is the nation in general, and the spirit we are concerned with is the spirit of the nation. But the spirits of nations differ in their own conceptions of themselves, in the relative superficiality or profundity with which they have comprehended and penetrated the nature of spirit. The right which governs the ethical existence of nations is the spirit's consciousness of itself; the nations are the concepts which the spirit has formed of itself. Thus it is the conception of the spirit which is realised in history. The

---

* The term Hegel uses here is *Bei-her-spiel*, a compound constructed by himself out of *beiher* (adverb, 'on the side', 'alongside') and *Beispiel* ('example').

national consciousness varies according to the extent to which the spirit knows itself; and the ultimate phase of its consciousness, on which everything depends, is the recognition that man is free. The spirit's own consciousness must realise itself in the world; the material or soil in which it is realised is none other than the general consciousness, the consciousness of the nation. This consciousness encompasses and guides all the aims and interests of the nation, and it is on it that the nation's rights, customs, and religion depend. It is the substance which underlies the spirit of the nation, even if individual human beings are unaware of it and simply take its existence for granted. It is a form of necessity, for the individual is brought up within its atmosphere and does not know anything else. But it is not to be identified with education or with the results of education; for this consciousness emanates from the individual himself and is not instilled into him by others: the individual **exists** within this substance. This universal substance is not of a worldly nature and no worldly agency can successfully oppose it. No individual can transcend it, and although the individual may be able to distinguish between himself and others of his kind, he can make no such distinction between himself and the spirit of the nation. He may surpass many others in resourcefulness, but he cannot surpass the spirit of the nation. Only those who know the spirit of the nation and shape their actions in accordance with it can be described as truly resourceful.* They are the great ones of the nation; they lead it in accordance with the dictates of the universal spirit. Thus, individuality falls outside our province, except in the case of those individuals who translate the will of the national spirit into reality. If we wish to treat history philosophically, we must avoid such expressions as 'this state would not have collapsed if there had been someone who...' etc. Individuals fade into insignificance beside the universal substance, and it creates for itself the individuals it requires to carry out its ends. But no individuals can prevent the preordained from happening.

On the one hand, the spirit of the nation is in essence particular, yet on the other, it is identical with the absolute universal spirit – for the latter is One. The **world spirit** is the spirit of the world as it reveals itself through the human consciousness; the relationship of men to it is that of single parts to the whole which is their substance. And this world spirit corresponds to the divine spirit, which is the absolute spirit. Since God is omnipresent, he is present in everyone and appears in everyone's

---

* Hegel's term is *geistreich* (literally, 'rich in spirit'). It is impossible to reproduce in English the relationship between *geistreich* and *Geist* ('spirit') which Hegel is here exploiting.

consciousness; and this is the world spirit. The particular spirit of a particular nation may perish; but it is a link in the chain of the world spirit's development, and this universal spirit cannot perish. The spirit of the nation is therefore the universal spirit in a particular form; the world spirit transcends this particular form, but it must assume it in so far as it exists, for it takes on a particular aspect as soon as it has actual being or existence. The particular character of the national spirit varies according to the kind of awareness of spirit it has attained. In everyday parlance, we say: 'This nation had such and such a conception of God, such and such a religion or system of justice, and such and such views on ethics.' We treat all these things as if they were external objects which a nation had in its possession. But we can tell even at a superficial glance that they are of a spiritual nature, so that the only kind of reality they can have is a spiritual one, i.e. through the spirit's consciousness of spirit.

But this, as already mentioned, is equivalent to self-consciousness, which can easily give rise to a misunderstanding, for I may wrongly imagine that, in the act of self-consciousness, it is my temporal individuality that I am conscious of. One of the difficulties of philosophy is that most people think it deals only with the particular and empirical existence of the individual. But spirit, in its consciousness of itself, is free; in this realisation, it has overcome the limits of temporal existence and enters into relationship with pure being, which is also its own being. If the divine being were not the essence of man and nature, it would not in fact be a being at all. Self-consciousness, then, is a philosophical concept, which can only attain its full determinate character in philosophical discourse. It we take this as established, we may further conclude that the determinate national consciousness is the nation's consciousness of its own being. The spirit is primarily its own object; but as long as it is this only in our eyes, and has not yet recognised itself in its object, it is not yet its own object in the true sense. Its ultimate aim, however, is the attainment of knowledge; for the sole endeavour of spirit is to know what it is in and for itself, and to reveal itself to itself in its true form. It seeks to create a spiritual world in accordance with its own concept, to fulfil and realise its own true nature, and to produce religion and the state in such a way that it will conform to its own concept and be truly itself or become its own Idea. (The Idea is the reality of the concept, of which it is merely a reflection or expression.) This, then, is the universal goal of the spirit and of history; and just as the seed bears within it the whole nature of the tree and the taste and form of its fruits, so also do the first glimmerings of spirit contain virtually the whole of history.

Given this abstract definition, we can say that world history is the record of the spirit's efforts to attain knowledge of what it is in itself. The Orientals do not know that the spirit or man as such are free in themselves. And because they do not know this, they are not themselves free. They only know that One is free; but for this very reason, such freedom is mere arbitrariness, savagery, and brutal passion, or a milder and tamer version of this which is itself only an accident of nature, and equally arbitrary. This One is therefore merely a despot, not a free man and a human being. The consciousness of freedom first awoke among the Greeks, and they were accordingly free; but, like the Romans, they only knew that Some, and not all men as such, are free. Plato and Aristotle did not know this either; thus the Greeks not only had slaves, on which their life and the continued existence of their estimable freedom depended, but their very freedom itself was on the one hand only a fortuitous, undeveloped, transient, and limited efflorescence, and, on the other, a harsh servitude of all that is humane and proper to man. The Germanic nations, with the rise of Christianity, were the first to realise that man is by nature free, and that freedom of the spirit is his very essence. This consciousness first dawned in religion, in the innermost region of the spirit; but to incorporate the same principle into secular existence was a further problem, whose solution and application require long and arduous cultural exertions. For example, slavery did not immediately [come to an end] with the adoption of Christianity; still less did freedom at once predominate in states, or governments and constitutions become rationally organised and founded upon the principle of freedom. This application of the principle to secular affairs, the penetration and transformation of secular life by the principle of freedom, is the long process of which history itself [is made up]. I have already drawn attention to this distinction between the principle as such and its application – i.e. its introduction and execution in the actual world of the spirit and of life – and we shall return to it again shortly. It is one of the basic articles of philosophical science, and its vital importance must not be overlooked. The same distinction applies not only to the Christian principle of the self-consciousness of freedom which I have mentioned provisionally here, it applies just as essentially to the principle of freedom in general. World history is the progress of the consciousness of freedom – a progress whose necessity it is our business to comprehend.

These general remarks on the different degrees of knowledge of freedom – firstly, that of the Orientals, who knew only that One is free, then that of the Greek and Roman world, which knew that Some are free, and finally, our own knowledge that All men as such are free, and that man is by nature free – supply us with the divisions we shall observe in our survey of world history and which will help us to organise our discussion of it. But these are only provisional remarks thrown out in passing; several other concepts must first be explained.

The spirit's consciousness of its freedom (which is the precondition of the reality of this freedom) has been defined as spiritual reason in its determinate form, hence as the destiny of the spiritual world, and – since the latter is the substantial world and the physical world [is] subordinated to it (or, in speculative terminology, has no truth in comparison with it) – as the ultimate end of the world in general. But that this freedom, as defined above, still remains an indefinite term which is capable of infinite interpretations, and that, since it is the highest concept of all, it is open to an infinite number of misunderstandings, confusions, and errors and covers every possible kind of extravagance – all this has never been known and experienced so fully as in the present age; but we must make do for the moment with this general definition. We have also stressed the importance of the infinite difference between the principle – i.e. that which exists only in itself – and its realisation. For freedom in itself carries with it the infinite necessity of attaining consciousness – for freedom, by definition, is self-knowledge – and hence of realising itself: it is itself the end of its own operations, and the sole end of the spirit.[21]

The substance of the spirit is freedom. From this, we can infer that its end in the historical process is the freedom of the subject to follow its own conscience and morality, and to pursue and implement its own universal ends; it also implies that the subject has infinite value and that it must become conscious of its supremacy. The end of the world spirit is realised in substance through the freedom of each individual.

The spirits of the nations are the links in the process whereby the spirit arrives at free recognition of itself. Nations, however, exist for themselves – for we are not concerned here with spirit in itself – and as such, they have a natural existence. In so far as they are nations, their principles are natural ones; and since their principles differ, the nations themselves are also naturally different. Each has its own principle which it seeks to realise as its end; if it has attained this end, it has no further task to perform in the world.

The spirit of a nation should thus be seen as the development of a principle; this principle is at first bound up with an indistinct impulse which gradually works its way out and seeks to attain objective reality. A natural spirit of this kind is a determinate spirit, a concrete whole; it must gain recognition in its determinate form. Since it is a spirit, it can only be understood in spiritual terms, by means of thought, and it is we who understand it in this way; the next step is for the national spirit to understand itself in turn by the same means. We must therefore examine the determinate concept or principle of the spirit in question. This principle is extremely rich in content, and it assumes many forms in the course of its development; for the spirit is living and active, and is concerned only with its own productions. The spirit, as it advances towards its realisation, towards self-satisfaction and self-knowledge, is the sole motive force behind all the deeds and aspirations of the nation. Religion, knowledge, the arts, and the destinies and events of history are all aspects of its evolution. This, and not the natural influences at work upon it (as the derivation of the word *natio* from *nasci* might suggest), determines the nation's character. In its active operations, the national spirit at first knows only the ends of its determinate reality, but not its own nature. But it is nevertheless endowed with an impulse to formulate its thoughts. Its supreme activity is thought, so that when it reaches the height of its powers, its aim is to comprehend itself. The ultimate aim of the spirit is to know itself, and to comprehend itself not merely intuitively but also in terms of thought. It must and will succeed in its task; but this very success is also its downfall, and this in turn heralds the emergence of a new phase and a new spirit. The individual national spirit fulfils itself by merging with the principle of another nation, so that we can observe a progression, growth and succession from one national principle to another. The task of philosophical world history is to discover the continuity within this movement.

The abstract mode of the development of the national spirit consists simply in the temporal process as perceived by the senses, which is the primary activity of the spirit; the more concrete process, however, is that of its spiritual activity. A nation makes internal advances; it develops further and is ultimately destroyed. The appropriate categories here are those of **cultural development,*** over-refinement, and degeneration; the latter can be either the product or the cause of the nation's downfall. But the word 'culture' tells us nothing definite about the substantial content of the national spirit; it is a formal category, and is always construed in terms of universal properties. A cultured man is one who

---

* The word *Bildung* is notoriously difficult to translate. In the following passage, it is rendered as 'cultural development' or 'culture', although it carries many of the associations of the English word 'education' as well. The same applies to the past participle *gebildet*, translated here as 'cultured'. For a detailed analysis of the concept of *Bildung* see W. H. Bruford, *Culture and Society in Classical Weimar 1775–1806*, Cambridge, 1962, pp. 4f. and *passim*.

knows how to impress the stamp of universality upon all his actions, who has renounced his particularity, and who acts in accordance with universal principles. Culture is the form of our thinking; it owes its existence to man's ability to control himself, and to the fact that he does not merely follow his desires and inclinations but subjects himself to a discipline. He thereby grants his object a position of independence, and habitually adopts a theoretical attitude. He is also in the habit of treating the various aspects of his object separately, of analysing the situation before him, of isolating individual aspects of it and abstracting from them, thereby directly conferring the imprint of universality upon them all. The cultured individual recognises the different facets of objects; all of them are present to him, and his fully developed powers of reflection have invested them with the form of universality. In his behaviour, too, he takes them all into account. The uncultured individual, on the other hand, may grasp the main point and at the same time inadvertently do violence to half a dozen others. But the cultured man takes in all the different aspects, and thus acts in a concrete manner; he is accustomed to act in the light of universal perspectives and ends. Culture can therefore be defined quite simply as the imposition of a universal quality upon a given content.

Since the development of spirit is the process which gives rise to culture, it must now be explained in more concrete terms. The universal property of spirit is that it actualises those determinants which it possesses in itself. This can also be interpreted in a subjective sense, in which case we call what the spirit is in itself its disposition; and when this disposition has been actualised, we speak instead of its qualities or abilities. In the latter case, the end product itself is also understood in a subjective sense. In history, however, it assumes the form of an object, deed, or work produced by the spirit. The national spirit is knowledge, and thought acts upon the reality of the national spirit in such a way that it knows its own work as something objective, and no longer merely as something subjective. We should note in connection with these determinations of the spirit that a distinction is often made between man's inner nature and his deeds. This does not apply in history; the man himself is the sum total of his deeds. One might imagine a case in which a person's intentions were excellent even though his actual deeds were worthless. And individual instances can certainly occur in which people conceal their real attitudes; but this is not the whole picture. The truth is that there is no difference between the inner and the outer. In history especially, there is no need to waste time puzzling over temporary differences between them. The character of the nation is that of its deeds, for the deeds represent the end it pursues.

The spirit's acts are of an essential nature; it makes itself in reality what it already is in itself, and is therefore its own deed or creation. In this way, it becomes its own object, and has its own existence before it. And it is the same with the spirit of a nation; its activity consists in making itself into an actual world which also has an existence in space. Its religion, ritual, ethics, customs, art, constitution, and political laws – indeed the whole range of its institutions, events, and deeds – all this is its own creation, and it is this which makes the nation what it is. Every nation feels this to be so. And then the individual finds his nation already in being, as a complete and firmly established world to which he must become assimilated. He must take over its substantial being as his own, so that his outlook and abilities are in accord with it, in order that he may himself become something in turn. The product is already there, and it is up to the individuals to adapt themselves to it and conform to it. If we examine a nation in its formative period, we find that its actions are calculated to further the end of its spirit; we describe it as moral, virtuous, and vigorous, because its actions are governed by the inner will of its spirit and it is also prepared, in its struggle to objectivise itself, to defend its achievements against external aggression. At this stage, the individuals are not yet separated from the whole, for this separation does not take place until later, when the period of reflection begins. Once the nation has created itself, the dichotomy between its essence (or what it is in itself) and its real existence is overcome, and it has attained satisfaction: it has created its own world out of its inner essence. The spirit now indulges itself in the world it has created.

The next stage begins after the spirit has attained its object. It is no longer aroused to activity, and its substantial soul is inactive. Its actions are now only remotely connected with its highest interests. I am interested in something only in so far as it is still out of my reach, or is necessary to some purpose which I have not yet fulfilled. Thus when a nation is fully developed and has attained its end, its profounder interests evaporate. The national spirit is a natural individual, and as such, it blossoms, grows strong, then fades away and dies. It lies in the nature of finite things that any limited spirit is ephemeral. Since it is a living thing, its business is to bring forth, to produce, and to realise itself. This involves an opposition in so far as reality does not match its concept, or in so far as its inner concept has not yet become conscious of itself. But as soon as the spirit has given itself an objective life, or as soon as it has fully worked out its concept and put it into practice completely, it reaches a stage of self-indulgence which is no longer activity but an unrestrained self-abandon. The period in which the spirit is still active is that of the nation's youth, the finest stage in its development; during this period, individuals feel impelled to preserve their fatherland and to implement their nation's end. When this is accomplished, life becomes a thing of habit; and just as man languishes through routine existence, so also does the national spirit through self-indulgence. When the spirit of the nation has fulfilled its function, its agility and interest flag; the nation lives on the borderline between manhood and old age, and enjoys the fruits of its efforts. Measures have been taken to satisfy the needs and wants of the past, and these have now ceased to exist. Then the measures themselves can be dispensed with in turn, and the present has no further needs left to satisfy. It may also be that the nation has relinquished certain aspects of its end and contented itself with more limited aims. Even if its imagination transcended these limits, it nevertheless abandoned its wider objectives if no opportunity of realising them presented itself, and restricted itself to what reality permitted. It then lives on with the satisfaction of having achieved its end, falls into fixed habits which are now devoid of life, and thus moves gradually on towards its natural death. It may still have much to do in war and in peace, and in internal and external affairs, for it may continue to vegetate over a long period. It still has movement; but this movement is only occasioned by the particular interests of individuals, and no longer by the interest of the nation itself. Its greatest and highest interest has vanished out of its life; for no interest is possible without some kind of opposition.

The natural death of the national spirit may take the form of political stagnation, or of what we call habit. The clock is wound up and runs on automatically. Habit is an activity with nothing to oppose it; it retains only the formal property of temporal continuity, and the depth and richness of its end need no longer be expressed. It is, so to speak, a superficial and sensuous kind of existence whose profounder significance has been forgotten. Thus both individuals and nations die a natural death. And even if the latter live on, their existence is devoid of life and interest; their institutions have become superfluous, because the needs which created them have been satisfied, and nothing remains but political stagnation and boredom. The negative element no longer assumes the form of dissension and conflict; this was the case with the old German Imperial Cities, for example, which lost their independence through no fault of their own and without realising what had befallen them. In a moribund state such as this, a nation may even prosper, although it no longer participates in the life of the Idea. It then serves as material for a higher principle, and becomes the province of another nation in which a higher principle is active. But the principle with which a nation is endowed has a real existence; even if it dies through habit, it still retains its spiritual nature and thus cannot be extinguished altogether, but moves on into a higher existence. The transience of everything may well distress us, but in a profounder sense, we realise that it is necessary in relation to the higher Idea of the spirit. For the spirit is such that it has to employ means of this kind to fulfil its absolute end, and this knowledge must reconcile us to the transient side of its existence.

The individual national spirit is subject to transience. It perishes, loses its world-historical significance, and ceases to be the bearer of the highest concept the spirit has formed of itself. For the nation whose concept of the spirit is highest is in tune with the times and rules over the others. It may well be that nations whose concepts are less advanced survive, but they exist only on the periphery of world history.

But since the nation is a universal, a collective, a further determinant comes into play. As a collective, the national spirit exists for itself; this also means that the universal aspect of its existence may assume a role of opposition. Its negative side manifests itself; thought rises above the nation's immediate functions. And thus its natural death also appears as a kind of suicide. Thus we see on the one hand how the national spirit brings about its own downfall. The phenomenon of national degeneration in fact takes on various forms. It may break out from within as appetites are unleashed, with individuals pursuing their own satisfaction to the detriment of the substantial spirit, which consequently disintegrates. Individual interests seize control of the powers and resources which were formerly dedicated to the whole. In this case, the negative side manifests itself as an internal degeneration, as a tendency towards particularism. It is usually associated with some external force which deprives the nation of its sovereignty, so that it ceases to exist as such. But this external force belongs only to the phenomenal world; no destructive force can prevail against the national spirit or within it unless it is already internally lifeless or dead.

But there is a further category beyond that of transience, for death is followed by new life. One might think in this context of life in the natural world, in which buds wither and fall and new ones take their place. But this is not the case in the spiritual world. The tree lives perennially, puts forth shoots, leaves, and blossoms, and produces fruit, and thus always starts again from the beginning. The annual plant does not survive its fruition, and although the tree can live for many decades, it too eventually dies. The reawakening of nature is merely the repetition of one and the same process; it is a tedious chronicle in which the same cycle recurs again and again. There is nothing new under the sun. But this is not so with the sun of the spirit. Its movement and progression do not repeat themselves, for the changing aspect of the spirit as it passes through endlessly varying forms is essentially progress. This progress is evident even when the national spirit destroys itself by the negativity of its thought, because its knowledge, its thinking apprehension of being, is the source and matrix from which a new form – and indeed a higher form, whose principle both conserves and transfigures it – emerges. For thought is of a universal and collective nature, so that it cannot die, but always retains its identity. Each determinate form which the spirit assumes does not simply fade away naturally with the passage of time, but is preserved* in the self-determining, self-conscious activity of the self-consciousness. Since this preservation† is an activity of thought, it is both a conservation and a transfiguration. Thus while the spirit on the one hand preserves‡ the reality and continuity of its own nature, it is at the same time enriched by the essence, the thought, the universal aspect of what was formerly its mere existence. Its principle is no longer the immediate content and end of its former existence, but their underlying essence.

As we trace the passage of one national spirit into the other, we should note that the universal spirit as such does not die; it dies only in its capacity as a national spirit. As a national spirit, it belongs to world history, and its task is to attain knowledge of its own function and to comprehend itself by means of thought. This thought or reflection eventually ceases to respect its immediate existence, for it realises that the principle behind it is a particular one; and as a result, the subjective spirit becomes divorced from the universal spirit. Individuals withdraw into themselves and pursue their own ends, and this, as already remarked, is the nation's undoing: each individual sets himself his own ends as his passions dictate. But as the spirit withdraws into itself, thought emerges as a reality in its own right, and the learned disciplines flourish. Thus learning and the degeneration or downfall of a nation always go hand in hand.

But at the same time, a new and higher principle emerges. Division contains and carries with it the need for unification, because the spirit is

---

* *aufgehoben* (cf. note to p. 20).   † *Aufheben.*   ‡ *aufhebt.*

itself one. It is a living thing, and is powerful enough to create the unity it requires. The opposition or contradiction between the spirit and the lower principle gives rise to a higher factor. For example, when their culture was at its height, the Greeks, for all the untroubled serenity of their manners, had no concept of universal freedom; they did have their καθῆκον, their idea of propriety, but they had no real morality or conscience. Morality, which rests on a reflexive movement of the spirit, a turning in of the spirit upon itself, did not yet exist; it dates only from the time of Socrates. But as soon as reflection supervened and individuals withdrew into themselves and dissociated themselves from established custom to live their own lives according to their own wishes, degeneration and contradiction arose. But the spirit cannot remain in a state of opposition. It seeks unification, and in this unification lies the higher principle. History is the process whereby the spirit discovers itself and its own concept. Thus division contains within it the higher principle of consciousness; but this higher principle also has another side to it which does not enter the consciousness at all. For there can be no consciousness of opposition until the principle of personal freedom is already present.

The result of this process is therefore that the spirit, as it objectivises itself and becomes aware of its objective being, destroys the determinate aspect of its being on the one hand and comprehends its universal aspect on the other, thereby giving its principle a new determination. This means that the substantial determination of the national spirit has altered, or to put it differently, that its principle has been absorbed into another and higher principle.

If we seek to understand history and to comprehend it by means of philosophy, the most important and distinctive feature of the whole undertaking – indeed its very essence – is that we should discover and recognise this idea of transition. The individual goes through various stages of development as a single unit and retains his individual identity; so too does the nation, at least up to the point at which its spirit enters its universal phase. We can see in this the inner or conceptual necessity by which such changes are governed. But, as already mentioned, the impotence of life is evident from the fact that its beginning and its end do not coincide. And this applies both to the life of individuals and to that of nations. The determinate national spirit is but a single individual in the course of world history. The life of the nation brings a fruit to maturity, for its activity is directed towards the fulfilment of its principle. This fruit does not, however, fall back into the womb from which it emerged; the nation itself is not permitted to enjoy it, but must taste it instead in the form of a bitter draught. It cannot refuse to drink it, for it has an infinite thirst for it, but the price of its satisfaction is its own annihilation (although it also heralds the birth of a new principle). The fruit again becomes the seed, but the seed of another nation, which it brings to maturity in turn.

The spirit is essentially the product of its own activity, and its activity consists in transcending and negating its immediacy and turning in upon itself.

The spirit is free; and the aim of the world spirit in world history is to realise its essence and to obtain the prerogative of freedom. Its activity is that of knowing and recognising itself, but it accomplishes this in gradual stages rather than at a single step. Each new individual national spirit represents a new stage in the conquering march of the world spirit as it wins its way to consciousness and freedom. The death of a national spirit is a transition to new life, but not as in nature, where the death of one individual gives life to another individual of the same kind. On the contrary, the world spirit progresses from lower determinations to higher principles and concepts of its own nature, to more fully developed expressions of its Idea.

The question at issue is therefore the ultimate end of mankind, the end which the spirit sets itself in the world, and which it is driven to realise incessantly and with irresistible power. The more specific implications of this ultimate end follow on from what has already been said with regard to the national spirit. We have seen that the spirit cannot be concerned with anything other than itself. Nothing is higher than the spirit, and nothing is more worthy of being its object. It cannot rest or occupy itself with anything else until it knows its own nature. This thought, which we have specified as the highest and only interest of the spirit, is, of course, of a general and abstract nature, and there is a wide gulf between it and that which constitutes the interests of nations and individuals as we observe them in history. On the empirical level, we see specific ends and particular interests with which nations have been occupied for centuries. We need only think, for example, of the antagonism between Rome and Carthage. And knowing these empirical phenomena is a far cry from recognising in them that process of thought which, as already said, constitutes their essential interest. We shall not discuss until later the opposition between the immediately obvious interests of the spirit and its absolute interest as specified above. At least it is not difficult to grasp the general significance of the idea that the relationship of the free spirit to itself is a necessary one, precisely because it is a free spirit; otherwise it would not be free at all but dependent. We have defined the goal of history as consisting in the spirit's development towards self-consciousness, or in its making the world conform to itself (for the two are identical). It might equally be said that the spirit produces its concept out of itself, objectivises it, and thus becomes the being of its own concept; it becomes conscious of itself in the objective world so that it may attain its salvation: for as soon as the objective world conforms to its internal requirements, it has realised its freedom. When it has determined its own end in this way, its progress takes on a more definite character in that it no longer consists of a mere increase in quantity. It may also be added that, even on the evidence of our own ordinary consciousness, we must acknowledge that the consciousness must undergo various stages of development before it becomes aware of its own essential nature.

The aim of world history, therefore, is that the spirit should attain knowledge of its own true nature, that it should objectivise this knowledge and transform it into a real world, and give itself an objective existence. The essential point to note is that this aim is itself a product of the spirit. The spirit is not a natural entity like an animal, for the animal is no more than its immediate existence. The spirit is such that it produces itself and makes itself what it is. Thus the first form it assumes in its real existence is the outcome of its own activity. Its essential being is actuosity, not static existence, for it has produced itself, it has come to exist for itself, and made itself what it is by its own agency. It can only be said to have a true existence if it has produced itself, and its essential being is process in the absolute sense. This process, in which it mediates itself with itself by its own unaided efforts, has various distinct moments; it is full of movement and change, and is determined in different ways at different times. It consists essentially of a series of separate stages, and world history is the expression of the divine process which is a graduated progression in which the spirit comes to know and realise itself and its own truth. Its various stages are stages in the self-recognition of the spirit; and the essence of the spirit, its supreme imperative, is that it should recognise, know, and realise itself for what it is. It accomplishes this end in the history of the world; it produces itself in a series of determinate forms, and these forms are the nations of world history. Each of them represents a particular stage of development, so that they correspond to epochs in the history of the world. Or on a more fundamental level, they are the principles in which the spirit has discovered itself, and which it is impelled to realise. There is therefore an essential connection between them in which the nature of the spirit alone is expressed.

World history is the expression of the divine and absolute process of the spirit in its highest forms, of the progression whereby it discovers its true nature and becomes conscious of itself. The specific forms it assumes at each of these stages are the national spirits of world history, with all the determinate characteristics of their ethical life, their constitutions, their art, their religion, and their knowledge. The world spirit has an infinite urge and an irresistible impulse to realise these stages of its development; for this sequence and its realisation are its true concept. World history merely shows how the spirit gradually attains consciousness and the will to truth; it progresses from its early glimmerings to major discoveries and finally to a state of complete consciousness. We have already discussed the ultimate end of this process. The principles of the national spirits in their necessary progression are themselves only moments of the one universal spirit, which ascends through them in the course of history to its consummation in an all-embracing totality.

This vision of a process whereby the spirit realises its aim in history clashes with a widespread attitude concerning the nature of ideals and their relationship to reality. For no opinion is more widely held or more frequently voiced than the lament that ideals cannot be translated into reality – be they ideals of the imagination or ideals of reason, so long as they claim to be ideals. In particular, we are told that the ideals of youth dissolve into dreams in the cold light of reality. Whatever ideals of this kind do founder on the rocks of harsh reality in the course of the voyage of life must be primarily subjective; they can belong only to individuals who consider themselves superior to and wiser than others. As such, they have no place in the present discussion. For the fancies of isolated individuals cannot become binding upon reality at large, just as the laws of the universe are not framed solely for the benefit of single individuals, who may in fact be most unfavourably affected by them. It may certainly happen that the ideals of individuals are not realised. Individuals often have their own peculiar opinions of themselves, of their lofty intentions, of the splendid deeds they hope to perform, and of their own supposed importance from which the world, as they think, must assuredly benefit. Be that as it may, such ideas merit no further attention here. The dreams of the individual are often no more than exaggerated estimates of his own personal significance. Furthermore, the individual may well be treated unjustly; but this is a matter of indifference to world history, which uses individuals only as instruments to further its own progress.

But these are not the only kind of ideals. There are also the ideals of reason, those ideas of the good, the true, and all that is best in the world;

and these have a genuine claim to be satisfied, for their non-fulfilment is generally recognised to be an objective injustice. Poets such as Schiller have expressed their grief over unfulfilled ideals with great pathos and emotion. But if we say that universal reason is fulfilled, this has of course nothing to do with individual empirical instances; the latter may fare either well or badly, as the case may be, for the concept has authorised the forces of contingency and particularity to exercise their vast influence in the empirical sphere. When we consider particular instances, we may well conclude that there is much injustice in the world, and there is certainly much to find fault with among individual phenomena. But we are not concerned here with empirical details; they are at the mercy of chance, which has no place in the present discussion. It is only too easy to indulge in criticism, and it helps to confirm men's estimates of their own superior knowledge and good intentions. Subjective criticism of this kind, directed solely at particular matters and their shortcomings – regardless of the universal reason behind them – is extremely facile; and inasmuch as it conveys an impression of good intentions towards the welfare of the whole, and lends itself an air of sincere benevolence, it can become extremely self-important and full of conceit. It is easier to perceive the shortcomings of individuals, states, and the course of world affairs than to understand their true import. For in passing negative judgements, one looks down on the matter in hand with a superior and supercilious air, without having gone into it thoroughly enough to understand its true nature, i.e. its positive significance. The criticism may well be justified, except that it is far easier to detect shortcomings than the true substance (as in works of art, for example). People often think they have done their job when they have found something which can be justly criticised; they are right, of course, in one respect; but they are also wrong in so far as they fail to recognise the positive factor. To see only the bad side in everything and to overlook all the positive and valuable qualities is a sign of extreme superficiality. Age, in general, takes a milder view, whereas youth is always dissatisfied; this is because age brings with it maturity of judgement, which does not simply tolerate the bad along with the rest out of sheer lack of interest, but has learnt from the seriousness of life to look for the substance and enduring value of things. And this is not so much equity as justice.

But to return to the true ideal, the Idea of reason itself, philosophy should help us to understand that the actual world is as it ought to be. It shows us that the rational will, the concrete good is indeed all-powerful, and that this absolute power translates itself into reality. The true good, the universal and divine reason, also has the power to fulfil its own purpose, and the most concrete representation of this goodness and reason is God. For goodness, not just as a general idea but also as an effective force, is what we call God. Philosophy teaches us that no force can surpass the power of goodness or of God or prevent God's purposes from being realised; it shows us that God's will must always prevail in the end, and that world history is nothing more than the plan of providence. The world is governed by God; and world history is the content of his government and the execution of his plan. To comprehend this is the task of the philosophy of world history, and its initial assumption is that the ideal is fulfilled and that only that which corresponds to the Idea possesses true reality. The pure light of this divine Idea, which is no mere ideal, dispels the illusion that the world is a collection of senseless and foolish occurrences. The aim of philosophy is to recognise the content and reality of the divine Idea, and to defend reality against its detractors. For it is through reason that we apprehend the work of God.

What is usually called reality is seen by philosophy as no more than an idle semblance which has no reality in and for itself. If we have the impression that the events of the past are totally calamitous and devoid of sense, we can find consolation, so to speak, in this awareness. But consolation is merely something received in compensation for a misfortune which ought never to have happened in the first place, and it belongs to the world of finite things. Philosophy, therefore, is not really a means of consolation. It is more than that, for it transfigures reality with all its apparent injustices and reconciles it with the rational; it shows that it is based upon the Idea itself, and that reason is fulfilled in it. For in reason, the divinity is present. The basic content of reason is the divine Idea, and its essence is the plan of God. In the context of world history, the Idea is not equivalent to reason as encountered in the subjective will, but to the activity of God alone. We conceive of reason as a means of perceiving the Idea, and even its etymology* suggests that it is a perception of something expressed, in other words, of the Logos – the true. The true acquires its truth in the created world. God expresses himself, and himself alone; he is that power whose nature is self-expression and whose expression can be perceived by reason. And what reason perceives is the truth and image of God. Thus philosophy concludes that nothing which is empty of significance can be an ideal, but only that which possesses reality, and that the Idea reveals itself to perception.

* Hegel is alluding to the etymological relationship between *Vernunft* (reason) and *vernehmen* (to perceive).

The immediate question which now presents itself is this: what means does the Idea employ to realise itself? This is the second point we have to consider here.

b. [*The means of its realisation*]

This question of the means whereby freedom creates a world for itself leads us to the phenomenon of history proper. Whereas freedom as such is primarily an internal concept, the means it employs belong to the external and phenomenal world which confronts us directly in history. An initial survey of history, however, would indicate that the actions of men are governed by their needs, passions, and interests, by the attitudes and aims to which these give rise, and by their own character and abilities; we gain the impression that, in this scene of activity, these needs, passions, interests, etc., are the sole motive forces. Individuals do at times pursue more general ends such as goodness, but the good they pursue is invariably of a limited character. Worthy patriotic sentiments are of this kind, for they may well be directed towards a country whose importance in relation to the world as a whole and to its universal end is negligible; and the same is true of love of one's family or friends, and indeed of moral rectitude in general. In short, all virtues come under this category. We may well see the ends of reason realised in the virtues of individual subjects and in their sphere of influence: but these are only isolated individuals who constitute but a small proportion of the mass of mankind when we compare them with all the others, and the extent to which their virtues are effective is relatively limited. But in many cases, passions, private interests, and the satisfaction of selfish impulses are the most potent force. What makes them powerful is [that] they do not heed any of the restraints which justice and morality seek to impose upon them, and the elemental power of passion has a more immediate hold over man than that artificial and laboriously acquired discipline of order and moderation, justice and morality.

When we contemplate this display of passions, and consider the historical consequences of their violence and of the irrationality which is associated with them (and even more so with good intentions and worthy aims); when we see the evil, the wickedness, and the downfall of the most flourishing empires the human spirit has created; and when we are moved to profound pity for the untold miseries of individual human beings – we can only end with a feeling of sadness at the transience of everything. And since all this destruction is not the work of mere nature[22] but of the will of man, our sadness takes on a moral quality, for the good spirit in us (if we are at all susceptible to it) eventually revolts at such a spectacle. Without rhetorical exaggeration, we need only compile an accurate account of the misfortunes which have overtaken the finest manifestations of national and political life, and of personal

68

virtues or innocence, to see a most terrifying picture take shape before our eyes. Its effect is to intensify our feelings to an extreme pitch of hopeless sorrow with no redeeming circumstances to counterbalance it. We can only harden ourselves against it or escape from it by telling ourselves that it was ordained by fate and could not have been otherwise. There is nothing we can do about it now, and we react against the lassitude into which such sorrowful reflections can plunge us and return to our customary attitudes, to the aims and interests of the present, which [call for] activity rather than laments over the past. Indeed, we retreat into that selfish complacency which stands on the calmer shore and, from a secure position, smugly looks on at the distant spectacle of confusion and wreckage. But even as we look upon history as an altar on which the happiness of nations, the wisdom of states, and the virtue of individuals are slaughtered, our thoughts inevitably impel us to ask: to whom, or to what ultimate end have these monstrous sacrifices been made? This usually leads in turn to those general considerations from which our whole enquiry began. From this beginning, we proceeded to define those same events which afford so sad a spectacle for gloomy sentiments and brooding reflection as no more than the means whereby what we have specified as the substantial destiny, the absolute and final end, or in other words, the true result of world history, is realised. From the very outset, we rejected the path of reflection as a means of ascending from the spectacle of historical detail to the universal principle behind it. Besides, such sentimental reflections have no real interest in transcending the attitudes and emotions which go along with them, or in solving the enigmas of providence to which they give rise. They are content instead to derive a lugubrious satisfaction from the empty and futile sublimities which the negative results of history evoke. Let us therefore return to the point of view we originally adopted; and the moments we shall discover within it will furnish us with the essential definitions we require in order to answer the questions which such scenes from history present.

The first thing we have to notice is[23] this: what we have hitherto called the principle, or ultimate end, or destiny, or the nature and concept of the spirit in itself, is purely universal and abstract. A principle, fundamental rule, or law is something universal and implicit, and as such, it has not attained complete reality, however true it may be in itself. Aims, principles, and the like are present at first in our thoughts and inner intentions, or even in books, but not yet in reality itself. In other words, that which exists only in itself is a possibility or potentiality[24] which has not yet emerged into existence. A second moment is necessary before it can attain reality – that of actuation or realisation; and its principle is the will,[25] the activity of mankind in the world at large. It is only by means of this activity that the original concepts or implicit determinations are realised and actualised.[26]

Laws and principles have no immediate life or validity in themselves. The activity which puts them into operation and endows them with real existence has its source in the needs, impulses, inclinations, and passions of man. If I put something into practice and give it a real existence, I must have some personal interest in doing so; I must be personally involved in it, and hope to obtain satisfaction through its accomplishment – in other words, my own interest must be at stake. To have an interest in something means to be implicated and involved in it, and an end which I am actively to pursue must in some way or other be my own end. It is my end which must be satisfied, even if the end for which I am working has many other sides to it which have nothing to do with me. This infinite right of the subject is the second essential moment of freedom, in that the subject must itself be satisfied by whatever activity or task it performs. And if men are to be interested in anything, they must be actively engaged in it; that is, they look for their own interest in whatever end they work for, and they wish to identify themselves with it and find their own self-esteem confirmed by it. But there is a possible misunderstanding here which we must take care to avoid: a common and justified form of censure or criticism is to say of someone that he is an interested party – in other words, that he is merely seeking some personal advantage and this alone; he is solely concerned with furthering his own cause, regardless of the common weal, and the latter interests him only in so far as he can turn it to his personal advantage, even at the expense of actively detracting from the general cause, jeopardising it, or sacrificing it altogether. But anyone who actively supports a cause is not just an interested party – he is interested in the cause itself.[27] *Language accurately reproduces this distinction. Thus nothing can happen, nothing can be accomplished unless the individuals concerned can also gain satisfaction for themselves as particular individuals. For they have their own special needs, impulses, and interests which are peculiar to themselves – peculiar to themselves inasmuch as they are separate individuals, although the same needs, impulses, and interests may be no different in content from those of others, and may in fact be shared by them. Such interests*[28] [29] *include not only those dictated by personal needs and volitions, but also those which arise out of personal beliefs and convictions (or at least out of personal conjectures and opinions) – provided, of course, that the desire to reflect, to analyse, and to think rationally is already awake. Under these conditions, people also expect that the cause for which they are supposed to act should appeal to them personally, and at all events, that they should be able to enter into it with the backing of their own opinions and convictions regarding its goodness, justice, utility, the reward they hope to reap from it, and so on. This moment is particularly applicable to our own age, in which people are much less inclined to accept things on trust or on the strength of external authority and wish to act in support only of those causes to which they can assent with their own understanding and their independent convictions and opinions.*

In world history, the object of our enquiry is the Idea as it expresses itself through the medium of the human will or of human freedom. The will thereby becomes the abstract basis of freedom, and gives rise to the entire ethical life of nations. The first principle of the Idea in this form, as already remarked, is the Idea itself as an abstract entity; and the second is that of human passion. These two are the warp and weft in the fabric of world history. The Idea as such is the reality, and the passions are the arm which serves it. These are the extremes, and the middle point at which the two coincide and in which they are united is the state of ethical freedom. Considered objectively, the Idea and the realm of particular things seem as completely opposed to one another as freedom and necessity, for we at once think in this connection of man's struggle against fate. But the necessity in question is not an external one like that of fate, but that of the divine Idea, so that we must now ask how this exalted Idea can be reconciled with human freedom. The will of the individual is free if he can determine his volitions absolutely, abstractly, and in and for himself. How, then, is it possible for the universal or the rational to determine anything whatsoever in history? This is not the place to discuss this paradox in all its ramifications, but the following points should at least be borne in mind.

A flame consumes air, and is at the same time fed by wood. Air is the sole condition for the growth of trees; but when wood enables the fire to consume the air, it is attacking its own existence and source; yet the oxygen in the air continues to exist as before, and the trees do not cease to flourish. In like fashion, if someone wishes to build a house, he is at liberty to do so; but all the elements must help him in his task. And yet the purpose of the house is to protect men against these very elements. In this instance, therefore, the elements are being used against themselves, although the universal law of nature is not thereby invalidated. The building of a house consists in the first place of an inner aim and intention. Opposed to this are the means employed, the particular elements and materials such as iron, wood, and stone. The elements are used to process these materials – fire to melt the iron, air to fan the flames, water to turn the wheels, to cut the wood, and so on. The final result is that the air which helped to build the house is shut out by the house itself, as are the torrents of rain and the ravages of fire (in so far as the house is fireproof). The stones and beams obey the law of gravity and press downwards, making it possible for high walls to be built. Thus the elements are utilised as their respective natures allow, and they act together to create a product which restricts their own activity. The human passions are satisfied in much the same way: they fulfil themselves and their ends in accordance with their specific nature, and thereby create the edifice of human society in which justice and order are given power over the passions themselves. In our daily existence, we can see that there is a system of justice which guarantees our security; and justice grows up of its own accord, for it is an essential characteristic of human behaviour (although it is often directed against the particular interests and aims of men). In individual instances, men pursue their particular ends in defiance of the universal justice, and behave as free agents. But this does not destroy the common ground, the underlying substance, the system of right. And the same applies to the world order in general; its ingredients are the passions on the one hand and reason on the other. The passions are the active force, and they are by no means always opposed to ethical values, for it is through them that the universal end is realised. As to their moral qualities, the passions admittedly do seek to further their own interests. Thus in one respect, they do appear base and selfish. But all active things are of an individual nature: I exist in my actions, and they are the ends which I seek to attain. But the end I pursue may well be morally good, or even universal. My interest may indeed be a particular one, but it does not follow from this that it is opposed to the universal interest. For the universal can only be realised by means of the particular.

Passion is usually regarded as something contrary to right and more or less base in nature, and man is expected not to have any passions. But passions is perhaps not quite the right word for what I am trying to express. I use it here to denote any human activity which is governed by particular interests, special aims, or, if you will, by selfish intentions; men dedicate the entire energy of their will and character to attaining such ends, and will sacrifice other possible ends and indeed all other things to this object. The particular content of such personal ends is so much a part of the individual's will that it determines it completely and is inseparable from it, and it is this which makes the individual what he is. For the individual exists as a determinate being, unlike man in general, who has no existence as such. The word 'character' also denotes this determinate aspect of the will and the intellect. But a person's character includes all his individual peculiarities, the way he behaves in his private relations, etc., and does not convey specifically the active functioning of his individuality. I shall therefore continue to use the word passion, by which I understand the determinate aspects of character and volition in so far as they do not have a purely private content but are the effective motive force behind actions whose significance is universal. I shall disregard all those intentions which can be classed as ineffectual subjective opinions, and with which persons of weak character are fond of making idle demonstrations.

We may therefore conclude that nothing whatsoever has been accomplished without the active interest of those concerned in it; and since interest can be described as passion (in so far as the whole individuality, to the exclusion of all other actual or possible interests and aims, applies itself to an object with every fibre of the will, and concentrates all its needs and resources on attaining its end), we may say without qualification that nothing great has been accomplished in the world without passion. Passion is the subjective or formal aspect of the energy of active volition – irrespective of its actual content or end – and this distinction between form and content also applies to all personal convictions, opinions, and conscience. For the content of my convictions and the end to which my passions are directed are of vital importance when it comes to deciding whether the one or the other is of a true and substantial nature. But conversely, if its nature is indeed such, it must inevitably attain real existence as that moment of the subjective will which includes all such factors as needs, impulses, and passions, as well as personal attitudes, opinions, and convictions.

From this examination of the second essential moment in the realisation of historical ends, it is evident – if we stop for a moment to consider the political implications – that a state will be well constituted and internally powerful if the private interest of its citizens coincides with the general end of the state, so that the one can be satisfied and realised through the other; this proposition is an extremely important one. But for the state to achieve this unity, numerous institutions must be set up and appropriate mechanisms invented, and the understanding must go through prolonged struggles before it discovers what is in fact appropriate. Conflicts with individual interests and passions are also inevitable, and the latter must be subjected to a long and rigorous process of discipline before the ultimate unity is achieved. The moment at which the state attains this unity marks the most flourishing period in its history, when its virtue, strength, and prosperity are at their height. But world history does not begin with any conscious end, as do all particular associations set up by men. Even man's social instinct entails the conscious purpose of securing his life and property, and as soon as a society has come into being, such purposes at once take on an even more definite shape. The aim is now to defend the city of Athens or Rome, for instance, and with every new evil or exigency which arises, the problem becomes more specific still. World history begins with its universal end – that the concept of the spirit should be realised – existing only in itself, i.e. as mere nature;[30] it is as yet only an inward, basic, unconscious impulse, and the whole activity of world history, as already mentioned, is a constant endeavour to make this impulse conscious. Thus, what we have called the subjective element – i.e. needs, impulses, passions, particular interests, and opinions or subjective ideas – is immediately present to itself from the beginning in the shape of natural being or natural will. This vast conglomeration of volition, interests, and activities is the sum total of instruments and means which the world spirit employs to accomplish its end, to make this end conscious and to give it reality; and its end is simply that of finding itself, of coming to terms with itself, and of contemplating its own actuality. All these expressions of individual and national life, in seeking and fulfilling their own ends, are at the same time the means and instruments of a higher purpose and wider enterprise of which they are themselves ignorant and which they nevertheless unconsciously carry out. This, however, may be open to question, and it has indeed been questioned and often denied altogether, or dismissed and condemned as pure fantasy or as a figment of mere philosophy. But I have made my position clear on this issue from the very beginning, and stated our initial assumption or belief (which I put forward only as anticipating the result of our enquiry, without any further pretensions for the moment) that reason rules the world, and consequently its history, and continues to do so. In relation to this universal substance which exists in and for itself, everything else is in a subordinate position and acts only as a means to serve its interests. This universal reason exists as an immanent principle within history, in which and through which it fulfils itself. That the union of the universal substance, which exists in and for itself, with the particular and the subjective, is the sole truth, is a speculative proposition which is dealt with in this general form by logic. But in the actual process of world history, seen as something as yet incomplete, we find that the subjective element or consciousness is [not] yet in a position to know the true nature of the ultimate end of history, the concept of the spirit. For the latter has not yet become the content of its needs and interests; and although the subjective consciousness is still unaware of it, the universal substance is nevertheless present in its particular

74

ends and realises itself through them. Since, as I have said, the speculative aspect of this relationship belongs to the province of logic, this is not the place for me to define and analyse its concept and to make it, so to speak, intelligible. But I can at least attempt, by means of examples, to give a clearer impression of its nature.

This relationship between the subjective consciousness and the universal substance is such that the actions of human beings in the history of the world produce an effect altogether different from what they themselves intend and accomplish, from what they immediately recognise and desire. Their own interest is gratified; but at the same time, they accomplish a further purpose, a purpose which was indeed implicit in their own actions but was not part of their conscious intentions. By way of analogy, let us imagine a man who, from motives of revenge – perhaps of justified revenge, in that he may himself have suffered unjustly – set light to someone else's house; this at once means that a connection is established between the immediate deed and a train of circumstances, albeit external circumstances, which have nothing to do with the original deed regarded purely in isolation. The deed as such consisted, let us say, in applying a small flame to a small portion of a beam. What this deed itself does not accomplish takes place of its own accord; the ignited portion is connected with further sections of the beam, these in turn are connected with the timberwork of the entire house, which is itself connected with other houses, and a widespread conflagration [results]; this conflagration destroys the property of many other people apart from that of the individual against whom the revenge was directed, and it may even cost many of them their lives. All this was not part of the original deed itself, nor of its perpetrator's intention. But the same action contains yet another[31] general implication: in the intention of its instigator, it was purely a means of gaining revenge on an individual by destroying his property; but it is also a crime, which carries its punishment with it. The perpetrator may not have been conscious of this, and it may not have been his remotest intention, but it is nevertheless the universal and substantial essence of the deed itself, and a necessary consequence of it.

The main purpose of this example is to show that an action may have implications which transcend the intention and consciousness of the agent. The above example has the further peculiarity [that] the substance of the act, and consequently the act itself in its entirety, reacts upon the individual who performed it; it recoils upon him and destroys him, thereby annulling the original act itself (inasmuch as it constitutes a crime) and restoring the authority of justice. But there is no need to stress this aspect here, as it applies only to a specific instance; and besides, I have already said that I wished only to establish an analogy.

But I should like to mention a further example, to which we shall have occasion to return later at the appropriate moment. As an actual historical instance, it exemplifies that combination of the universal and the particular, of an apparently necessary determination and an apparently contingent purpose, in the peculiar form with which we are at present chiefly concerned. Caesar, in danger [of losing] the position to which he had ascended – a position in which he was not yet superior to the others who stood at the head of the state, but at least on an equal footing with them – opposed his rivals with the intention of preserving himself, his position, his honour, and his security. He was in danger [of succumbing] to those who [were] on the point of becoming his enemies, but who at the same time had the formal constitution of the state (and hence the authority of outward legality) on the side of their own personal ends. But since their power gave them sovereignty over the provinces of the Roman Empire, his victory over them simultaneously enabled him to conquer the whole empire itself. He thereby became the sole ruler of the state, although he left the form of the constitution intact. But the means by which he achieved his own (originally negative) end, i.e. the undivided sovereignty of Rome, was at the same time an inherently necessary determination in the history of Rome and of the world. Thus not just his own personal advantage was involved, for his work was the product of an impulse which accomplished the end for which his age was ready. Such are the great men of history: the substance of their own particular ends is the will of the world spirit. Their true power resides in this inner content, which is present in the universal unconscious instinct of mankind. All men are driven on by an inward compulsion, and they are incapable of resisting the individual who has taken it upon himself to execute one of the ends of history in the course of furthering his own personal interests. On the contrary, the nations flock to his standard, for he reveals to them and carries out what is already their own immanent impulse.

A nation consists on the one hand of distinct moments which combine to give it its general character; on the other, it also embodies the opposite principle of individuality, and these two principles together constitute the reality of the Idea. In a nation or state, everything depends on the nature of these two elements, on the way in which they differ, and the way in which they unite. They create between them the living process from which the Idea itself derives its life. The Idea is at first an internal and inactive principle, the inner essence of the nation which exists only in thought and representation, but not yet in reality; and that which implements and externalises this universal principle and gives it reality is the activity of individuality, which translates the inner essence into reality.

It thereby brings what is wrongly described as reality, i.e. the world of mere externals, into conformity with the Idea.

Individuality itself, in so far as it is as yet devoid of spirit or not yet fully developed, comes under this category of mere externality; individual things become progressively more authentic the more completely they enter in their totality into the universal substance and the more completely the Idea enters into them. Everything depends on this relationship between the universal and the subjective; the underlying substance must become part of the national consciousness, so that the nation is conscious of the truth as the essential element which has eternal being in and for itself. But this development towards living consciousness, whereby being in and for itself gains recognition, does not immediately attain its proper form, the form of universality. So long as it remains internal and dormant, the will is still only a natural will which has not yet discovered the rational. Justice and the sense of right as such do not yet exist for it. No truly ethical existence is possible until individuals have become fully conscious of their ends. They must attain knowledge of the unmoved mover, as Aristotle calls it, of the unmoved motive force by which all individuals are activated. For this force to become effective, the subject must have developed to a condition of free individuality in which it is fully conscious of the eternally unmoved mover, and each individual subject must be free and independent in its own right. From this point of view, the individual members of a nation can be seen as analogous to the nations themselves in their independent development throughout the history of the world.

The Idea contains the inner determination of self-knowledge and activity. For the Idea is the eternal inner life of God, the logical nexus which is present, as it were, even before the creation of the world. Initially, it still lacks the form of immediate being, for it is as yet purely general, an inner representation. The second stage in the development of the Idea is that it must acknowledge the rights of the opposite principle which is at first only ideally present within it – in short, it must posit its own antithesis. The antithesis in question is that between the Idea in its free and universal mode, in which it is entirely self-sufficient, and the Idea as purely abstract internal reflection. Thus, while the universal Idea retains its primary position, it proceeds to determine its opposite pole as that of formal being-for-itself, of formal freedom, of abstract unity of self-consciousness, of infinite internal reflection, and of infinite negativity: the ego which, as an individual atom, is diametrically opposed to all fulfilment, is the ultimate extreme within this opposition, the antithesis of the total fullness of the Idea. The universal Idea accordingly exists as substantial fullness on the one hand, and as the abstract quality of free volition on the other. God and the whole of existence are divided up into discrete elements, and each of these is posited as a separate entity; but the knowing subject, the ego, is also in a position to recognise the existence of other things. If we pursue this development further, we can see that the creation of independent minds, and of the world itself, etc., is implicit within it. This dimension of otherness, of the individual atom which is at the same time a plurality, constitutes the world of finite things. Each separate entity exists for itself only in so far as it excludes the other, which is accordingly restricted and limited by it in turn so that it is itself of a finite nature. This reflection of the subject upon itself is individual self-consciousness; it is the complete antithesis of the Idea, and is therefore absolutely finite.

But in relation to the divine glory, as the absolute Idea which perceives the ultimate destiny of everything, this finite realm of maximal freedom, this world of formal knowledge, is the soil in which the spiritual moment of knowledge as such takes root. It is therefore itself an aspect of the absolute, but only of its formal reality. To comprehend this antithetical relationship in absolute terms is the profound concern of metaphysics. For the ego, the other is present both in the divinity, as the object of religion, and also in the world at large, as the universal aggregate of finite things. Within the world of finite things, the ego too sees itself in finite terms; it conceives of itself in this context as something finite, and its perspective is accordingly one of finite ends and of the phenomenal world. The freedom of internal reflection, in an abstract and general sense, is the formal moment in the activity of the absolute Idea. In the first instance, the self-conscious subject wills only itself, and it wills itself in everything; its certainty of itself is such that it seeks its own self-conscious subjectivity in all objective things. This may be called an impulse of reason in so far as it is the sole content of subjectivity – just as the sole concern of religious piety is the salvation of the subject. Thus the ego does not will itself primarily as a knowing subject, but as a finite and immediate entity, and this is the sphere of its phenomenal existence. It wills itself in its own particularity, and it is at this point that the passions come into play, and that individuality realises its own particular nature. If it succeeds in realising its finite nature, it has in fact doubled itself; and when the atom has thus reconciled itself with its other, the individual has attained that state which we call **happiness**. For a man is said to be happy if he has found harmony within himself. It is possible to consider history from the point of view of happiness, but history is not the soil in which happiness grows. The periods of happiness in it are the blank pages of history. There are certainly moments of satisfaction in the history of the world, but this satisfaction is not to be equated with happiness: for the aims which are satisfied transcend all particular interests. All ends of importance in world history must be secured by means of abstract volition and energy. The world-historical individuals who have pursued such ends may well have attained satisfaction, but happiness was certainly not their object.

This moment of abstract activity should be regarded as an intermediate link, a middle term between the universal Idea, which remains at rest in the innermost recesses of the spirit, and the world of external things. It stands for everything which the Idea projects out of itself into external existence. As soon as the universal is externalised, it takes on a particular character. In isolation, the inward dimension of the Idea would remain a lifeless abstraction, and it is only by means of activity that it acquires real existence. Conversely, activity elevates the world of empty objectivity into a manifestation of being in and for itself. So far, we have considered one aspect of the diremption of the Idea – its division into the Idea on the one hand and the atom – the thinking atom – on the other. The atom exists for the other, and the other exists for it; its nature is therefore pure activity and infinite agitation. As a specific entity, it stands out in isolation; but it is at the same time an immediate existence whose task it is to translate everything from the realm of matter into that of universality and vice versa, so that the absolute will may be recognised and fulfilled. This infinite impulse towards unity, this reconciliation of division, is the other aspect of the diremption of the Idea. The perspective of finite existence is that of individual activity, whereby the universal acquires a real existence and realises its inner determinations. It consists, on the one hand, of activity as such, inasmuch as all individuals endeavour to accomplish their real and finite volitions and to gratify their own particular natures. But on the other hand, universal ends such as goodness, justice, and duty are also manifest within it. If this is not the case, a state of barbarism and arbitrariness prevails; but we are here concerned with a higher level than this. The ethical education of the subject consists in learning to generalise from the particular, and it is this alone which makes ethical existence possible. This universal quality in particular things is the particular form of the universal good, in which it attains a specific ethical existence. Its creation is really no more than a conservation of what is already there, in so far as all conservation is productive and not just a lifeless perpetuation of what already exists. This conservation (of ethical norms and recognised standards of right) is of a particular nature, and is not to be equated with goodness in general, which is an abstraction. Duty requires that men should defend not just whatever country they choose but their own particular fatherland. This requirement is the criterion by which the ethical activity of all individuals is measured; it is the source of all the recognised duties and laws which are known to every individual, and the objective basis on which each individual's position rests. For there is no room in living reality for empty notions like that of pursuing goodness for its own sake. If someone intends to act, it is not enough for him simply to pursue the good; he must also know whether this or that specific thing is good. For the everyday contingencies of private life, definitions of what is good and bad or right and wrong are supplied by the laws and customs of each state, and there is no great difficulty in recognising them.

The worth of individuals is measured by the extent to which they reflect and represent the national spirit, and have adopted a particular station within the affairs of the state as a whole. And one of the conditions of freedom in a state is that this decision should be left to the individual, and that the occupation he takes up should not be laid down in advance by any kind of caste system. The individual's **morality** will then consist in fulfilling the duties imposed upon him by his social station; these can be recognised without difficulty, and their particular form will depend on the particular class to which the individual belongs. The substantial nature of such relationships, i.e. the rational element they embody, is universally known, and its expression is what we call duty. To try to define duty in itself is idle speculation, and to regard morality as something difficult to attain may even indicate a desire to exempt oneself from one's duties. Every individual has his **station** in society, and he is fully aware of what constitutes a right and honourable course of action. If someone declares that, in ordinary private existence, it is not at all easy to decide what is right and good, and if he considers that moral excellence consists in finding it extremely difficult to be moral and in having all kinds of scruples about being so, we can only attribute this to his evil or malevolent will which is looking for excuses to escape its duties; for it is by no means hard to recognise what these duties are. Failure to do so suggests at the very least that one's powers of reflection are in abeyance, and that, receiving too little stimulus from a pusillanimous will, they have become preoccupied with other things and have lapsed into moral complacency. The nature of a relationship governed by moral considerations is determined by its underlying substance and by the precepts of duty. Thus, the nature of the relationship between children and their parents simply prescribes that their actions should accord with this relationship. Or to take a legal relationship, let us suppose that I owe someone money. By rights, I must act as the nature of the transaction requires and pay the money back. There is no difficulty here. Duty is rooted in the soil of civil life: individuals follow their appointed profession, and hence also their appointed duty; and their morality consists in acting in accordance with this duty.

Thus, the union of the two extremes – i.e. the translation of the universal Idea into immediate reality and the elevation of the particular to universal truth – is approached from an initial state in which the two sides must be assumed to be completely distinct and indifferent towards one another. The individual agents pursue finite ends and particular interests in their activity; but they are also knowing and thinking beings. For this reason, the content of their ends is interwoven with universal and essential determinations of justice, goodness, duty, and the like. For mere desires and barbarous or uncultivated forms of volition fall outside the sphere of world history and play no part in it. These universal determinants, which also serve as guidelines for the aims and actions of individuals, have a particular content. Each individual is the son of his own nation at a specific stage in this nation's development. No one can escape from the spirit of his nation, any more than he can escape from the earth itself. The earth is the centre of gravity, and if we imagine a body abandoning its own centre, we can only conceive of it as disintegrating in the air. And the same applies to the individual. By his very nature, the individual must accord with his own substance; he must become conscious within himself of the will which his nation demands, and give expression to it. The individual does not invent his content, but merely activates the substantial content which is already present within him.

But this universal substance which every individual must translate into activity, an activity by which the whole of ethical life is sustained, is countered by a second universal which expresses itself in history as a whole and which makes it difficult for the individual to comply with the precepts of ethics. I have already discussed the origin of this second universal in connection with the development of the Idea. It does not fall within the limits of the ethical community; within the latter, there may well be particular occurrences (such as vices, deceptions, and the like) which violate its own particular universal, but these are soon suppressed. Since, however, an ethical whole is of a limited nature, it has above it a higher universal which creates a dichotomy within it. The transition from one phase of the spirit to another can only take place in so far as an earlier universal is overcome* and recognised in its particularity through the activity of thought. The higher universal which supersedes it is, so to speak, the next variety of the previous species, and is already inwardly present within it, although it has not yet come into its own; and it is this which makes the present reality unstable and fragmentary.

One of the essential moments in history is the preservation of the individual nation or state and the preservation of the ordered departments of its life. And the activity of individuals consists in participating in the common cause and helping to further it in all its particular aspects; for it is by this means that ethical life is preserved. But the second moment in history is that the further existence of the national spirit is interrupted (inasmuch as it has exhausted itself and worked itself out to its conclusion) in order that world history and the world spirit may continue in their course. Neither the position of individuals within the ethical whole nor their moral attitudes and duties need be discussed here, for we are concerned only with the development, progress, and ascent of the spirit towards a higher concept of itself. But this is accompanied by the debasement, fragmentation, and destruction of the preceding mode of reality which had already developed its concept to the full. All this takes place to some extent automatically through the inner development of the Idea; yet, on the other hand, the Idea is itself the product of factors outside itself, and it is implemented and brought to its realisation by the actions of individuals. It is precisely at this point that we encounter those great collisions between established and acknowledged duties, laws, and rights on the one hand, and new possibilities which conflict with the existing system and violate it or even destroy its very foundations and continued existence, on the other (although their content may well appear equally good and for the most part propitious, essential, and necessary). These new possibilities then become part of history. They incorporate a universal of a different order from that on which the continued existence of a nation or state is based. For the universal they embody is a moment of the productive Idea itself, of that truth which works its way on to its own realisation.

The great individuals of world history, therefore, are those who seize upon this higher universal and make it their own end. It is they who

_____
* *aufgehoben.*

realise the end appropriate to the higher concept of the spirit. To this extent, they may be called **heroes**. They do not find their aims and vocation in the calm and regular system of the present, in the hallowed order of things as they are. Indeed, their justification does not lie in the prevailing situation, for they draw their inspiration from another source, from that hidden spirit whose hour is near but which still lies beneath the surface and seeks to break out without yet having attained an existence in the present. For this spirit, the present world is but a shell which contains the wrong kind of kernel. It might, however, be objected that everything which deviates from the established order – whether intentions, aims, opinions, or so-called ideals – is likewise different from what is already there. Adventures of all kinds have such ideals, and their activities are based on attitudes which conflict with the present circumstances. But the fact that all such attitudes, sound reasons, or general principles differ from existing ones does not mean to say that they are justified. The only true ends are those whose content has been produced by the absolute power of the inner spirit itself in the course of its development; and world-historical individuals are those who have willed and accomplished not just the ends of their own imagination or personal opinions, but only those which were appropriate and necessary. Such individuals know what is necessary and timely, and have an inner vision of what it is.

It is possible to distinguish between the insight of such individuals and the realisation that even such manifestations of the spirit as this are no more than moments within the universal Idea. To understand this is the prerogative of philosophy. World-historical individuals have no need to do so, as they are men of practice. They do, however, know and will their own enterprise, because the time is ripe for it, and it is already inwardly present. Their business is to know this universal principle, which is the necessary and culminating stage in the development of their world, to make it their end, and to devote their energy to its realisation. They derive the universal principle whose realisation they accomplish from within themselves; it is not, however, their own invention, but is eternally present and is merely put into practice by them and honoured in their persons. But since they draw it from within themselves, from a source which was not previously available, they appear to derive it from themselves alone; and the new world order and the deeds they accomplish appear to be their own achievement, their personal interest and creation. But right is on their side, for they are the far-sighted ones: they have discerned what is true in their world and in their age, and have recognised the concept, the next universal to emerge. And the others, as already remarked, flock to their standard, for it is they who express what the age requires. They are the most far-sighted among their contemporaries; they know best what issues are involved, and whatever they do is right. The others feel that this is so, and therefore have to obey them. Their words and deeds are the best that could be said and done in their time. Thus, the great individuals of history can only be understood within their own context; and they are admirable simply because they have made themselves the instruments of the substantial spirit. This is the true relationship between the individual and his universal substance. For this substance is the source of everything, the sole aim, the sole power, and the sole end which is willed by such individuals; it seeks its satisfaction through them and is accomplished by them. It is this which gives them their power in the world, and only in so far as their ends are compatible with that of the spirit which has being in and for itself do they have absolute right on their side – although it is a right of a wholly peculiar kind.

The state of the world is not yet fully known, and the aim is to give it reality. This is the object of world-historical individuals, and it is through its attainment that they find satisfaction. They can discern the weakness of what still appears to exist in the present, although it possesses only a semblance of reality. The spirit's inward development has outgrown the world it inhabits, and it is about to progress beyond it. Its self-consciousness no longer finds satisfaction in the present, but its dissatisfaction has not yet enabled it to discover what it wants, for the latter is not yet positively present; its status is accordingly negative. The world-historical individuals are those who were the first to formulate the desires of their fellows explicitly. It is not easy for us to know what we want; indeed, we may well want something, yet still remain in a negative position, a position of dissatisfaction, for we may as yet be unconscious of the positive factor. But the individuals in question knew what they wanted, and what they wanted was of a positive nature. They do not at first create satisfaction, however, and the aim of their actions is not that of satisfying others in any case. If this were so, they would certainly have plenty to do, because their fellows do not know what the age requires or even what they themselves desire. But to try to resist these world-historical individuals is a futile undertaking, for they are irresistibly driven on to fulfil their task. Their course is the correct one, and even if the others do not believe that it corresponds to their own desires, they nevertheless adopt it or acquiesce in it. There is a power within them which is stronger than they are, even if it appears to them as something external and alien and runs counter to what they consciously believe they want. For the spirit in its further evolution is the inner soul of all individuals, although it remains in a state of unconsciousness until great men call it to life. It is the true object of all men's desires, and it is for this reason that it exerts a power over them to which they surrender even at the price of denying their conscious will; they follow these leaders of souls because they feel the irresistible power of their own inner spirit pulling them in the same direction.

If we go on to examine the fate of these world-historical individuals, we see that they had the good fortune [to be] the executors of an end which marked a stage in the advance of the universal spirit. But as individual subjects, they also have an existence distinct from that of the universal substance, an existence in which they cannot be said to have enjoyed what is commonly called happiness. They did not wish to be happy in any case, but only to attain their end, and they succeeded in doing so only by dint of arduous labours. They knew how to obtain satisfaction and to accomplish their end, which is the universal end. With so great an end before them, they boldly resolved to challenge all the beliefs of their fellows. Thus it was not happiness that they chose, but exertion, conflict, and labour in the service of their end. And even when they reached their goal, peaceful enjoyment and happiness were not their lot. Their actions are their entire being, and their whole nature and character are determined by their ruling passion. When their end is attained, they fall aside like empty husks. They may have undergone great difficulties in order to accomplish their purpose, but as soon as they have done so, they die early like Alexander, are murdered like Caesar, or deported like Napoleon. One may well ask what they gained for themselves. What they gained was that concept or end which they succeeded in realising. Other kinds of gain, such as peaceful enjoyment, were denied them. The fearful consolation that the great men of history did not enjoy what is called happiness – which is possible only in private life, albeit under all kinds of different external circumstances – this consolation can be found in history by those who are in need of it. It is needed by the envious, who resent all that is great and outstanding and who accordingly try to belittle it and to find fault with it. The existence of such outstanding figures only becomes bearable to them because they know that such men did not enjoy happiness. In this knowledge, envy sees a means of restoring the balance between itself and those whom it envies. Thus, it has often enough been demonstrated even in our own times that princes are never happy on their thrones; this enables men not to grudge them their thrones, and to accept the fact that it is the princes rather than they themselves who sit upon them. The free man, however, is not envious, for he readily acknowledges and rejoices in the greatness of others.

But such great men are fastened upon by a whole crowd of envious spirits who hold up their passions as weaknesses. It is indeed possible to interpret their lives in terms of passion, and to put the emphasis on moral judgements by declaring that it was their passions which motivated them. Of course, they were men of passion, for they were passionately dedicated to their ends, which they served with their whole character, genius, and nature. In such individuals, then, that which is necessary in and for itself assumes the form of passion. Great men of this kind admittedly do seem to follow only the dictates of their passions and of their own free will, but the object of their will is universal, and it is this which constitutes their pathos. Passion is simply the energy of their ego, and without this, they could not have accomplished anything.

In this respect, the aim of passion and that of the Idea are one and the same; passion is the absolute unity of individual character and the universal. The way in which the spirit in its subjective individuality here coincides exactly with the Idea has an almost animal quality about it.

A man who accomplishes something excellent puts his whole energy into the task; he is not sufficiently dispassionate to vary the objects of his will or to dissipate his energy in following various separate ends, but is entirely dedicated to the one great end to which he truly aspires. His passion is the energy of the end itself and the determinate aspect of his will. That a man can thus devote his whole energy to a particular cause suggests a kind of instinct of an almost animal quality. We also describe such passions as zeal or enthusiasm, but we only use the term enthusiasm when the ends in question are of a more ideal and universal nature. The man of politics is not an enthusiast, for he must possess that clear circumspection which we do not normally attribute to enthusiasts. Passion is the prerequisite of all human excellence, and there is accordingly nothing immoral about it. And if such zeal is genuine, it remains cool and reflecting; the theoretical faculty retains a clear view of the means by which its true ends can be realised.

We must further note that, in fulfilling their grand designs as necessitated by the universal spirit, such world-historical individuals not only attained personal satisfaction but also acquired new external characteristics in the process. The end they achieved was also their own end, and the hero himself is inseparable from the cause he promoted, for both of these were satisfied. One may, however, attempt to distinguish the hero's self-satisfaction from the success of the cause itself and to show that the great men in question were really pursuing their own ends, and then conclude that it was only their own ends which they were pursuing. Such men did indeed win fame and honour, and were recognised both by their contemporaries and by posterity – at least so long as the latter has not succumbed to the temptations of criticism, and of envy in particular. But it is absurd to believe that anyone can do anything without wishing to obtain satisfaction from doing so. Nevertheless, since the subjective factor is of a purely particular character, and since its ends are purely finite and individual, it must necessarily subordinate itself to the universal. But in so far as it implements the Idea, it must also help to sustain the underlying substance.

To make a distinction of this kind, however, is simply psychological pedantry. Those who indulge in it label every passion as a lust, and thereby cast doubt on the morality of the individuals in question. In so doing, they present the results of such individuals' actions as their actual ends, and reduce the deeds themselves to the position of means, declaring that those concerned acted solely out of lust for fame, lust for conquest, and the like. Thus the aspirations of Alexander, for example, are characterised as lust for conquest, which lends them a subjective colouring and presents them in an unfavourable light. This so-called psychological approach contrives to trace all actions to the heart and to interpret them subjectively, with the result that their authors appear to have done everything because of some greater or lesser passion or lust, and, on account of such passions and lusts, cannot have been moral men. Alexander of Macedonia partly conquered Greece, and then Asia; therefore he was filled with a lust for conquest. He acted from a lust for fame and conquest, and the proof that these were his motives is that his actions brought him fame. What schoolmaster has not demonstrated of Alexander the Great or Julius Caesar that they were impelled by such passions and were therefore immoral characters? – from which it at once follows that the schoolmaster himself is a more admirable man than they were, because he does not have such passions (the proof being that he does not conquer Asia or vanquish Darius and Porus, but simply lives and lets live). These psychologists are particularly apt to dwell on the private idiosyncrasies of the great figures of history. Man must eat and drink; he has relationships with friends and acquaintances, and has feelings and momentary outbursts of emotion. The great men of history also had such idiosyncrasies; they ate and drank, and preferred this course to another and that wine to another (or to water). 'No man is a hero to his valet de chambre' is a well known saying. I have added – and Goethe repeated it two years later[32] – 'not because the former is not a hero, but because the latter is a valet'. The valet takes off the hero's boots, helps him into bed, knows that he prefers champagne, etc. The hero as such does not exist for the valet, but for the world, for reality, and for history. Historical personages who are waited upon in the history books by such psychological valets certainly come off badly enough; they are reduced to the same level of morality as these fine connoisseurs of humanity, or rather to a level several degrees below theirs. Homer's Thersites, the critic of kings, is a stock figure in all ages. Admittedly, not every age belabours him – in the sense of thrashing him with a stout cudgel – as happened to him in Homer's time; but his envy and obstinacy are the thorn which he carries in his flesh, and the undying worm which eats at him is the tormenting knowledge that all his excellent intentions and criticisms have no effect whatsoever upon the world. We may even derive a malicious satisfaction from the fate of Thersites and his kind.

Besides, psychological pedantry of this variety is not even internally consistent. It depicts the honour and fame of great men as faults, as if honour and fame had been the objects they aimed for. Yet, on the other hand, we are told that the designs of great men must have the assent of others, that is, that their subjective will should be respected by their fellows. But the very fact that they rose to honour and fame implies that they did meet with this required assent and that their aims were recognised by others as correct. The ends which world-historical individuals set themselves in fact correspond to what is already the inner will of mankind. Yet the assent which they are supposed to receive from others is treated as a fault after they have received it, and they are accused of having coveted the honour and fame they achieved. To this we may reply that they were not at all concerned with honour and fame, for the ordinary and superficial appearances which had previously been revered are precisely what they would have treated with derision. And only by so doing were they able to fulfil their task, for otherwise they would have remained within the ordinary channels of human existence, and someone else would have accomplished the will of the spirit.

Yet, on the other hand, they are again censured for not having sought the approval of others and for having flaunted their opinions. It is perfectly true that they rose to honour by treating accepted values with contempt. Since the innovation they brought into the world was their own personal goal, they drew their conception of it from within themselves, and it was their own end that they realised. It was this which gave them their satisfaction. They willed their own end in defiance of others, and were satisfied in the process. The aim of great men was to obtain satisfaction for themselves, and not for the well-meaning intentions of others. They learnt nothing from others, and if they had followed their advice, it would only have limited them and led them astray. They themselves knew what was best. Caesar had formed an extremely accurate impression of the so-called Roman Republic, for he realised that the supposed laws of *auctoritas* and *dignitas* had fallen into abeyance and that it was right and proper to put an end to the latter as a source of individual arbitrariness. He succeeded in doing so because this course was the correct one. If he had followed Cicero, he would never have achieved anything. Caesar knew that the republic was a lie, and that Cicero's words were empty. He knew that this hollow structure had to be replaced by a new one, and that the structure he himself created was the necessary one. Thus such world-historical individuals, in furthering their own momentous interests, did indeed treat other intrinsically admirable interests and sacred rights in a carefree, cursory, hasty, and heedless manner, thereby exposing themselves to moral censure. But their position should be seen in an altogether different light. A mighty figure must trample many an innocent flower underfoot, and destroy much that lies in its path.

The particular interests of passion cannot therefore be separated from the realisation of the universal; for the universal arises out of the particular and determinate and its negation. The particular has its own interests in world history; it is of a finite nature, and as such, it must perish. Particular interests contend with one another, and some are destroyed in the process. But it is from this very conflict and destruction of particular things that the universal emerges, and it remains unscathed itself. For it is not the universal Idea which enters into opposition, conflict, and danger; it keeps itself in the background, untouched and unharmed, and sends forth the particular interests of passion to fight and wear themselves out in its stead. It is what we may call the cunning of reason that it sets the passions to work in its service, so that the agents by which it gives itself existence must pay the penalty and suffer the loss. For the latter belong to the phenomenal world, of which part is worthless and part is of positive value. The particular is as a rule inadequate in relation to the universal, and individuals are sacrificed and abandoned as a result. The Idea pays the tribute which existence and the transient world exact, but it pays it through the passions of individuals rather than out of its own resources. Caesar had to do what was necessary to overthrow the decaying freedom of Rome; he himself met his end in the struggle, but necessity triumphed: in relation to the Idea, freedom was subordinate to the external events.

But although we may accept that individuals, their aims, and the satisfaction of these aims are sacrificed, that their entire happiness is given up to the realm of natural forces – and hence to the realm of contingency to which it belongs – and that individuals in general come under the category of means rather than ends, there still remains one aspect of individuality which we should hesitate to view in this light, even in relation to the universal itself, for it is definitely not of a subordinate nature. It is an essentially eternal and divine principle which is present in all individuals, and it manifests itself in morality, ethics, and religiosity. In my earlier remarks on how the end of reason is put into operation by individuals, I have already mentioned that their subjective aim – i.e. their interest as a whole and that of their needs and impulses, opinions and convictions – although representing only the formal aspect of their activity, itself has an infinite right to be satisfied. When we speak of a means, we think of it primarily as something wholly external to the end and as having no part in the latter. But in fact, even natural objects and the commonest inanimate materials, if used as means, must be suited to their end and have something in common with it. And the relationship of human beings to the end of reason is least of all that of a means in this purely external sense; for in fulfilling the end of reason, they not only simultaneously fulfil their own particular ends (whose content is quite different from that of the universal end), but also participate in the end of reason itself, and are therefore ends in their own right. They are ends in themselves not only in a formal sense, as are all living things[33] *(although their individual life is by its very nature subordinate to that of man and is rightly used by him as a means); individual human beings are also ends in themselves by virtue of the content of the end which they serve. And under this heading we must include all that we would exempt from the category of means, namely morality, ethics, and religiosity. Man is an end in himself only by virtue of that divine principle within him which we have all along referred to as reason (or, in so far as it is internally active and self-determining, as freedom); and although we cannot discuss its further implications here, we may nevertheless assert that religiosity, ethics, etc., have their roots and source in this principle and are therefore essentially elevated above external necessity and chance. But it must be remembered that we are only concerned with these factors in so far as they exist within individuals, that is, in so far as they are subject to the discretion of individual freedom; from this point of view, the individuals themselves can be blamed for any decline, corruption, or loss of religious and moral values.*

This is the hallmark of the sublime and absolute destiny of man – that he knows what good and evil are, and that it is his will which chooses either the one or the other. In short, he can be held responsible, for good as well as for evil, and not just for this or that particular circumstance and for everything around him and within him, but also for the good and evil which are inherent in his individual freedom. Only the animal can truly be described as totally innocent. But to prevent or remove all the misunderstandings to which this usually gives rise (for example, the fallacy that innocence, in the sense of complete unconsciousness of evil, is hereby debased and devalued) would require an extensive disquisition, a disquisition no less extensive than a complete treatise on freedom itself.

But when we consider the fate which overtakes virtue, morality, and even religiosity in history, we must not fall into a litany of lamentations to the effect that the good and the pious often, or indeed in most cases, fare badly in the world, while the evil and the wicked prosper. The idea of prosperity can be interpreted in very many different ways, for example in the sense of wealth, outward honour, and the like. But when we are discussing an end which exists in and for itself, the so-called prosperity or misfortune of some particular individuals or other cannot and should not be regarded as an essential moment within the rational order of the universe. There is more justification for requiring that the universal end should allow good, just, and moral ends to seek fulfilment and protection within it and under it than for expecting it to provide individuals with happiness and good fortune. What makes men morally discontented (and they may even take a certain pride in this discontent) is that they find the present unsuited to their ideas, principles, and opinions concerning ends of a more universal content, which they consider to be right and good (among which we must nowadays include ideals of political constitutions in particular), or to their predilection for constructing their own ideals on which to lavish their enthusiasm.* They contrast existence as it is with their own view of how things by rights ought to be. In this case, it is not particular interests or passions which demand satisfaction, but reason, justice, and freedom; and, equipped with this title, such demands give themselves an air of authority and can easily take the form not just of discontent with the condition and events of the world but of actual rebellion against them. To appreciate such feelings and attitudes correctly, we should have to make a thorough examination of the demands themselves and of the highly peremptory views and attitudes which accompany them. Never before have so many general propositions and ideas been advanced on such matters, and with such great pretension, as in our own times. Whereas history usually presents itself as a conflict of passions, in the present age – although the

---

* This sentence is grammatically and syntactically incoherent in Hegel's original German.

passions are not absent – it appears, on the one hand, primarily as a conflict of ideas vying with one another to justify themselves and, on the other, as a conflict of passions and subjective interests, but essentially under the guise of the higher principles which are used to justify them. These rights, demanded in the name of what we have described as the absolute end of reason and as self-conscious freedom, are thereby classed as absolute ends like those of religion, ethics, and morality.

We shall turn in a moment to the state, at which all such demands are directed. But as for the corruption, violation, and destruction of religious, ethical, and moral purposes and affairs in general, it must at least be[34] *said – although we shall examine the question in more detail later – that such spiritual forces are indeed absolutely justified; nevertheless, although their inward and universal aspect is infinite, the forms they assume, their content, and their development towards realisation may be of a limited character, and hence subject to the realm of external nature and of contingency. In this respect, therefore, they too are transient and subject to decay and injury. Religion and ethics, as intrinsically universal essences, have by definition (and hence in the true sense) the quality of being present in the individual soul, even if they do not develop to their fullest extent in it and are not applied to situations of great complexity. The religiosity and ethicality of a restricted sphere of life (for example, that of a shepherd or peasant), in their concentrated inwardness and limitation to a few simple situations of life, have infinite worth; they are just as valuable as those which accompany a high degree of knowledge and a life with a wide range of relationships and actions.*[35] *This inner centre, this simple source of the rights of subjective freedom, the seat of volition, resolution, and action, the abstract content of conscience, that in which the responsibility and worth of the individual and his eternal court of judgement are contained – all this remains untouched and [protected] from the noisy clamour of world history, and not only from external and temporary changes, but also from those produced by the absolute necessity of the concept of freedom itself. But as a general rule, we must take it as established that whatever in the world can justly claim glory and nobility is nevertheless subject to something even higher than itself. The right of the world spirit transcends all particular rights; it shares in the latter itself, but only to a limited extent, for although these lesser rights may partake of its substance, they are at the same time fraught with particularity.*

These remarks may suffice in respect of the means which the world spirit employs in order to realise its concept. In simple abstract terms, the means it employs is the activity of individual subjects in which reason is present as their inherent substantial essence; but this basis is as yet indistinct and concealed from their view. The problem becomes more complex and difficult, however, when we consider individuals not merely from the point of view of their[36] actions and of those particular ends which are confined to them alone, but in more concrete terms with reference to the determinate content of their[37] religion and ethical life; for this content partakes of reason itself and hence also of its absolute rights. In the latter instance, the relation of a mere means to an end disappears. The principal considerations which arise in connection with the absolute end of the spirit have, however, already been briefly discussed.

c. [*The material of its realisation*]

The third point to be considered is the nature of the end to be realised by these means, in other words, the form it assumes in reality. We have spoken hitherto of means, but in the realisation of a subjective and finite end we must also take account of the material which is available or which has to be procured in order that the end may be realised. The question we must answer is accordingly this: what is the material in which the ultimate end of reason is realised?

The changes in historical existence presuppose a medium within which such changes occur. But as we have seen, it is the subjective will which implements them. Thus, in this case too, the first part of our answer is once again the subject itself, the needs of men, and the realm of subjectivity in general. The rational attains existence within the medium of human knowledge and volition. We have seen how the subjective will has an end which represents the truth of a reality (in so far as it embodies some great passion of world-historical significance). When its passions are limited, however, the subjective will is dependent, and it can only satisfy its particular ends within this position of dependence. But as already pointed out, it too has a substantial life, a reality in which it moves as in its essential being and which constitutes the aim of its existence. This essential being, the unity of the subjective will and the universal, is the ethical whole, and its concrete manifestation is the **state**. The state is the reality within which the individual has and enjoys his freedom, but only in so far as he knows, believes in, and wills the universal. This, then, is the focal point of all the other concrete aspects of the spirit, such as justice, art, ethics, and the amenities of existence. Within the state, freedom becomes its own object and achieves its positive realisation. But this does not mean that the subjective will of the individual is implemented and satisfied through the universal will, and that the latter is merely a means to the end of the former. Nor is the universal will merely a community of human beings within which the freedom of all individuals has to be limited. To imagine that freedom is such that the individual subject, in its co-existence with other subjects, must limit its freedom in such a way that this collective restriction, the mutual constraint of all, leaves everyone a limited area in which to act as he pleases, is to interpret freedom in purely negative terms; on the contrary, justice, ethical life, and the state, and these alone, are the positive realisation and satisfaction of freedom. The random inclinations of individuals are not the same thing as freedom. That kind of freedom on which restrictions are imposed is mere arbitrariness, which exists solely in relation to particular needs.

Only in the state does man have a rational existence. The aim of all education is to ensure that the individual does not remain purely subjective but attains an objective existence within the state. The individual can certainly make the state into a means of attaining this or that end. But the truth is realised only in so far as each individual wills the universal cause itself and has discarded all that is inessential. Man owes his entire existence to the state, and has his being within it alone. Whatever worth and spiritual reality he possesses are his solely by virtue of the state. For as a knowing being, he has spiritual reality only in so far as his being, i.e. the rational itself, is his object and possesses objective and immediate existence for him; only as such does he possess consciousness and exist in an ethical world, within the legal and ethical life of the state. For the truth is the unity of the universal and the subjective will, and the universal is present within the state, in its laws and in its universal and rational properties.

The subjective will – or passion – is the activating and realising principle; the Idea is the inner essence, and the state is the reality of ethical life in the present. For the state is the unity of the universal, essential will and the will of the subject, and it is this which constitutes ethical life. The individual who lives within this unity has an ethical existence, and his value consists solely in this substantiality. Sophocles' Antigone says: 'The divine commands are not of yesterday, nor of today; no, they live eternally, and no one could say whence they came.' The laws of ethics are not contingent, for they are the rational itself. The aim of the state is that the substance which underlies the real activity and dispositions of men should be recognised and made manifest, and that it should ensure its own continuity. The absolute interest of reason requires that this ethical whole should be present; and it is from this interest of reason that the justification and merit of those heroes who have founded states – however primitive the latter may have been – are derived. The state does not exist for the sake of the citizens; it might rather be said that the state is the end, and the citizens are its instruments. But this relation of end and means is not at all appropriate in the present context. For the state is not an abstraction which stands in opposition to the citizens; on the contrary, they are distinct moments like those of organic life, in which no one member is either a means or an end. The divine principle in the state is the Idea made manifest on earth.

The essence of the state is ethical life. This consists in the unity of the universal and the subjective will. The will is activity, and within the subjective will, it encounters its opposite in the external world. The principle of the will is that of being for itself; but this entails exclusivity and limitation. It is often said that man is unlimited in his will and limited in his thought, although quite the reverse is true. But if we take the will in its essential being in and for itself, we must conceive of it as liberated from its opposition to the external world, and as completely universal in this respect too. Thus, the will is a power in its own right and the essence of universal power in both nature and the spirit. We may choose to think of this essential being as 'the Lord', the Lord of nature and of the spirit. The Lord as a subject, however, is merely one entity as against other entities. But the absolute power is not Lord over other things, but Lord over itself, reflection within itself, or personality. This inward reflection is simple self-relatedness with an existence of its own; for power, thus internally reflected, is immediate reality. But this is equivalent to knowledge, or, more precisely, to the bearer of knowledge – in other words, to human individuality. The universal spirit is essentially present as human consciousness. Knowledge attains existence and being for itself in man. The spirit knows itself and exists for itself as a subject, and its nature is to posit itself as immediate existence: as such, it is equivalent to human consciousness.

It is customary to act in accordance with the universal will and to make one's aim a universal one which is recognised within the state. Even in primitive states the will is subordinated to another will, although this does not mean that the individual has no will of his own, but only that his particular will has no authority. The whims and fancies of individuals are not taken into account; even in primitive political conditions, the particular aspects of the will are disregarded, and the universal will is alone essential. The particular will is at least suppressed, and it accordingly turns in upon itself. This is the first necessary moment in the existence of the universal – the element of knowledge and thought which emerges at this point within the state. Only in this environment, i.e. within the state, can art and religion exist. The nations we are concerned with here have acquired a rational internal organisation, and world history takes account only of those nations which have formed themselves into states. But we must not imagine that this can occur on a desert island or in a completely isolated community. It is certainly true that all great men have developed in solitude, but they have done so only by assimilating to their own ends what the state had already created. The universal must be more than just the opinions of individuals. It must have an existence of its own, and as such, it is to be found in the state itself in the shape of all that is generally recognised. In the state, the internal becomes reality. Reality, of course, is outwardly varied, but in this case, we are considering its universal qualities.

The universal Idea attains phenomenal reality in the state. As regards the expression **phenomenal**, it should be noted that its meaning in the present context is not the same as in everyday thinking. In everyday usage, we distinguish between forces and phenomena, as if the former were essential and the latter inessential and external. But even the category of force does not contain a concrete determination. In the case of the spirit or concrete concept, however, the phenomenon itself is the essential. The differentiation of spirit is the work of the spirit itself, and it is the product of its own activity. Man, too, is his own product; he is the sum total of his own deeds, and has made himself what he is. Spirit, therefore, is essentially energy, so that it is impossible in this case to abstract from the phenomenon itself. The phenomenal aspect of the spirit is its self-determination, which is the element of its concrete nature: the spirit which does not determine itself is merely an abstraction of the understanding. The self-determination of the spirit is its phenomenal aspect, which we have to consider here in the shape of states and individuals.

The spiritual individual, the nation – in so far as it is internally differentiated so as to form an organic whole – is what we call the state. This term is ambiguous, however, for the state and the laws of the state, as distinct from religion, science, and art, usually have purely political associations. But in this context, the word 'state' is used in a more comprehensive sense, just as we use the word 'realm' to describe spiritual phenomena. A nation should therefore be regarded as a spiritual individual, and it is not primarily its external side that will be emphasised here, but rather what we have previously called the spirit of the nation, i.e. its self-consciousness in relation to its own truth and being, and what it recognises as truth in the absolute sense – in short, those spiritual powers which live within the nation and rule over it. The universal which emerges and becomes conscious within the state, the **form** to which everything in it is assimilated, is what we call in general the nation's **culture**. But the determinate **content** which this universal form acquires and which is contained in the concrete reality which constitutes the state is the **national spirit** itself. The real state is animated by this spirit in all its particular transactions, wars, institutions, etc. This spiritual content is a firm and solid nucleus which is completely removed from the world of arbitrariness, particularities, caprices, individuality, and contingency; whatever is subject to the latter is not part of the nation's character: it is like the dust which blows over a town or a field or hangs above it without changing it in any essential way. Besides, this spiritual content is the essential being of each individual, as well as constituting the spirit of the nation. It is the sacred bond which links men and spirits together. It remains one and the same life, one great object, one great end, and one great content, on which all private happiness and all private volition depend.

Thus, the state is the more specific object of world history in general, in which freedom attains its objectivity and enjoys the fruits of this objectivity. For the law is the objectivity of the spirit, and the will in its true expression; and only that will which obeys the law is free: for it obeys itself and is self-sufficient and therefore free. When the state or fatherland constitutes a community of existence, and when the subjective will of men subordinates itself to laws, the opposition between freedom and necessity disappears. The rational, as the substance of things, is necessary, and we are free in so far as we recognise it as law and follow it as the substance of our own being; the objective and the subjective will are then reconciled, forming a single, undivided whole. For the ethical character of the state is not that of individual morality, which is a product of reflection and subject to personal conviction; reflective morality is more accessible to the modern world, whereas the true ethics of antiquity are rooted in the fact that everyone adhered to his prescribed duty. An Athenian citizen did virtually by instinct what was expected of him; if I reflect on the object of my activity, however, I must be conscious that my will has assented to it. But ethical life is duty, the substantial right, or second nature (as it has justly been called); for man's first nature is his immediate animal existence.

The nature of the state has now been described. We have also seen that, in present-day theories, various misconceptions concerning the state are prevalent. These have acquired the status of established truths, and have become fixed prejudices. We will cite only a few of them here, with particular reference to those which have some relationship to the aim of our study of history.

The first fallacy we encounter stands in direct contradiction to our concep-
tion of the state as the realisation of freedom. According to the view in question,
man is by nature free, but in society and the state – which he must of necessity
enter – he must limit this natural freedom. That man is by nature free is
perfectly true in the sense that he is free by the inherent concept of his nature,
but only in relation to his destiny, i.e. to what he is in himself; for it must
be acknowledged that the nature of an object is equivalent to its inherent
concept. But the above proposition is also supposed to provide information
regarding man's natural and immediate mode of existence. In this way, a
state of nature is postulated in which man is allegedly in full possession of
his natural rights, with unrestricted exercise and enjoyment of his freedom.
This assumption does not exactly claim the status of historical fact – and if it
did seriously make such pretensions, it would be difficult to show that such a
condition actually existed either in the present or at any time in the past.
States of savagery can certainly be encountered, but they are obviously
associated with brutal passions and deeds of violence; and no matter how
primitive they are, they are also accompanied by social institutions which – to
use the common expression – impose restrictions on freedom. This assumption
is one of those nebulous constructions which theory produces as a necessary
consequence of its operations, and to which it then attributes a real existence
without seeking any historical justification for doing so.

It is customary to present history as beginning with a state of nature
or state of innocence. But according to our present conception of the
spirit, its initial condition is not a state of freedom at all but a state in
which the spirit as such has no reality. The opposite view is based on a
misunderstanding. If the word 'nature' denotes the being or concept of a
thing, then the state of nature or the law of nature is that state or law
which is appropriate to man by virtue of his inherent concept and of the
inherent concept of spirit. But this must not be confused with what the
spirit is in its natural condition; for the latter is a condition of servitude
in which man lives by the intuitions of his senses: Exeundum est e statu
naturae (Spinoza). We shall therefore not begin with those traditions
which tell of man's original condition (the Mosaic tradition, for example),
but will touch on them only at that point of time at which the prophecies
they embodied were fulfilled. For only then do the latter have a historical
existence; before that time, they had not yet become part of their national
cultures.

States of nature as we encounter them in empirical existence do indeed
conform to the concept of a purely natural state. Freedom as the ideal condition
of what is as yet purely immediate and natural does not itself possess an

immediate and natural existence. It still has to be earned and won through the endless mediation of discipline acting upon the powers of cognition and will. For this reason, the state of nature is rather a state of injustice, of violence, of uncontrolled natural impulses, and of inhuman deeds and emotions. It does involve some restrictions imposed by society and the state, but such restrictions are imposed only on those brutal emotions and crude impulses already referred to, on reflected inclinations, on the needs which arise with the progress of culture, and on arbitrariness and passion. Restrictions of this kind are part of that process of mediation whereby the consciousness of freedom and the will to realise it in its true (i.e. rational and essential) form are engendered. The concept of freedom is such that justice and ethical life are inseparable from it, and these are universal essences, objects, and aims which exist in and for themselves, which can be discovered only through the activity of thought (as it distinguishes itself from the realm of the senses and develops itself in opposition to the latter), and which must in turn be assimilated and incorporated into the (primarily sensuous) will in defiance of its own inclinations. To regard freedom in a purely formal and subjective sense, abstracted from its absolutely essential objects and aims, is a perennial misunderstanding; for it means that impulses, desires, and passions – which pertain by their nature exclusively to the particular individual – and arbitrariness and random inclinations are identified with freedom, and that any restrictions imposed upon these are seen as restrictions on freedom itself. On the contrary, such restrictions are the indispensable conditions of liberation; and society and the state are the only situations in which freedom can be realised.

We must also mention a second point of view which conflicts with the development of justice towards a law-governed state. The **patriarchal** *condition is regarded – either in relation to the human species as a whole or at least to some branches of it – as that state in which both justice and the ethical and emotional aspects of life receive their due, and in which justice itself, in conjunction with these other elements, is truly realised in all its implications. The patriarchal condition is based on the family relationship, the earliest expression of ethical life, to which the second (consciously developed) institution of the state is subsequently added. The patriarchal relationship is a transitional stage in which the family has already grown into a tribe or nation. The family bond has therefore already ceased to be simply a bond of love and trust, and has become an association of mutual service.*

We must first define the ethical principle of the family. The family is nothing more than a single person; its members have either mutually surrendered their individual personality (and hence also their legal status as

individuals and all their other particular interests and selfish inclinations),
as in the case of the parents, or they do not yet have a personality of their
own, as in the case of the children, who remain for the time being in that
state of nature described above. They accordingly live in a union of feeling,
love, trust, and faith towards one another. Within a love relationship, the
individual is conscious of himself through the consciousness of another; he
renounces his own self, and in this mutual renunciation, each gains not only
the other self but also his own self in return, for the latter is united with that
of the other. The further interests which arise out of the exigencies and external
concerns of life, as well as the internal development of the family (which takes
place through the children) lend it a common purpose. The spirit of the
family – the Penates – constitutes a single substantial being just as much as
the spirit of the nation within the state, and ethical life consists in both cases
in a common sentiment, a common consciousness, and a common volition
which are not confined to individual personalities and interests. But in the
family, this unity is essentially one of feeling, and it remains on a purely
natural plane. Family piety must be treated with the highest respect by the
state; for it is thanks to it that the state has as its members individuals who
already have an explicitly ethical existence (which, as individual persons,
they do not possess), and who bring with them as a sound basis of political life
the ability to feel that they belong to a larger whole. But the expansion of the
family into a patriarchal unit transcends the ties of blood relationship and
the purely natural aspect of the original family, beyond which individuals must
assume the status of independent personalities.

To examine the wider implications of the patriarchal condition would also
lead us to consider the form of theocracy, for the head of the patriarchal
tribe is also its priest. If the family is still completely at one with society and
the state, religion has not yet been divorced from it either, the less so since
family piety is itself a deeply subjective form of emotion.

Situations of this kind are certainly to be encountered in the world, and
states also originate in part from the union of families. The family itself
is an ethical whole, although it is in love as such that the spirit manifests
itself within it. In the family as well as in the nation, each member knows
that he is a member of the whole; he does not work selfishly for his own
ends, but for those of the whole family. But the spirit of the state is
different from the ethic of the family, the spirit of the Penates. In the
state, the spirit does not assume the form of love and emotion, but of
consciousness, volition, and knowledge. The state has the universal of
ethical life already present within it as a natural world, for its ethics
appear as an immediate form of ethical existence. But a state requires

laws, which means that its ethicality is present not only in an immediate form, but also in a universal form as an object of knowledge. It is the fact that this universal is known which lends the state its spiritual quality. The individual obeys the laws and knows that he owes his freedom to this obedience; his relationship to his own will is governed by it. This unity is therefore consciously willed. Thus, individuals enjoy a position of independence within the state; for they are knowing subjects, in that they can distinguish between their own ego and the universal. Such independence is not to be found within the family, for it is a natural impulse which binds the members of the family together. Only within the state are their powers of internal reflection developed; for in the state, a division arises between that which confronts the individuals as their object, and the position of independence which they occupy in face of it. This is the moment of rationality whereby the state exists as an inherently concrete entity.

We must now consider more closely the further determination of the national spirit, its internal differentiation, and the essentially necessary phenomena in which the spirit appears as self-activating and self-determining: for these are the qualities which make it what it is. When we speak of a nation, we must analyse those powers in which the spirit particularises itself. These powers are religion, the constitution, the system of justice (including civil right), industry, trade, arts and science, and the military world, the world of valour, by which one nation is distinguished from the other. The relationship between these distinct moments is of particular relevance to our present discussion. All the features which stand out in the history of a nation are intimately connected with one another. The history of a nation consists solely of that process whereby the nation impresses on all the spheres of its activity the spirit's concept of its own nature. In other words, the state, religion, art, the system of justice, and the relationship of the nation to other nations – all of these are aspects in which the spirit's concept of itself is realised, in which the spirit contrives to perceive itself and to know itself as an existent world, and to have itself as its own object. As such, it is like an artist who is impelled to project his own being outside himself and to satisfy himself in his own work. The products of the national spirit, as already mentioned, include religion, etc.; but they also include the stages in its destiny and the deeds which it performs: for these are nothing more than the expression of its inherent concept. A nation's religion, its laws, its ethical life, the state of its knowledge, its arts, its judiciary, its other particular aptitudes and the industry by which it satisfies its needs, its entire destiny, and its relations with its neighbours in war and peace – all these are extremely closely connected. **Montesquieu** in particular was a firm advocate of this view, which he expressed and elaborated with great ingenuity. Its importance is manifold, for it enables us to perceive, for example, that Indian religion is incompatible with the spiritual freedom of the Europeans, and that political constitutions, which are often widely different, are themselves incompatible with an alien religion. On the other hand, the proposition that all aspects of national life are related is an overworked one. A multitude of sayings to this effect is in common use, and they fill whole pages and indeed books without conferring any real content upon them. For example, there are nations in which many arts have attained a high degree of perfection, as in China and India. But although the Chinese invented gunpowder, they did not know how to use it, while the Indians produced superb gems of poetry without any corresponding advances in art, freedom, and law. If, on the strength of these particular achievements, we were to pass the superficial judgement that their culture was uniform in every respect, it would at once be evident how seriously our initial proposition concerning the relatedness of all branches of national life can be misunderstood. What matters most is that the real nature of the relationship in question should be defined. But this side of the problem has been neglected, as if it were enough to note simply that the various moments of national life were generally related; there is, however, one principle basic to them all, the spirit of their determinate character which permeates every one of them. This principle is the nation's **self-consciousness**, the active force at work in the destinies of all nations. The various aspects of a nation's culture are the spirit's relationships to itself; it is the spirit which shapes the nations, and we can only know these relationships if we recognise the spirit itself. In this way, the substance of the national spirit should be seen as a kind of Hermes, who leads the souls to the underworld, as the guide and leader of all individuals within the nation. This is what is meant by the idea that it is important to have the individuals present to us.

*The living reality of the state within its individual members is what we have called its **ethical life**. The state and its laws and institutions belong to these individuals; they enjoy their rights within it, and they have their external possessions within its nature, its soil, its mountains, its air, and its waters, for it is their land, their fatherland. The history of their state, its deeds and the deeds of their forefathers, are theirs too; this past heritage lives in their memory as having created what now exists, and it is to them that it* *belongs. All this is their property, just as they are its property; for it is their very substance and being. Their ideas are fulfilled within it, and their will affirms the laws of their fatherland.* If he is asked, any Englishman will say of himself and his fellow citizens that it is they who rule the East Indies and the oceans of the world, who dominate world trade, who have a parliament and trial by jury, etc. It is deeds such as these which give the nation its sense of identity. *This spiritual totality constitutes a single being, the spirit of the nation. Since it is of a spiritual nature, and since all its determinate attributes are parts of one simple entity, it must become fixed as one power and one being; Athena, for example, has a double significance;* [*she is the city of Athens itself in its totality, and the goddess as the spirit by which this totality is animated*]. *The individuals belong to this spirit; each of them is the son of his nation, and also, in so far as the state to which he belongs is still developing, the son of his age – for no one can remain behind the age he lives in, let alone transcend it. This spiritual being is his being, and he is its representative; he arises out of it and exists within it.* It is this which constitutes the objective element in all men, and everything else is purely formal.

The national spirit is a determinate spirit, and, as I have just said, it is also determined by the stage of historical development it has reached. This same spirit is likewise the foundation and content of the other forms of spiritual awareness mentioned above. For in its self-consciousness, the spirit must be its own object, and its objective reality directly entails the emergence of differences which together make up the totality of the various spheres of the objective spirit; in the same way, the soul exists only as a system of distinct components which, joining together into a simple unit, produce the soul itself. *The spirit is a single individual; in religion, its essential being is represented, revered, and assimilated as the divine being or God; in art, it is depicted as an image and intuition;* * *and in philosophy, it is recognised and comprehended by thought. The forms which it assumes, because of the original identity of their substance, their content, and their object, are indivisibly united with the spirit of the state, so that this particular form of state can only exist in conjunction with a particular religion, and only this or that particular philosophy and art can exist within it.*

The foregoing remarks are particularly important in view of the foolish attempts made in our own times to devise and implement constitutions independently of religion. The Catholic religion, although it is akin to Protestantism in so far as they are both forms of Christianity, does not

* *Anschauung.*

103

permit that internal justice and ethicality in politics which the more profound principle of Protestantism embodies. The peculiar nature of a religion which does not acknowledge the independent and substantial existence of justice and ethical life does make it necessary for the political constitution to be separated from religion itself; but if political principles and institutions are divorced from the realm of inwardness, from the innermost shrine of conscience, from the still sanctuary of religion, they lack any real centre and remain abstract and indeterminate.

We have, then, distinguished two separate moments: the Idea of freedom as the absolute and ultimate end, and the means by which it is realised, the subjective aspect of knowledge and volition with all its life, movement, and activity. We have recognised that the state is the totality of ethical life and the realisation of freedom, and hence the objective unity of the two moments in question. For although the two aspects may be distinguished for the purposes of discussion, we must not forget that they are intimately connected, and that this connection is implicit in each of them even if they are considered in isolation. On the one hand, we have recognised that the Idea in its determinate form is equivalent to freedom which knows and wills its own existence and whose sole end is itself: and it is also the simple concept of reason and what we have described as the subject, or self-consciousness, or the spirit in its worldly existence. If, on the other hand, we consider subjectivity itself, we find that subjective knowledge and volition are the same thing as thought. But if I know and will something as a thinking being, the object of my will is the universal substance of reason which exists in and for itself. It is therefore evident that the objective aspect, i.e. the concept, and the subjective aspect, are implicitly united. The objective existence of this union is the state, which is accordingly the basis and focus of the other concrete aspects of national life – of art, justice, ethics, religion, and science. The sole end of all spiritual activity is to attain consciousness of this union, and hence of freedom. Of all the forms which this conscious union assumes, **religion** occupies the first place. In it, spirit in its worldly existence becomes conscious of the absolute spirit, and in this consciousness of the being which exists in and for itself, the human will relinquishes its particular interests; it puts them aside in a spirit of devotion in which it can no longer occupy itself with particulars. Through sacrifice, man expresses his renunciation of his property, his will, and his particular emotions. The religious concentration of the mind takes the form of feeling, but it also passes over into contemplation: for worship is an external manifestation of contemplation. The second form which the spiritual union of the objective and the subjective assumes is **art**: art enters more fully into the world of sensuous reality than does religion, and its worthiest occupation is to portray, if not the spirit of God, at least the form of the deity, and the divine and the spiritual in general. The aim of art is to make the divine immediately perceptible and to present it to the imagination and intuition.* But truth is present not only to the powers of representation† and feeling, as in religion, and to intuition, as in art, but also to the thinking mind: and this brings us to the third form of spiritual union, that of **philosophy**, which, in its own way, is the highest, freest, and wisest of the three.

That content of the state which exists in and for itself is the national spirit. The real state is animated by this spirit, but the real state is also occupied with determinate interests and particular matters such as wars, institutions, and the like. But these are not the only things which man must know, for through them, he must also know himself and become expressly conscious of his original unity with the universal spirit. The real spirit of this consciousness and the focal point of this knowledge is **religion**. It is the primary mode of self-consciousness, the spiritual consciousness of the national spirit itself, of the universal spirit which exists in and for itself, but in its determinate role as the spirit of a nation; it is the consciousness of truth in its purest and most undivided determination. And everything else which can be defined as true is the concern of all men in so far as it has a corresponding principle within religion. To this extent, religion, which is the representation of God, constitutes the universal horizon and foundation of the nation's existence. It is in terms of religion that a nation defines what it considers to be true. The definition of an object, or the laws which govern it, contain everything which belongs to that object by virtue of its inner essence. This definition is equivalent to the nature of the object as a whole, reduced to a simple determination of thought by means of which all its individual properties can be said to be explained; in short, it is the soul of all particular things. In this way, we can deduce all the particular positions of the heavenly bodies from the laws which govern their movement.

Religion is the nation's consciousness of its own being and of the highest being. This knowledge is in fact the universal being. A nation conceives of God in the same way as it conceives of itself and of its relationship to God, so that its religion is also its conception of itself. A nation which worships nature cannot possess freedom; for only if it sees

---

* *Anschauung.*   † *Vorstellung.*

God as a spirit which transcends nature can it itself become a spirit and attain freedom. But when we consider spiritual religions themselves, everything depends on whether they know the truth – i.e. the Idea – only in its divided form, or in its true unity. In the former case, God is regarded as the highest being in an abstract sense, as Lord of heaven and earth, who exists above and beyond the world and from whom human reality is excluded. In the latter, God is seen as the unity of the universal and the particular, for within him, even the particular takes on a positive significance in the idea of the Incarnation. Within the divine Idea, the unity and universality of spirit and of consciousness in its true existence have their being; in other words, the finite and the infinite are united. Where the two are separate, the infinity of the understanding is dominant. But in the Christian religion, the divine Idea is revealed as the unity of divine and human nature. This is the true Idea of religion. It is the object of worship, which is simply the means whereby the individual consciousness becomes united with the divinity. The understanding of the modern age has made God into an abstraction, into something which lies beyond the self-consciousness of man, into a bare iron wall against which man can only beat his head in vain. But the ideas of reason are totally different from the abstractions of the understanding.

The object of religion is the truth, the unity of the subjective and the objective. But in particular religions, the absolute often becomes separated again from the finite, even where the former already goes under the name of spirit; in such cases, spirit is no more than an empty name. This applies to the Jews, to the Mohammedans, and to the modern religion of the understanding, which in this respect has reverted to the Turkish attitude. It is also possible to conceive of this abstract universal as a mere work of nature of an elemental variety such as fire; but it can also be interpreted as a spiritual universal, as in the Jewish religion. If man equates this universal with nature, his religion is one of pantheism. But pantheism has no content, for God, as a subject, disappears, because the subject no longer has any distinct existence. Another possibility is to conceive of God as united with the world: this applies to the Indian doctrine of incarnation, to the art of the Greeks, and, in a much more refined sense, to the Christian religion, in which the unity of divine and human nature is made manifest in Christ. The Christian incarnation is not presented in an anthropomorphic form unworthy of the deity, but points instead to the true Idea of God.

To show in more detail how the religious consciousness progressively acquires a greater understanding of the nature of spirit is the task of the philosophy of religion, and we can only touch upon it in passing here. For we are equally concerned with the other aspects of the spirit, with the remaining forms into which the national spirit is differentiated. The real spirit of this consciousness is religion, and art and secular knowledge can be regarded as its individual aspects or forms. The content of art is the same as that of religion, except that its medium is the intuition of the senses. Knowledge κατ' ἐξοχήν, i.e. philosophy, also treats of the same object, but through the medium of thought. The other branches of knowledge do not possess an absolute content, and so far as the state is concerned, their content is finite and comes under the heading of human needs. In religion, therefore, the national principle receives its simplest expression, and it is on religion that the nation's entire existence is based.

In this respect, religion is intimately associated with the principle of the state. It is a representation* of the spirit of the state in absolute universality, but it is such that the real spirit in which it is represented has, in its religious capacity, rid itself of all external contingencies. Conscious freedom can only exist when all individual things are recognised as having their positive existence within the divine being and when subjectivity is related to the divine being itself. This freedom, as an object of knowledge, existed among the Greeks, and – in a more highly developed form – in the Christian world. From this point of view, it can rightly be said that the state is based on religion. The relationship between the two is such that, although worldly existence, being of a temporal order, is relative and without any inherent justification in itself, it does receive its justification in so far as the universal soul or principle which animates it is itself absolutely justified; and the latter can only be justified if it is recognised as the particular form and existence of the divine being. It is in this sense, therefore, that the state is based upon religion. The principle of the state must have its own immediate justification, whereas finite interests remain purely relative. The universal principle gains its absolute justification through being recognised as a moment or determination of the divine nature itself. Thus, the principle of the state, the universal on which its existence depends, is recognised as an absolute, as a determination of the divine being itself. We often hear it said in our own times that the state is based on religion, and this usually means simply that pious individuals are the more ready and willing to do their duty because obedience towards the ruler and towards the law can so easily be linked with religious piety. It is admittedly true that such piety, inasmuch as it exalts the universal

* *Vorstellung.*

above the particular, can turn against the particular, become fanatical, and visit fire and destruction on the state and on all its works and institutions. For this reason, it is often maintained, piety should be kept within the bounds of sobriety and retain a certain coolness, lest it should rise in turmoil against that which it ought to protect and preserve, and sweep it away altogether. Such violence does at least exist as a latent possibility within it.

But even those who have rightly realised that the state is based on religion approach the latter as if the state were already present but religion itself were not. They believe that, in order to support the state, religion should be imported into it by the bushel or bucketful and instilled into the minds of men. It is perfectly correct that men should be educated towards religion, but not as if it were something which did not yet exist. Man is educated towards what is already there, and not to that which does not yet exist. For although we may say that the state is founded on religion and has its roots in it, this really means that it has emanated from religion and continues to do so, now and always, and that each particular state has emerged from its own particular religion. As already remarked, the principles of the state must be regarded as valid in and for themselves, and this is not possible unless they are recognised as determinations of the divine nature. Thus the state and its constitution will correspond to the religion which underlies them; for the state really has grown out of religion, so that the Athenian or Roman state, for example, was possible only in conjunction with the specific form of paganism practised by the nations in question, just as a Catholic state will have a different spirit and constitution from a Protestant one.

If, as it would often seem, those noisy appeals and agitations which set out to implant religion in the state are really expressions of fear and distress in face of the threat that religion has already disappeared from the state or is about to disappear completely, the situation is certainly grave, and in fact even worse than the cries of distress would imply; for such appeals still assume that the evil can be counteracted by propagating and inculcating religion. But religion is not something which can be artificially created in this way, for it creates itself at a much more profound level.

The state, then, shares a common principle with religion. Religion is not something introduced from outside in order to regulate the workings of the state and the conduct of individuals towards it from within; on the contrary, it is the original inner principle which determines and activates itself within the state. Men must indeed be educated to religion, and religion must be continually fostered, just as science and art have to be imparted through instruction. But we must not imagine that the relationship is such that religion has to be added as an afterthought; for, as already pointed out, the true sense of this relationship is that the state has already grown out of a definite religion, that it shares the same principle with it, and that its entire political, artistic, and learned life are dependent upon it.

Superficial objections can easily be raised against these arguments. But we must not simply pick upon any so-called nation at random if we wish to discover whether this relationship is present within it. We must look instead to those states which have attained maturity, and to nations which have reached the fullest stage of development – but not, for example, to pastoral nations, whose constitutions will be the same however much their religions may vary. Undeveloped states of this kind have not yet reached that degree of advancement at which the principle of the national spirit realises itself in a determinate form and can become an object of determinate knowledge. When a nation is fully developed, all the departments and ways of life within it make up a single unity; but in those nations whose condition is still primitive or which have not yet attained autonomy and independence (or which at least do not owe their constitution and power to their independent position), these different areas of national life may still exist in isolation. Such nations either have not yet developed fully within themselves, or they do not enjoy a position of independence. Athens had a democratic constitution, but so, for example, does Hamburg; the religions of the two states are completely different, although their constitutions are the same. These examples would seem to weigh against our contention that there is an essential link between certain religions and certain constitutions. But the phenomenon in question can be explained by the fact that the commercial element is paramount in Hamburg; this means that the city is indeed independent, but not in the same way as a major European state. Similarly, we must disregard those nations which, though possessing the outward capacity, have not yet developed it freely to its fullest extent. The North American states began from the sea and laid the foundations of commerce; they are now expanding internally, but have not yet reached that degree of development and maturity which is the prerogative of the older European states.

Religion should accordingly be seen as necessarily inseparable from the political constitution, from secular government, and from secular life. The universal principle is present in the world and must be realised within it, for the world is the object of its knowledge. The deeper the spiritual principle descends into itself – i.e. the more refined the religion is – the less it is concerned with worldly things. This can be seen, for example, in the Christian religion. Religion differs from secular wisdom in that it enjoins indifference towards honour, valour, and property, whereas the latter takes more part in worldly affairs, aspires to honour, and praises valour and bravery: for these are worldly values. It is well known that religion can be extremely unfruitful. For this reason, it is often said that religion must dwell in the hearts of men as well as in their minds, that the whole of their actual lives should be an expression of their religion, and that morality and righteousness should be an essential part of them. And while, in the case of individuals, we may have the impression that the principle of truth is not always translated into reality, we see that it cannot fail to be realised in nations as a whole. For the universal principle of truth permeates all the particular areas of national life, so that the latter becomes imbued with a practical religious consciousness of truth. Thus, the political constitution, the system of justice, ethical life in general, art, and science are all manifestations of truth in particular areas of national existence. As we have repeatedly pointed out, the spirit must realise its consciousness of itself and become its own object, for it is only a spirit in so far as it knows itself and has itself as its object. But in order to attain objectivity, it has to become finite; distinctions must emerge within it, just as an organism requires a series of separate members. As soon as the spirit enters into relations with an object, its differentiation is posited; and when it enters into relations with itself, divides itself into separate parts, and becomes the single living soul within the various members, it is internally conscious of itself and results in itself as the expression of its particular parts within its own particular sphere. The spirit should not be seen merely as a beginning, however; for it creates itself and is its own end and product, so that the end result is identical with the beginning. But it gives itself reality through the mediating process of self-objectification. Religion as such must give itself essential reality; it must create a world for itself so that the spirit may become conscious of itself as a real spirit.

In religion, everything depends on the extent to which the spirit's consciousness of its own nature is really contained within it. And if this consciousness of the nature of spirit also includes a consciousness of the nature of truth, i.e. of the concept of spirit, all the aspects of its existence are truly posited and invested with the determination of truth – but this can only occur within the true religion. Unless they are based upon religion, all other aspects of life will remain barren, for they will not be determined by truth. But even then, certain areas will be given over to arbitrariness and remain in a state of lawlessness in which the truth is not yet realised. The aim of these deliberations is to show how religion is the common denominator of all the particular areas of existence.

It has been said that religion as such often proves unfruitful in the case of individuals. The system of national life, on the other hand, must develop in accordance with religion. Religions will differ profoundly according to whether or not their principle is such that everything which comes under the category of spirit has a common basis in the religious principle itself and has acquired a determinate principle of its own. Unless the spirit is grasped in all its true profundity, there will, as already remarked, be aspects of national existence which are irrational, a prey to arbitrary forces, or in some way lacking in freedom. For example, the religion of the Greeks, the principle of the Greek spirit, or the concept which the spirit had formed of itself within the Greek nation, was deficient, for the Greeks had to resort to oracles both in public affairs (as in the conclusion of treaties) and in their private business. This meant that an essential aspect of the spirit had fulfilled itself in a false and unfree manner before it had been accorded its proper place within the substantial principle of religion. And the same applies to Mohammedanism. The fanaticism of its adherents impelled them to conquer the world, but it was incapable of producing a state with a differentiated organic life and a system of laws framed in the interest of freedom. But if, as in Christianity, a religion has the absolute concept of the spirit as its principle, the development of its whole world must be governed by this concept. The transformation of reality in the light of this principle requires prolonged exertions, and could not be accomplished immediately; at the beginning of the Christian era, we shall in fact discover an enormous discrepancy between the Christian principle and the barbarism and lawlessness which at first prevailed among the Christian nations.

Art, both as a supplier of materials for practical requirements and as a creator of works of beauty, is much affected by the determinate nature of whatever religion it is associated with. There can be no art for the understanding – except perhaps that of sublimity, in which form is so attenuated that the individual disappears altogether. Where the spirit, as opposed to man, is seen as something devoid of form (as with the Jews and Mohammedans), no place is left for visual art. What is recognised by such religions as the truth is not amenable to visual representation, and it is not supposed to be apprehended through the medium of external forms. In such religions, the imagination is not the appropriate faculty for comprehending what the spirit has recognised as truly valid. But art is essentially fine art, and its presence is accordingly necessary wherever the formative imagination is the supreme faculty and where God is not yet recognised as the universal spirit. Thus, it had its necessary function among the Greeks, whose vision of the divine universality took the form of natural subjectivity. Such a nation has to comprehend and depict the universal and the divine by means of direct intuitions of the senses. Art is also an essential part of Christianity, for Christianity does not treat the divine as an abstraction of the understanding either. But art can no longer be the highest vehicle of expression for us as it was for the Greeks, who saw it as a means of representing and comprehending the truth; its position is now a subordinate one. That form which art can alone confer does not possess unconditional truth for us; it is not the form in which the absolute can become manifest. Artistic form is purely finite, and is therefore incommensurate with the infinite content which it is meant to represent.

The learned disciplines come closest of all to religion. Admittedly, their content is extremely varied, and is often no more than a collection of known facts; but at least the principle of thought and cognition is recognised in all of them. They are useful to all areas of reality; religion, the state, and justice are useful too, but truth serves other purposes as well. One might even argue that God is useful; but this would be a profane and inappropriate manner of speaking, for God's usefulness is the goodness with which he grants independence to other things and sacrifices himself to them. But the learned disciplines should not really be measured by this subordinate criterion of utility, because, like religion, they are an end in and for themselves, and are themselves their own ultimate end. Since they belong to the province of thought – and this applies particularly to disciplines such as philosophy which practise free intellectual enquiry – they exist within the peculiar medium and soil of the spirit. A nation comprehends its concept of itself and of the truth by means of scientific thought, i.e. thought whose form corresponds to the concept of the spirit itself. If we attain an abstract comprehension of the deepest regions of the spirit, we do so by means of thought. The object is in this case commensurate with the nature of the spirit. To this extent, the learned disciplines are the supreme culmination of a nation's life, for the nation's highest impulse is to comprehend itself and to realise in every area of its existence the concept it has formed of itself. The most important element is neither that of physical need, whatever its nature may be, nor that of formal justice, but of thought and intelligence as such. Free, disinterested, dispassionate consciousness is the highest achievement of the nation, and the same is true in art. But the content of this consciousness does not appear in a tangible medium as in art, for the element in which it expresses its concept is that of thought. To cultivate the learned disciplines does a nation credit. It is the discipline of philosophy in particular which thinks and comprehends that content which appears in religion in the form of sensuous and spiritual representation. Christianity expresses it in the doctrine that God has brought forth a Son. This is not a conceptual relationship but a natural one. What religion grasps as a living relationship by means of representational thought is grasped by philosophy by means of rational comprehension, so that the content remains the same but appears in the latter instance in its highest, worthiest, and most vivid form. Philosophy is the highest means by which a nation can attain consciousness of the truth and realise the absolute mode of the spirit. Thus the position of philosophy in world history is similar to that of visual art. Concrete philosophy can only occur among the Greeks and the Christians, whereas abstract philosophy can also be found among the Orientals, who do not, however, achieve a synthesis between the finite and the divine.

As against this ideal mode of existence, the state has a second dimension in the content of its external appearance. Whatever its particular nature may be, this content is likewise illuminated by the universal.

The first material of this class is everything that pertains to the ethics and customs of nations. This includes the **natural phase of ethical life** or the **family relationship**, which is determined by the nature of the state – for example, by the forms which marriage assumes, such as polygamy, polyandry, or monogamy. In Christian states, the only recognised form of marriage is that of one man with one woman, since this is the only form in which both partners can receive their full rights. It also includes the relationship between children and their parents, which may be one of slavery or which may allow the children to be free owners of property. The second mode of ethical life is that which relates to the conduct of individuals towards one another, even down to the level of ordinary politeness. One need only think of such differences in etiquette as that between Europeans and Asiatics in their behaviour towards superiors. These customs are derived from substantial relationships, and they express what men think about them. They have a symbolic value, although they also contain much that is purely contingent; for not everything in them is equally significant.

Another item which comes under the category of external appearance is the practical comportment of men in relation to nature and to the way in which they satisfy their finite needs. Their **industry** comes under this heading, for it reveals the way in which men behave in their dependence upon and relationship to nature, and how they satisfy their needs in this direction in order to obtain various kinds of enjoyment. The natural impulse which this involves is part of man's particular qualities; the essential aspect as such, i.e. religion and the constitution of the state, is therefore only remotely connected with this particular sphere. But the universal principle of the spirit is also essentially present in the nation's attitude towards industry, trade, and commerce. The purpose of such activities is that the individual should look after himself and apply his diligence, understanding, energy, and skill to satisfying his needs – which can, incidentally, be multiplied and refined upon ad infinitum. Among these activities, that of agriculture is necessarily dependent upon nature. What is properly called industry takes up raw material in order to process it, and derives its subsistence from what it can produce by dint of intelligence, reflection, and application. All this belongs to the particular sphere, to which there are no inherent limits, because the accumulation of wealth and the refinement of techniques can continue indefinitely. But there is a great difference between a situation in which industry is restricted or tied to social castes so that it cannot expand, and one in which the individual is completely unrestricted and can extend the sphere of his activity without limit. The latter situation presupposes a completely different national spirit – and hence also a completely different religion and constitution – from that in which diligence, though equally necessary, is placed within fixed and final limits.

In this same category we must also include the weapons which men use against animals and against each other, as well as the ships in which they sail. For example, ancient legend has it that iron was first discovered by the Asiatic peoples. The invention of gunpowder should not be regarded as fortuitous, however, for it could only have been discovered and applied at a specific time and in a specific culture. But a whole host of such commodities is independent of the specific character of the national spirit – for example luxuries, which can appear in much the same form at any time and in any culture.

The third item in this class is that of **private right**, i.e. the rights of individuals in relation to those finite needs which have already been mentioned. This raises the question of personal freedom and its development, and hence of whether slavery is prohibited and property freely owned or not. Full personal freedom and complete freedom of ownership can only occur in states which are governed by a determinate principle. For the principle of justice is directly connected with the universal principle itself. The universal principle of the Christian religion, for example, is, firstly, that there is one spirit, which is the truth, and secondly, that individuals have infinite worth and should be received in grace into absolute spirituality. A consequence of this is that the individual personality is recognised as infinite, as absolutely self-conscious and free. The Oriental religions do not acknowledge the principle that the human being, as a human being, has infinite worth. It is therefore only under Christianity that men become personally free, i.e. capable of owning property in freedom.

Finally, a word must be said about the science of finite things. Mathematics, natural history, and physics also demand a certain level of culture. For only when the individual has gained inner freedom does he accord the object an existence of its own and react to it not simply in terms of desire but in a theoretical manner. In this case too, the ancient and modern worlds are different, for the former did not have this kind of interest in nature and its laws. Such an interest requires a higher and more concrete assurance, a strength of intellect which is capable of looking at the objects in their finite aspects. The intellect can only achieve this abstraction when it has reached a higher degree of self-consciousness.

These, then, are the principal areas into which the spirit becomes differentiated as it realises itself to form a state. In a fully developed state in which these various aspects have a distinct existence and in which each has received its due, they must correspond to different social classes. On the one hand, the individual *can* participate in all of these aspects, and on the other, he is *obliged* to do so, at least indirectly, as in the case of religion, justice, the constitution, and science. But these areas also correspond to particular social classes to which different groups of individuals belong, and it is these classes which determine the individual's profession. For the differences which are inherent in the various aspects in question must crystallise into particular spheres, each with its own peculiar preoccupations. It is this which determines the difference between the social classes as found within an organised state. For the state is an organic whole, and these subdivisions are just as necessary to it as they would be within an actual organism. The state is an organic whole, but of an ethical nature. Freedom is not envious; it allows its various aspects to assume different forms, while the universal remains strong enough to preserve the unity between itself and its particular determinations.

d. [*Its reality*]

The points hitherto discussed have concerned the abstract moments which occur within the concept of the state. But it is the constitution which puts this concept into execution and adopts measures to ensure that all that happens within the state is in accord with its nature. [*Some may consider it*] *superfluous for a nation to have a constitution,* [*and argue that the form of the state*] *is self-evident. But this simply means that the absence of a constitution is itself regarded as a kind of constitution, just as a sphere is regarded as a shape.*

If the principle of the **individual** *will is taken as the sole determination of political freedom, and it is accepted that all individuals should consent to everything that is done by and for the state, there is, strictly speaking, no constitution. The only institution required would be a central body with no will of its own, which took note of what appeared to be the needs of the state and made its opinion known; and then a mechanism would have to be set up to call the individuals together, to register their votes, and to perform the arithmetical operation of counting and comparing the number of votes in favour of the different propositions, at which point the decision would already have been taken.*

The state itself is an abstraction which has its purely universal reality in the citizens who belong to it; but it does have reality, and its purely universal existence must take on a determinate form in the will and activity of individuals.[38] *The need arises for some kind of government and political administration; it becomes necessary to single out and separate from the rest those who are heavily occupied with political affairs, who take political decisions and determine how they are to be put into practice, and who issue instructions to those citizens who have to implement them. For example, even if it is the nation as a whole which decides upon war in a democratic state, a general still has to be placed at the head of the army in order to conduct the war. The state as an abstraction only acquires life and reality through the constitution; but as it does so, a difference arises between those who command and those who obey, those who rule and those who are ruled. Yet obedience seems incompatible with freedom, and those who command would seem to be doing the opposite of what is required by*[39] *the very basis of the state, the concept of freedom. But if, as is often maintained, the distinction between commanding and obeying is necessary because the state could not function without it – and this would indeed appear to be no more than a form of compulsion, an external necessity which actually conflicts with freedom in the abstract sense – the constitution should be so organised that the minimum of obedience is required of the citizens and the minimum of arbitrariness is permitted to those who issue the commands; and the content of whatever makes these commands necessary should in the main be determined and resolved upon by the people, by the will of many or all of the individual citizens – although the state as a reality, as an individual unity, must at the same time retain its vigour and strength.*

The first determination of all within the state is the distinction between rulers and ruled, and constitutions in general have rightly been divided into monarchy, aristocracy, and democracy. But we should also note, firstly, that monarchy must be further divided into despotism and monarchy proper; secondly, that in all classifications derived from the concept of the state, only the basic determination of each category is specified, which does not imply that the latter is necessarily exhausted in its concrete application [by] any single form, variety, or kind; and thirdly, the most important point of all is that [the concept] admits of a large number of particular modifications, not only within the general types of constitution mentioned above, but also in the shape of combinations of several of these essentially distinct types, which are consequently amorphous, unstable, and internally inconsistent structures. [Thus, the first determination within the state is the distinction between rulers and ruled,] together with the institutions which follow from it, and the sense and aim which underlies them. This collision raises the question of what is the best constitution, that is, by what arrangement, organisation, or mechanism of political power the aim of the state can most surely be fulfilled.

*This aim can admittedly be interpreted in various ways – for example, as the peaceful enjoyment of civic life, or as universal happiness. It is aims of this kind which have given rise to the so-called **ideal constitutions**, and particularly to ideal schemes of princely education (cf. Fénelon)[40] or of the education of rulers in general, i.e. of the aristocracy (cf. Plato). For, in all such cases, the main emphasis falls on the character of those who govern the state, and the ideal constitutions tell us nothing about the organic institutions of the state itself. The question of what is the best constitution is often treated as if not only the theory itself were the business of free subjective deliberation, but as if the actual implementation of a constitution recognised as the best (or at least as superior to others) would automatically follow from a purely theoretical decision of this kind – as if the variety of constitution adopted were a matter of completely free choice, determined solely by reflection. It was in this thoroughly naïve spirit that the noblemen of Persia (although not the Persian nation as a whole), having successfully conspired to overthrow the pseudo-Smerdis and the Magi, deliberated on the kind of* *constitution they should introduce in Persia in the light of the fact that no member of the ruling family* was still alive; and Herodotus gives an equally naive account of these deliberations.*

Nowadays, people no longer imagine that the constitution of a country and nation is so completely a matter of free choice. The fundamental but still abstractly formulated definition of freedom has led to the very widespread theory that the republic is the only just and authentic constitution. There have even been many, who, while holding high political office under monarchic constitutions (e.g. Lafayette),[41] have made no attempt to oppose such opinions or have actually adopted them themselves; but they have nevertheless perceived that such a constitution, though it may well be the best, cannot always be realised, and that, men being what they are, we must content ourselves with a lesser degree of freedom. Under the given circumstances, and with the moral condition of the people as it is, the monarchic constitution would therefore seem the most advantageous one. This same way of thinking also makes the need for a particular constitution dependent upon the prevailing situation as something purely external and contingent. Conceptions of this kind are based on the distinction which the reflective understanding makes between the concept and its reality, in that it fastens upon a purely abstract and hence unauthentic concept and fails to grasp the Idea itself; or, what amounts to the same thing in substance, if not in form, it fails to attain a concrete perception† of the nation and state. We have already noticed how the constitution of a nation forms a single substance and a single spirit with its religion, art, and philosophy – or at least with the attitudes and thoughts which go along with its culture in general – not to mention the further external influences of its climate, its neighbours, and its position in the world at large. Every state is an individual totality, from which it is impossible to select and isolate any particular aspect, however important the latter may be (as in the case of the constitution), and to consider it solely in relation to itself. For not only is the constitution intimately associated with and dependent upon those other spiritual powers, but the determinate form of its whole spiritual individuality, including all the powers it embodies, is only one moment in the history of the whole, occupying its predetermined place within its development; and it is this which gives the constitution its supreme sanction and necessity.

But it should not be forgotten that, when we are dealing with constitutions, we must not rest content with abstract distinctions such as the

---

* Hegel uses the proper name *Pischdadier* (plural) for the royal house of Persia. If an English equivalent of this name exists, I have been unable to trace it.
† *Anschauung.*

well known classification, already referred to, of democracy, aristocracy, and monarchy. Besides, no one will deny that it is hard to find an unmixed democracy from which the aristocratic principle is completely absent. Furthermore, monarchy is a constitution which comprehends and contains the other two moments within it. But when we come to consider constitutions, i.e. the essential political condition of nations, totally different considerations come into play.

The essential determination of the constitution amidst all the various aspects of political life can be expressed in the following proposition: the best state is that in which the greatest degree of **freedom** prevails. But this raises the question of what constitutes the reality of freedom. Freedom is usually thought of as a state in which the subjective will of all individuals is involved in the most important affairs of the state. In this case, the subjective will is regarded as the ultimate and decisive factor. But the nature of the state is the unity of the objective and the universal will, and the subjective will is raised to the point at which it renounces its particularity. The common conception of the state tends to make a division between the government on the one hand and the people on the other, so that the former is equated with the concentrated activity of the universal and the latter with the many subjective wills of the individual citizens. Thus, the government and people are treated as separate entities. It is thought that a good constitution is one in which the two elements – the government in its universal function and the people in its subjective will – are secured against one another; the two are thus expected to impose mutual restraints on one another. This form of constitution does indeed have its place in history; but the opposition it contains is overcome* in the concept of the state. There is something perverse about such contrasts between the people and the government, a malicious artifice designed to imply that the people, divorced from the government, themselves constitute the whole. So long as such ideas are countenanced, it cannot be said that the state – which is the unity of the universal and the particular will – is really present. On the contrary, the state still has to be created. The rational concept of the state has left such abstract antitheses behind it; and those who treat them as if they were necessary know nothing of the nature of the state. For the state has this unity as its basis, and it is this which constitutes its being and its substance.

But this does not mean that its substance is fully developed within itself. For as such, it is a system of organs, of distinct spheres, of parti-

* *aufgehoben.*

cular universalities which are intrinsically independent but whose function is to create the whole and thereby to annul* their own independence. In the organic world, there can be no question of any such opposition between particular independent functions; in animal life, for example, the universal property of life is present in every smallest particle, and when it is removed, only inorganic matter remains. The constitutions of states, however, vary according to the form which the totality assumes. The state is rationality made manifest in the world, and the various constitutions accordingly succeed one another, each with its distinct principle; and it invariably happens that the earlier forms are superseded† by those which follow them.

The state is the spiritual Idea externalised in the human will and its freedom. All historical change is therefore essentially dependent upon the state, and the successive moments of the Idea appear within it as distinct constitutional principles. The constitutions under which the world-historical nations have blossomed are peculiar to them, and should not therefore be seen as universally applicable. Their differences do not simply consist in the particular way in which they have elaborated and developed a common basis, but in the distinct nature of the principles which underlie them. No lessons can therefore be drawn from history for the framing of constitutions in the present. For the latest constitutional principle, the principle of our own times, is not to be found in the constitutions of the world-historical nations of the past. In knowledge and art, however, it is altogether different. For, in their case, the earlier principles are the absolute foundation of all that follows; for example, the philosophy of antiquity is so fundamental to modern philosophy that it is necessarily contained within the latter and constitutes its entire basis. The relation here is one of unbroken development within one and the same edifice, whose foundation stone, walls, and roof have always remained the same. In art, it might even be said that the art of the Greeks, in its original form, remains the supreme model. But with political constitutions, it is quite different; for ancient and modern constitutions have no essential principle in common. Abstract determinations and doctrines of just government to the effect that wisdom and virtue should rule supreme are of course common to both. But it is quite mistaken to look to the Greeks, Romans, or Orientals for models of how constitutions ought to be organised in our own times. The Orient affords us fine spectacles of the patriarchal system, of paternal government, and of

---

* *aufzuheben.*   † *aufgehoben.*

popular devotion, and the Greeks and Romans furnish us with accounts of popular freedom. For in Greece and Rome the concept of a free constitution was so construed that all citizens were expected to participate in discussions and decisions concerning the affairs and laws of the state. In our own times, this still remains the general opinion, but with the qualification that, since our states are so large and the number of citizens so vast, the latter should not give their assent directly to decisions on matters of public concern, but through the indirect method of representation; in short, for the purposes of legislation in general, the people should be represented by deputies. The so-called representative constitution is the form with which we associate the idea of a free constitution, so much so that this has become a hardened prejudice. But the most important point is that freedom, if it is determined by the concept itself, does not have as its principle the subjective will and its arbitrary inclinations, but the insights of the universal will; and the system of freedom consists in the free development of its various moments. The subjective will is a purely formal determination which does not tell us what it is that is willed. The rational will alone is the universal principle which determines and develops itself independently and unfolds its successive moments as organic members. But the last phase of all is that of rational freedom, a Gothic edifice whose substance is the universal. Of such Gothic cathedral building the Ancients knew nothing, for it is an achievement of the Christian era. An infinite dichotomy has arisen, and it is only resolved when individuals recognise that their freedom, independence, and essential being reside in their unity with the underlying substance, and when the latter coincides with the form of their activity – for everything depends on this last phase in the development of the substance. This is the higher sense in which nations and their constitutions differ from one another.

Seen in the light of this higher principle, what is usually taken to be the most important factor in a constitution – i.e. whether the individual citizens have given their subjective assent to it or not – appears as a distinction of subordinate significance. It must first be established whether the individuals are regarded as persons in their own right, and whether the substance is present as spirit, as that essential being of which the individuals are conscious. Among the Chinese, for example, no form of individual assent whatsoever is required; if they were taken to task for this as a deficiency in their constitution, they would consider it just as absurd as if children of all ages were asked to participate in a family council. The Chinese are not yet conscious of their own nature as free subjectivity; they do not yet realise that the essential property of ethicality and justice is contained within the latter, which is not yet present to them as their end, their product, and their object. With the Turks, on the other hand, we see the subjective will expressing itself in a completely uncontrolled manner. The Janissaries, for example, have their independent will and exercise it; it is a savage will which is determined in part by religion but at the same time unrestrained in its desires. It is wrongly imagined that their personal will is therefore free, although it is not in fact integrated into the rational and concrete will. It knows nothing of the latter, which is neither its object, its interest, nor its motivating principle, and when it does impinge on a universal, this universal is not something organic, but merely an abstraction of a purely fanatical nature; it is destructive of all organisation, ethical existence, and justice of every kind. In European states, the position is different again, for here, on the whole, discernment is universal. Systematic education and the pursuit of universal ends and principles are the property of everyone; they are shared by the citizens with the government, and by the government with the citizens (in so far as all branches of the administration are included within the concept). In such circumstances, the consent of each particular individual is again more or less superfluous, for individuals in general cannot contribute any particular wisdom to the common cause, but have in fact less to offer than those who are expressly concerned with political matters. Nor would their particular interests bring favourable consequences with them either; for the decisive factor is that there is a common weal to which all individual interests must yield. If freedom is defined as a state to which all individuals must give their assent, it is easily seen that no law can be upheld unless everyone agrees to it. This in turn gives rise to the principle that the minority must yield to the majority, so that the majority in fact makes the decisions. But as J. J. Rousseau has already observed, this can no longer be described as freedom, for the will of the minority is no longer respected. In the Polish diet, every individual had to give his assent to all decisions, and it was this very freedom which led to the downfall of the state. Besides, it is a dangerous and mistaken assumption that the people alone possess reason and discernment and know what is right and proper; for every popular faction can set itself up as representing the people as a whole. What constitutes the state is in fact the business of those who possess education and knowledge, and not that of the people at large.

The differences between political constitutions concern the form in which the totality of political life is manifested. The first form is that in which this totality is not yet clearly defined and in which its various particular spheres have not yet attained an independent existence; the second is that in which these particular spheres – and hence the individual citizens – have gained a greater degree of freedom; and the third and last form is that in which they have attained independence and at the same time function in such a way as to create the universal. We can see how every country and the history of the world as a whole go through each of these phases in turn. At first, we find in every state a kind of patriarchal kingdom, either peacefully or belligerently inclined. During this first phase in its evolution, the state is imperious and ruled by instinct. But even obedience and force and fear of a ruler involve a relation of the will. At the next stage, the particular becomes dominant; aristocrats, distinct spheres of interest, democrats, and individuals hold sway. From among these individuals, a fortuitous aristocracy is precipitated, and this in turn gives way to a new kingdom or monarchy. The final stage is accordingly that at which the particular is subordinated to a power whose nature is necessarily such that the particular spheres can exist independently outside it – in other words, a monarchy. We must therefore distinguish between primary and secondary varieties of monarchy. This, then, is the abstract but necessary process whereby states develop towards true independence; and in every case, we encounter a definite constitution which is not a matter of free choice but invariably accords with the national spirit at a given stage of its development.

All constitutions will depend on the internal development of the rational (i.e. political) condition of the state in question, on the liberation of the successive moments within the concept. The particular powers within the state become differentiated and complete within themselves, but at the same time they freely collaborate towards the realisation of a single purpose by which they are all sustained: in short, they form an organic whole. Thus, the nature of the state is rational freedom which knows itself objectively and exists for itself. For freedom only attains an objective existence when its moments are present not just ideally but in their own peculiar mode of reality, and when they become absolutely effective in relation to reality itself; and as a result, the totality, the soul, the individual unity, is created.

It must also be remembered, however, that the state has **relationships with other states**, although it is itself independent and self-sufficient. The nation's honour in fact consists in its position of independence. But to define these factors more precisely would call for a long explanation which can well be dispensed with here. It is, however, important that we should not confuse the principles which govern relations between states with the principle which governs their position within the history of the world. For in world history, the sole authority is the **right of the absolute spirit**, and the only relations which matter are those in which a higher spiritual principle asserts itself. But this is a right to which no state can appeal. Individual states recognise one another as independent individuals, and the independence of each is only respected in so far as the independence of the others is also recognised. Such relationships can be defined in treaties, in which case legal considerations are at least supposed to decide the issue. But in world history, a higher right comes into play. In fact, this is even recognised in reality in those situations where civilised nations come into contact with barbarian hordes. And in wars of religion, one of the parties involved will invariably claim to be defending a sacred principle in relation to which the rights of other nations are secondary and of lesser validity. This was true of the Mohammedans in former times, and in theory even today. The Christians likewise, in making war on heathen nations with a view to converting them, have claimed that their religion invests them with superior rights. In situations such as these, it is not a question of abstract rights and wrongs; but such situations can only arise where a law-governed state has not yet come into force. And whatever obtains under these conditions cannot be applied to a situation in which states enjoy true independence in their reciprocal relations. Conversely, whatever obtains within a state of right cannot be applied to a situation which cannot yet be described as law-governed. We are therefore not concerned here with those political principles which come under the heading of international law. Instead, we shall look to the right of the world spirit as against that of individual states.

C
The course of world history

a. [*The principle of development*]

Historical change in the abstract sense has long been interpreted in general terms as embodying some kind of progress towards a better and more perfect condition. Changes in the natural world, no matter how great their variety, exhibit only an eternally recurring cycle; for in nature there is nothing new under the sun, and in this respect its manifold play of forms produces an effect of boredom. Only in those changes which take place in the spiritual sphere does anything new emerge. This peculiarity of spiritual phenomena has given rise to the idea that the destiny of man is quite different from that of merely natural objects. For in the latter we always encounter one and the same determination and a constantly stable character to which all change can be reduced, and from which all change follows as a secondary consequence; whereas man displays a real capacity for change, and, as already remarked, for progress towards a better and more perfect condition – in short, he possesses an impulse of perfectibility. This principle, which reduces change itself to a law-governed process, has met with disfavour both from religions – for example Catholicism – and from states, which claim a genuine right to a fixed (or at least stable) position. Although it is generally conceded that worldly things, including the state, are subject to change, an exception is made in the case of religion – as the religion of truth – on the one hand; and on the other, it is always possible to ascribe changes, revolutions, and the destruction of legitimate institutions to accidents or errors of judgement, but above all to the levity, depravity, and evil passions of man. In fact, perfectibility is almost as indeterminate a concept as that of change in general; it is without aim or purpose, and the better and more perfect condition to which it supposedly tends is of a completely indefinite nature.

It is important that we should recognise that the development of the spirit is a form of progress, for although this idea is widespread enough, it is just as frequently attacked (as we have already noticed). For it may well appear incompatible with the idea of peaceful stability and of a permanent constitution and legislation. Stability is a value which must certainly be accorded the highest respect, and all activity ought to contribute to its preservation. The idea of progress is unsatisfactory simply because it is usually formulated in such a way as to suggest that man is perfectible, i.e. that it is possible and even necessary for him to become increasingly perfect. From this point of view, stability does not appear as the highest value; on the contrary, the highest value is that of change itself. For the sole consideration here is that of ever increasing perfection, which is so indefinite that we are left only with the idea of change in general; we are offered no criterion whereby change can be measured, nor any means of assessing how far the present state of affairs is in keeping with right and with the universal substance. We have no principle which can help us to exclude irrelevant factors, and no goal or definite end is in sight; and the only definite property which remains is that of change in general. Lessing's idea of the education of the human race is an ingenious one, but it is only remotely connected with what we are discussing here. For such doctrines invariably present progress in quantitative terms – as a constant growth of knowledge, as increasing refinement of culture, and other such comparatives; one can go on in this manner at great length without ever reaching any definite conclusions or making any qualitative pronouncements. The object in hand, the qualitative element, is given from the start, but no indication is given of the goal which is supposed to be ultimately reached; the goal itself remains completely indefinite. If, however, we wish to discuss progress in definite terms, we must realise that the idea of quantitative change is devoid of intellectual content. We must know the goal which is supposed to be ultimately attained, because the activity of the spirit is such that its productions and changes must be presented and recognised as variations in quality.

But the principle of development has further implications, for it contains an inner determination, a potentially present condition which has still to be realised. This formal determination is an essential one; the spirit, whose theatre, province, and sphere of realisation is the history of the world, is not something which drifts aimlessly amidst the superficial play of contingent happenings, but is in itself the absolute determining factor; in its own peculiar destiny, it is completely proof against contingencies, which it utilises and controls for its own purposes. But organic entities in the natural world are also capable of development. Their existence is not just an immediate one which can be altered only by external influences; on the contrary, it has its source within itself, in an unchanging inner principle, a simple essence whose own existence as a germ is at first equally simple, but which subsequently develops distinct parts. These then enter into relations with other objects and consequently undergo a continuous process of change – although this process itself leads to the very opposite of change, in that it takes on the new function of conserving the organic principle and the forms it creates. Thus the individual organism produces itself: it makes itself actually what it already was potentially; and the spirit too is only what it makes itself, for it likewise makes itself actually what it already was potentially. But the development of natural organisms takes place in an immediate, unopposed, and unhindered fashion, for nothing can intrude between the concept and its realisation, between the inherently determined nature of the germ and the actual existence which corresponds to it. But it is otherwise in the world of the spirit. The process whereby its inner determination is translated into reality is mediated by consciousness and will. The latter are themselves immersed at first in their immediate natural life; their primary object and aim is to follow their natural determination as such, which, since it is the spirit which animates it, is[42] nevertheless endowed with infinite claims, power, and richness. Thus, the spirit is divided against itself; it has to overcome itself as a truly hostile obstacle to the realisation of its end. That development which, in the natural world, is a peaceful process of growth – for it retains its identity and remains self-contained in its expression – is in the spiritual world at once a hard and unending conflict with itself. The will of the spirit is to fulfil its own concept; but at the same time, it obscures its own vision of the concept, and is proud and full of satisfaction in this state of self-alienation.

Development, therefore, is not just a harmless and peaceful process of growth like that of organic life, but a hard and obstinate struggle with itself. Besides, it contains not just the purely formal aspect of development itself, but involves the realisation of an end whose content is determinate. And we have made it clear from the outset what this end is: it is the spirit in its essential nature, i.e. as the concept of freedom. This is the fundamental object, so that the guiding principle of development endows the development itself with meaning and significance; thus, in Roman history, Rome is the object which guides our consideration of the events, and, conversely, the events have their source in this object alone, so that their entire significance and import are derived from it. In the history of the world, there have been several great periods of development which have come to an end without any apparent continuation; whereupon,[43] *in fact, the whole enormous gains of past culture have been destroyed, with the unfortunate result that everything had to start again from the beginning, in the hope of regaining – perhaps with some help from fragments salvaged from the lost treasures of the past and with an incalculable new expenditure of time and energy, crimes and sufferings – one of the provinces of past culture which had originally been conquered long ago. But there have also been unbroken processes of development, structures and systems of culture existing in their own peculiar elements, rich in quality and radiating in every direction. The formal principle of development in general can neither assign to one product superiority over another, nor help us to comprehend the purpose which underlies the destruction of earlier periods of development; instead, it must regard such happenings – or more precisely, the retrogressions they embody – as external contingencies, and it can only evaluate the gains by indeterminate criteria (which, since development is the ultimate factor, are relative rather than absolute ends).*

The concept of the spirit is such that historical development must take place in the temporal world. But time entails the property of negativity. A given entity or event has a positive existence for us, but its opposite is equally possible, and this relation to non-existence is a function of time; it is a relation which exists not only for thought, but also for our immediate perception. Time, then, is the completely abstract dimension of the sensory world. If non-existence does not encroach upon something, we describe it as permanent. If we compare spiritual changes with those of nature, we observe that, in the natural world, individual things are subject to change, whereas the species themselves are enduring. Thus a planet, for example, leaves each particular position it occupies, although its orbit as a whole is constant. And the same is true of animal species. For change is a cyclic process, a repetition of identical phases. Thus, everything moves in cycles, and it is only within these, in the world of particular things, that change takes place. In nature, the life which arises from death is itself only another instance of particular life; and if the species is taken as the substantial element behind this change, the destruction of particular things will appear as a relapse on the part of the species into particularity. Consequently, the survival of the species consists purely in a uniform repetition of one and the same mode of existence. But with spiritual forms, it is otherwise; for in this case, change occurs not just on the surface but within the concept, and it is the concept itself which is modified. In the natural world, the species does not progress, but in the world of the spirit, each change is a form of progress. Admittedly, the hierarchy of natural forms also constitutes a gradual sequence, extending from light at the one extreme to man at the other, so that each successive step is a modification of the preceding one, a higher principle which arises out of the dissolution* and destruction of its predecessor. But in nature, this sequence is fragmented, and all its individual elements coexist simultaneously; the transitions between them are only apparent to the thinking mind, which comprehends their overall relationship. Nature cannot comprehend itself, so that the negation of the forms it creates does not exist for it. But in the case of spiritual phenomena, higher forms are produced through the transformation of earlier and less advanced ones. The latter accordingly cease to exist; and the fact that each new form is the transfiguration of its predecessor explains why spiritual phenomena occur within the medium of time. Thus, world history as a whole is the expression of the spirit in time, just as nature is the expression of the Idea in space.

But in one respect, the nations of history, which are spiritual forms, are also natural entities. Accordingly, the various patterns they assume appear to coexist indifferently in space, i.e. to exist perennially. For if we cast our eyes around the world, we can discern three main principles in the older continents: the Far Eastern (i.e. Mongolian, Chinese, or Indian) principle, which is also the first to appear in history; the Mohammedan world, in which the principle of the abstract spirit, of monotheism,

* *Aufheben.*

128

is already present, although it is coupled with unrestrained arbitrariness; and the Christian, Western European world, in which the highest principle of all, the spirit's recognition of itself and its own profundity, is realised. This universal series has been described here as existing perennially; but in world history we encounter it as a sequence of successive stages. For although these great spiritual principles coexist perennially, this does not mean that all the forms which have come and gone with the passage of time should also endure permanently. We might expect, for example, to find a Greek nation with its noble paganism etc. still existing in the present, or a Roman one of the same kind. But these nations belong to the past. Similarly, we encounter in every nation forms which have disappeared while the nation itself continued to exist. Why they disappear and do not likewise endure permanently in space can only be explained by their own peculiar nature, which only allows them to exist within the medium of world history itself. And it will at the same time emerge that only the most general forms endure, and that the more specific ones must inevitably disappear as soon as they have expressed themselves in restless activity.

All progress takes the form of following the successive stages in the evolution of consciousness. Man begins life as a child, and is only dimly conscious of the world and of himself; we know that he has to progress through several stages of empirical consciousness before he attains a knowledge of what he is in and for himself. The child starts out with sensory emotions; man next proceeds to the stage of general representations, and then to that of comprehension, until he finally succeeds in recognising the soul of things, i.e. their true nature. In spiritual matters, the child lives at first by relying on its parents and its environment, and is aware of their efforts to guide it in the ways of rectitude, which appear to it to have been laid down arbitrarily. A further stage is that of youth; its distinctive feature is that the human being now looks for independence within himself, that he becomes self-sufficient, and that he recognises that what is right and ethically proper, what is essential for him to perform and accomplish, is present in his own consciousness. And the consciousness of the adult contains even more principles regarding what is essential. Since progress consists in a development of the consciousness, it is not just a quantitative process but a sequence of changing relationships towards the underlying essence.

The[44] history of the world accordingly represents the successive stages in the development of that principle whose substantial content is the consciousness of freedom. This development is gradual, not only because the spirit appears in it in a mediate rather than an immediate form – in that the spirit mediates itself with itself; but also because it is internally differentiated, for it involves a division or differentiation of the spirit within itself. The more specific determination of these various stages in their universal form belongs to the province of logic, but in its concrete aspect it is part of the philosophy of spirit. As regards its abstract qualities, it need only be mentioned here that, during the first and immediate stage in the process, the spirit, as already pointed out, is still immersed in nature, in which it exists in a state of unfree particularity (only One is free). But during the second stage it emerges into an awareness of its own freedom. The first departure from nature is, however, imperfect and partial – only Some are free – for it is derived indirectly from a state of nature, and is therefore related to it and still encumbered with it as one of its essential moments. The third stage witnesses the ascent of the spirit out of this as yet specific form of freedom into its purely universal form – man as such is free – in which the spiritual essence becomes conscious of itself and aware of its own nature.

Thus, the first stage we shall consider in the spirit's development can be compared with the spirit of childhood. In it, that so-called unity of the spirit with nature which we encounter in the **Oriental World** still prevails. This natural spirit is still immersed in nature and is not yet self-sufficient; it is therefore not yet free, and has not undergone the process by which freedom comes into being. Even at this initial stage in the spirit's evolution, we find states, arts, and the rudiments of learning already in existence; but they are still rooted in the soil of nature. In this early patriarchal world, spirituality is still an underlying substance to which the individual is related only as an accidental property. In relation to the will of the One, all the others are in the position of children or subordinates.

The second phase of the spirit is that of separation, in which the spirit is reflected within itself and in which it emerges from a position of mere obedience and trust. This phase is made up of two distinct parts. The first is the youthful age of the spirit, in which it possesses freedom for itself, but a freedom which is still bound up with the underlying substance. Freedom has not yet been reborn from within the depths of the spirit. This youthful age is that of the **Greek World**. The second part of this phase is that of the spirit's manhood, in which the individual has his own ends for himself, but can only attain them in the service of a universal, of the state. This is the **Roman World**. In it, the personality of the individual and service towards the universal stand in opposition.

Then fourthly, there follows the Germanic age, the **Christian World**. If it were possible to compare the spirit's development to that of the individual in this case too, this age would have to be called the old age of the spirit. But it is a peculiarity of old age that it lives only in memories, in the past rather than in the present, so that the comparison is no longer applicable. In his negative aspects, the individual human being belongs to the elemental world and must therefore pass away. The spirit, however, returns to its concepts. In the Christian age, the divine spirit has come into the world and taken up its abode in the individual, who is now completely free and endowed with substantial freedom. This is the reconciliation of the subjective with the objective spirit. The spirit is reconciled and united with its concept, in which it had developed from a state of nature, by a process of internal division, to be reborn as subjectivity. All this is the a priori structure of history to which empirical reality must correspond.

These stages are the basic principles which underlie the universal process; but to show in detail how each of them contains within itself a further process whereby it achieves specific form, and what constitutes the dialectic of transitions between them, must be left to the later part of this investigation.

*We must merely note for the present that the spirit begins in a state of infinite potentiality – but no more than potentiality – which contains its absolute substance as something as yet **implicit**, as the object and goal which it only attains as the end result in which it at last achieves its realisation. In actual existence, progress thus appears as an advance from the imperfect to the more perfect, although the former should not be understood in an abstract sense as merely imperfect, but as something which at the same time contains its own opposite, i.e. what is commonly called perfection, as a germ or impulse: just as potentiality – at least in terms of reflection – points forward to something which will eventually attain reality, or – to take a more specific example – just as the Aristotelian **dynamis** is also **potentia**, i.e. power and strength. Thus the imperfect, in so far as it contains its own opposite within itself, is a contradiction; and although it certainly exists, it must just as surely be overcome* and resolved. It is the drive and inherent impulse of spiritual life to break through[45] the shell of natural and sensory existence, of all that is alien to it, and to arrive at the light of consciousness, i.e. at its own true nature.*

b. [The beginning of history]

In connection with the idea of a state of nature in which freedom and justice are – or were – supposedly present in perfect form, we have already remarked

---

* *aufgehoben.*

in general terms on how the commencement of the history of spirit should be interpreted in relation to the concept which underlies it. But the idea of a state of nature was merely an assumption as far as historical existence is concerned, an assumption made in the twilit regions of hypothetical reflection. But a claim of an altogether different kind – i.e. one put forward not as an assumption based on thought but as a historical fact guaranteed by a higher authority – is made by another idea which is now frequently advanced in certain quarters. It takes up the old doctrine of the primitive paradisiac condition of man, which the theologians originally elaborated after their own fashion (for example, in the theory that God conversed with Adam in Hebrew), but adapts it to suit other requirements. For it has been argued (by **Schelling**, for example; cf. also **Schlegel's** *On the Language and Wisdom of the Indians*) that a primitive nation once existed, and that all our knowledge and art has simply been handed down to us from it. This original nation, it is contended, existed before mankind proper had come into being, and is immortalised in ancient legends under the image of the gods; distorted fragments of its highly developed culture are allegedly also to be found in the myths of the earliest nations. And the condition of the earliest nations, as described in history, is represented as a gradual decline from the high level of culture which preceded it. All this is put forward with the claim that philosophy requires that it should be so, and that it is also supported by historical evidence. *The high authority to which appeal is made in the first instance is that of the biblical narrative. But on the one hand, this narrative portrays the primitive condition only in its few well known characteristics, and on the other, it describes it and its various changes either in relation to mankind at large – i.e. as part of human nature in general – or, in so far as Adam is to be taken as a single individual or at most as two people, as present and complete only in this one individual or in a single human couple. The biblical account does not justify us in imagining that a nation and its historical condition actually existed in that primitive form, let alone in inferring that it had developed a perfect knowledge of God and of nature. Nature, so the fiction runs, originally lay open and transparent like a bright mirror of God's creation before the clear eye of man,[46] and the divine truth was equally transparent to him. It is also hinted – albeit in an indefinite and obscure manner – that in this primeval condition, man was in possession of a definite and already extensive knowledge of religious truths, revealed to him directly by God. Furthermore, all religions had their historical origin in this primitive condition, although they subsequently adulterated and obscured the original truth with figments of error and depravity. But in all the mythologies which error has created, traces of that* *original state and of the early doctrines of religious truth are present and can still be recognised. It is accordingly claimed that the study of the history of ancient peoples gains its essential interest from the fact that it is possible to follow it back to the point where such fragments of the earliest revealed knowledge can still be encountered in a purer form.*[47]

We certainly owe very much that is valuable to the interest which has fired such historical research, but this same research can also be indicted on its own direct testimony. For it sets out to prove by historical methods that whose historical existence it has already presupposed. Besides, it begins with a highly concentrated amalgam of historical data, and even these are eventually lost sight of altogether. Neither that advanced state of theological knowledge, or of other scientific (e.g. astronomical) knowledge (such as astronomers themselves, including Bailly,[48] have fancifully attributed to the Indians), nor the assumption that such a state of affairs prevailed at the beginning of history or that the religions of the various nations were traditionally derived from it and subsequently developed by a process of degeneration and deterioration (as is claimed by the crudely conceived so-called 'system of emanation') – none of these assumptions has any historical foundation, nor – if we may contrast their arbitrary and purely subjective origin with the true concept of history – can they ever hope to attain one.

This notion of a perfect primeval condition does, however, contain a philosophical element – namely the realisation that man cannot have originally existed in a state of animal insensibility. This is perfectly correct; man cannot have developed from a state of animal insensibility, although he may well have developed from a state of human insensibility. Animal humanity is altogether different from animality proper. The spirit is present from the beginning; but the spirit at first exists only in itself, as natural spirit, on which the character of humanity is nevertheless already imprinted. The child has no rationality, but it does have the real capability of becoming rational. The animal, on the other hand, is incapable of attaining self-consciousness. Even the simple movements of the child have a human quality about them; its first movement of all, its crying, is of a completely non-animal nature. For man is from the start an intelligent being; but those who persist in believing that man, in his original condition, lived in pure consciousness of God and of nature – surrounded, as it were, by everything which we have to acquire through laborious efforts, and in the centre of all arts and sciences – have failed to appreciate what intelligence and thought are. They cannot have understood that spirit is that infinite movement, ἐνέργεια, ἐντελέχεια (energy, activity) which never rests, that it abandons its original condition and is drawn on to a new one which it works upon in turn, discovering itself through the work it performs: for it is through this work alone that the spirit externalises its universal concept and attains a real existence. This, accordingly, is not the first but the last stage in its development. The customs, laws, institutions, and symbols of ancient nations are indeed the vessels of speculative ideas, for they are products of the spirit. But this inner reality of the Idea and its recognition of itself in the form of the Idea are two quite different things. The speculative Idea as an object of knowledge cannot have come first; on the contrary, it is the fruit of the spirit's highest and most abstract endeavours.

The only appropriate and worthy method of philosophical investigation is to take up history at that point where rationality begins to manifest itself in worldly existence – i.e. not where it is still a mere potentiality in itself but where it is in a position to express itself in consciousness, volition, and action. The inorganic existence of the spirit or of freedom – i.e. unconscious indifference (whether savage or mild in temper) towards good and evil, and hence towards laws in general, or, if we prefer to call it so, the perfection of innocence – is not itself an object of history. The natural (and at the same time religious) form of ethical life is family piety. In a society where this prevails, ethical life consists in the members behaving towards each other not as individuals or distinct persons with a will of their own; and for this very reason, the family in itself lies outside that development from which history takes its source. But if this spiritual unit steps beyond the sphere of emotion and natural love and attains a consciousness of personality, we have before us that dark and impenetrable intermediate zone in which neither nature nor spirit is open and transparent, and for which nature and spirit can become open and transparent only through a further process whereby the will, which has now become conscious of itself, develops over a protracted period of time. The quality of openness pertains solely to consciousness, and it is to consciousness alone that God – and indeed all other things too – can be revealed; in their true and universal form, which exists in and for itself, they can only be revealed to a consciousness which has become capable of reflective thought. Freedom is nothing more than a knowledge and affirmation of such universal and substantial objects as law and justice, and the production of a reality which corresponds to them – i.e. the state.

Nations may have had a long history before they finally reach their destination – i.e. that of forming themselves into states – and may even have developed considerably in some respects before they attain this goal. But, as already indicated, this pre-historical period lies outside the scope of our present investigation, irrespective of whether a real history followed it or whether the nations in question never finally succeeded in forming themselves into states. A great historical discovery, like the discovery of a new world, has been made in the last twenty [years] or upwards in connection with the Sanskrit language and its affinities with the languages of Europe. In particular, it has given us an insight into the historical links between the Germanic nations and those of India, an insight which carries as much certainty with it as can ever be achieved in such matters. Even at the present time, we know of peoples which scarcely form a society, let alone a state, but which have long been known to exist; and with others again, although it is primarily their advanced condition which interests us, their traditions extend beyond the history of their first constitution, and they underwent numerous changes before this epoch began. In the above-mentioned connection between the languages of nations so widely separated in space and so very different in religion, constitutions, ethics, and in every variety of spiritual and even physical culture (differences which have existed not only in the present, but also in the already remote ages in which they first became known to us), we have before us a result which proves as an irrefutable fact that these nations spread outwards from a centre in Asia and developed in disparate ways from an original family relationship; and this is not a fact established by the favourite method of combining and reasoning from circumstances of greater and lesser import – a method which has enriched history with so many fabrications given out as facts, and which, since alternative combinations of the same circumstances (either among themselves or with others) are equally possible, will continue to enrich it in the same fashion. But all these events, whose range appears so extensive, lie outside history proper: they in fact preceded it.

In our language, the word 'history'* combines both objective and subjective meanings, for it denotes the historia rerum gestarum as well as the res gestae themselves, the historical narrative and the actual happenings, deeds, and events – which, in the stricter sense, are quite distinct from one another. But this conjunction of the two meanings should be recognised as belonging to a higher order than that of mere external contingency: we must in fact suppose that the writing of history and the actual deeds and events of history make their appearance simultaneously, and that they emerge together from a common source. Family memorials and patriarchal traditions have an interest only within the family or tribe itself. The uniform course of their existence is not an object worthy of commemoration, although distinct deeds or turns of fate may well inspire Mnemosyne to retain their images, just as love and

---

* *Geschichte*, from the verb *geschehen* (to happen).

religious emotion impel the imagination to confer shape upon impulses which are initially lacking in form. But it is the state which first supplies a content which not only lends itself to the prose of history but actually helps to produce it. Instead of the merely subjective dictates of authority – which may suffice for the needs of the moment – a commonwealth in the process of coalescing and raising itself up to the position of a state requires formal commandments and laws, i.e. general and universally valid directives. It thereby creates a record of its own development, and an interest in intelligible, determinate, and – in their results – enduring deeds and events, on which Mnemosyne, for the benefit of the perennial aim which underlies the present form and constitution of the state, is impelled to confer a lasting memory. All deeper emotions such as love, as well as religious contemplation and the forms it creates, are wholly immediate and satisfying in themselves; but the external existence of the state, despite the rational laws and principles it contains, is an incomplete present which cannot understand itself and develop an integrated consciousness without reference to the past.

Those periods – whether we estimate them in centuries or millennia – which elapsed in the life of nations before history came to be written, and which may well have been filled with revolutions, migrations, and the most violent changes, have no objective history precisely because they have no subjective history, i.e. no historical narratives. It is not that the records of such periods have simply perished by chance; on the contrary, the reason why we have no records of them is that no such records were possible. It is only within a state which is conscious of its laws that clearly defined actions can take place, accompanied by that clear awareness of them which makes it possible and necessary to commit them to posterity. It is obvious to anyone with even a rudimentary knowledge of the treasures of Indian literature that this country, so rich in spiritual achievements of a truly profound quality, nevertheless has no history. In this respect, it at once stands out in stark contrast to China, an empire which possesses a highly distinguished and detailed historical record going back to the earliest times. India not only has ancient religious books and splendid works of poetry, but also ancient books of law – and the latter have already been mentioned as a prerequisite for the growth of history proper; nevertheless, it still does not have a history. But in this particular case, the incipient organisation which first created social distinctions immediately became petrified into natural determinations – i.e. the caste system – so that, although the laws are concerned with civil rights, they make these very rights dependent on distinctions of natural origin; their principal aim is to define the duties (in terms of wrongs rather than rights) of these classes towards one another, i.e. the privileges of the higher over the lower. The ethical element is thereby excluded from the splendour of Indian life and from every one of its provinces. Given this state of bondage in an order based firmly and permanently on nature, all social relations are wild and arbitrary, an ephemeral activity – or rather madness – with no ultimate end in the shape of progress and development: thus, no intelligent recollection, no object worthy of Mnemosyne presents itself, and a profound but extravagant fantasy drifts at random over a region which ought to have had a fixed purpose – a purpose rooted at least in substantial (i.e. implicitly rational, if [not] yet also subjective) freedom and reality – and thereby rendered itself worthy of history.

Since such conditions must be fulfilled before history is possible, it has happened that so rich and immeasurable an enterprise as the growth of families into tribes and of tribes into nations, which have then spread out in space as a result of their increase in size (a process which, as one can imagine, has led to innumerable complications, revolutions, and catastrophes) has taken place without giving rise to history; and what is more, that the concomitant expansion and development of the realm of spoken sounds has itself remained dumb, and has taken place in a silent and surreptitious manner. It is a fact attested by the monuments of literature that languages spoken by uncivilised nations have attained a high degree of development, and that the human understanding, by an intelligible process, has fully acquainted itself with this theoretical region. A full and consistent grammar is the product of thought, and the categories of thought are apparent within it. It is also a fact that, as society and the state become progressively more civilised, this systematic completeness of the understanding is gradually eroded, and, in this respect, language becomes correspondingly poorer and less refined – for it is a peculiar phenomenon that progress towards greater spirituality, although it promotes and cultivates rationality, allows the elaborate and precise constructions of the understanding to fall into neglect, seeing them as an obstruction and finally dispensing with them altogether. Language is the activity of the theoretical intelligence in the proper sense, for it is through language that it receives its external expression. The activities of memory and of the imagination, if not expressed in language, are no more than internal utterances. But this whole theoretical activity, together with its further development and the more concrete process which accompanies it – i.e. the dissemination of peoples, their separation from one another, their interminglings and their migrations – remains buried in the obscurity of a voiceless past; these are not acts of a will becoming conscious of itself, of freedom giving itself an external embodiment and a proper reality. Since they do not partake of this true substance, all such changes – regardless of the linguistic advances which accompany them – have not attained the status of history. The precocious development of language and the progress and diffusion of nations have acquired their significance and interest for concrete reason partly in so far as the nations in question have had contact with other states, and partly as they have begun to form political constitutions of their own.

c. The course of development[49]

After these remarks concerning the beginning of world history and that pre-historical period which lies outside it, we must now define more precisely the nature of its course— but for the present only in its formal aspects; the further definition of its concrete content is a problem of detailed classification.

World history,[50] as already pointed out, represents the development of the spirit's consciousness of its own freedom and of the consequent realisation of this freedom. This development is by nature a gradual progression, a series of successive determinations of freedom which proceed from the concept of the material in question, i.e. the nature of freedom in its development towards self-consciousness. The logical – and even more so the dialectical – nature of the concept in general, i.e. the fact that it determines itself, assumes successive determinations which it progressively overcomes,* thereby attaining a positive, richer, and more concrete determination – this necessity, and the necessary series of pure abstract determinations of the concept, are comprehended by means of philosophy.[51] All that need be noted here is that each step in the process, since it is different from all the others, has its own peculiar determinate principle. In history, such principles constitute the determinate characteristics of the spirit of a nation. Each historical principle, in its concrete form, expresses every aspect of the nation's consciousness and will, and indeed of its entire reality; it is the common denominator of its religion, its political constitution, its ethical life, its system of justice, its customs, its learning, art, and technical skill, and the whole direction of its industry. These special peculiarities should be interpreted in the light of the general peculiarity, the particular principle of the nation in question, just as this general peculiarity can be detected in the factual details with which history presents us. The question of whether this or that particular characteristic actually constitutes the distinctive principle of a nation is one which can only be approached empirically and demonstrated by historical means. To accomplish this, a trained capacity for abstraction and a thorough familiarity with ideas are necessary; one must have, so to speak, an a priori knowledge of the entire sphere to which the principles in question belong, just as Kepler – to name

---

* *aufhebt.*

the greatest exponent of this mode of cognition – had to have an a priori knowledge of ellipses, cubes, and squares and of the ideas concerning their relations before he could discover his immortal laws from the empirical data at his disposal; and the laws themselves consist of definitions borrowed from the above-mentioned class of conceptions. Anyone who approaches such matters without a knowledge of these elementary general principles, however long he may contemplate the heavens and the movements of the celestial bodies, can no more understand these laws than he could hope to formulate them himself. This ignorance of ideas concerning the gradual development of freedom is responsible for some of the objections commonly levelled against the philosophical approach to a subject which usually confines itself to empirical matters – objections to its so-called a priori method and to its alleged attempts to foist ideas on to the data of history. In the eyes of the objectors, these determinations of thought appear as something alien and extraneous to the object in hand. To a subjectively conditioned mind which is unfamiliar with ideas and unaccustomed to using them, they will indeed appear alien, and they have no place in the conceptions and theories which so limited an intellect forms of its object. It is this which has given rise to the saying that philosophy does not understand such subjects. Philosophy must indeed admit that it does not have the kind of understanding which prevails in other disciplines, i.e. that it does not proceed according to the categories of the understanding, but according to the categories of reason – although it is fully acquainted with the understanding and with its value and position. In the process of scientific understanding – just as in philosophy itself – the essential must be separated from the so-called inessential and clearly distinguished from it. But this is impossible unless we know what is essential, and in relation to world history in general, the essential is precisely that consciousness of freedom and those determinate phases in its development which we have already mentioned. The relationship of all particular things to these categories is their relationship to the truly essential.

Among the more direct kinds of objection levelled against the interpretation of any determinate object in a universal sense, some instances can usually be traced back to an inability to grasp and understand Ideas. If, in natural history, some monstrous and abnormal specimen or hybrid is cited as an instance against clearly defined species and genera, we can rightly reply with that saying which is so often used in an imprecise sense: namely that the exception proves the rule, i.e. that the exception reveals either the particular conditions under which the rule applies, or the deficiency and hybridism which occur in deviations from the norm. Nature is not strong enough to preserve its general classes and species from the influence of other elemental factors and agencies. But although the organisation of man, for example, is defined by the concrete form it assumes, and the brain, the heart, etc., are specified as essential ingredients of it, it is quite possible to adduce some wretched abortion or freak which possesses a generally human form (or at least parts of it) and which has been conceived in a human body, lived in it, been born from it, and drawn the breath of life, but which lacks either a brain or a heart. If such a specimen is quoted against the defining properties of an authentic human constitution, we can proceed no further than the abstract name of man and its superficial definition, from which the idea of a real, concrete human being is of course altogether different: for the latter must have a brain in its head and a heart in its breast.

A similar situation arises when it is maintained – quite correctly – that genius, talent, moral virtues, moral sentiments, and piety can be encountered in every region, under all constitutions, and in all political circumstances; and there is no lack of examples to prove this assertion. But if this is meant to imply that those distinctions which arise out of the degree of self-consciousness which freedom has attained are unimportant or inessential in relation to the above-mentioned qualities, reflection remains tied to abstract categories and lacks any determinate content, for which no principles are provided by the categories in question. The intellectual attitude which adopts such formal points of view certainly affords unlimited scope for ingenious questions, scholarly opinions, striking comparisons, and seemingly profound reflections and declamations; their brilliance may in fact seem to increase in proportion to their capacity for indefiniteness, and they may be the more readily refurbished and modified the less their attempts to achieve great results lead to anything of rational substance. From this point of view, one might well compare the familiar Indian epics, as they are called, with those of Homer, and argue that, since imaginative greatness is the true test of poetic genius, they are superior to the latter; in the same way, similarities between certain imaginary traits or attributes of the deities have led some to feel justified in identifying figures of Greek mythology with those of India. Similarly, the philosophy of China, in so far as it takes the One as its basis, has been equated with what later appeared as the Eleatic philosophy or the system of Spinoza; and since it also expresses itself in abstract numbers and lines, some have claimed to detect Pythagorean philosophy or even Christian dogma in it. Examples of bravery, indefatigable courage, qualities of magnanimity, self-denial and self-sacrifice, etc., which are encountered in the most savage and the most faint-hearted of nations, are deemed sufficient evidence for the view that there is as much – or even more – virtue and morality in such nations as in the most civilised Christian states, and so on. With such examples in mind, some have seen fit to doubt whether men have become better with the progress of history and of culture in general, and whether their morality has increased – the assumption being that morality depends upon the agent's subjective intentions and insights, on what he considers as justice or injustice, good or evil, and not on what is considered to be just and good or unjust and evil in and for itself or within a particular religion which is generally recognised as true.

We can spare ourselves the task of analysing the formalism and error of such attitudes here, and of establishing the true principles of morality – or rather of ethical life – in opposition to false morality. For world history moves on a higher plane than that to which morality properly belongs, for the sphere of morality is that of private convictions, the conscience of individuals, and their own particular will and mode of action; and the latter have their value, imputation, and reward or punishment within themselves. Whatever is required and accomplished by the ultimate end of the spirit, which exists in and for itself, and whatever providence does, transcends the obligations, liability, and responsibility which attach to individuality by virtue of its ethical existence. Those who, on ethical grounds (and hence with a noble intention), have resisted what the progress of the Idea of the spirit required, stand higher in moral worth than those whose crimes have been transformed by a higher order into the instruments of realising its will. But in revolutions of this kind, both parties alike stand within the same circle of corruptible existence, so that it is merely a formal kind of justice, abandoned by the living spirit and by God, which those who have the existing law on their side defend. The deeds of the great men who are the individuals of world history thus appear justified not only in their inner significance (of which the individuals in question are unconscious), but also in a secular sense. But from this latter point of view, no representations should be made against world-historical deeds and those who perform them by moral circles to which such individuals do not belong. The litany of private virtues – modesty, humility, charity, liberality, etc. – must not be raised against them. World history might well disregard completely the sphere to which morality and the much discussed and misunderstood dichotomy between morality and politics belong – and not merely by refraining from judgements (for the principles of world history and the necessary relationship of men's actions to these principles themselves constitute the judgement), but by ignoring individuals altogether and leaving them unmentioned; for what it has to record is the activity of the spirit of nations, and the individual forms which the spirit has assumed in the sphere of external reality could well be left to the attention of ordinary historians.

The same kind of formalism as that practised in morality also makes use of the indefinite notions which surround genius, poetry, and even philosophy, and likewise manages to discover them in everything. These notions are products of reflective thought, and the ability to manipulate such generalities – which do signalise and designate essential distinctions, but without bringing out the true depth of their significance – is what we call culture;* it is a purely formal property, in that its sole aim, irrespective of the content it has before it, is to analyse the latter into its component parts and to comprehend these in forms and definitions of thought. Culture as such does not contain that free universality which would enable it to make itself the object of its own consciousness. Such a consciousness of thought itself and of the forms of thought taken in isolation from any particular material, is philosophy, for whose existence culture is admittedly a prerequisite; but the function of culture consists merely in clothing whatever content it has before it in the form of universality, so that the two are inseparably united within it – so inseparably that it regards its content (which, through the analysis of one conception into a multitude of subordinate conceptions, can be enlarged to an immeasurable degree of richness) as a purely empirical element in which thought plays no part whatsoever. It is nevertheless just as much an act of thought – or, more specifically, of the understanding – to reduce to a simple conception (such as earth, man, etc., or Alexander or Caesar) an object which itself encompasses a rich and concrete content and to designate it by a single word, as it is to analyse it into its separate parts, to isolate the determinations which such a conception contains, and to bestow particular names on each of them. All this [had to be said] to avoid the risk of making indefinite and empty pronouncements on culture. But to return to the view which originally provoked the above remarks, it is at least clear that, just as reflection produces the universal notions of genius, talent, art, science, etc., and equally general observations concerning their nature, formal culture, at every stage of spiritual evolution, not only can but also must make its appearance, grow, and blossom out to the full; for each stage in the process must develop itself into a state, and advance from this basis of civilisation to reflective understanding and to forms of generalisation, both in laws and in all other things. Political life as such inevitably gives rise to formal culture, and hence also to learning and to a fully developed poetry and art in general. Besides, what we call the plastic arts, even in their technical aspects, presuppose a civilised community of men. Poetry, which has less need of external means and accessories and whose medium is the voice, the instrument of the spirit's immediate self-

---

* *Bildung;* cf. note to p. 56 above.

expression, emerges in all its boldness and with highly developed powers of expression even in nations which have not yet reached the stage of uniting to form a law-governed community; for as already remarked, language attains a high level of reflective development in its own right even before civilisation has emerged.

Philosophy, too, must make its appearance as soon as political life is established. For that which confers the property of culture upon any given content is, as already mentioned, the form proper to thought itself; whereas philosophy is merely the consciousness of this form, the thinking of thinking, so that the material which it requires for its own peculiar edifice is already prepared for it through the general progress of culture. And in the development of the state itself, periods must occur in which the spirit of nobler natures is forced to flee from the present into ideal regions, and to find in them that reconciliation with itself which it can no longer enjoy in an internally divided reality; for the reflective understanding attacks all those sacred and profound elements which were artlessly introduced into the religion, laws, and customs of nations, and debases and dilutes them into abstract and godless generalities. Thought is then impelled to become thinking reason, and to pursue and accomplish in its own element the undoing of that destruction which had previously overtaken it.

Thus, in all world-historical nations, we do indeed encounter poetry, plastic art, science, and even philosophy. But these differ not only in their tone, style, and general tendency, but even more so in their basic import; and this import involves the most important difference of all, i.e. that of rationality. It is pointless for a presumptuous aesthetic criticism to insist that their subject-matter, i.e. the substantial part of their content, should not be determined by the pleasure we derive from it, and to argue that beauty of form as such, imaginative greatness, and the like, are the aims of fine art and the only factors which should be registered and appreciated by a liberal disposition and cultivated mind. If the substance itself is insignificant, or wild and fantastic or absurd, a healthy common sense cannot bring itself to abstract from it in such a way as to derive enjoyment from the work in question. For even if one ranks the Indian epics as highly as Homer's on account of numerous formal qualities of this kind – greatness of invention and imagination, vividness of imagery and sentiments, beauty of diction, etc. – they nevertheless remain infinitely different in their import and hence in their very substance; and the latter involves the interest of reason, which is directly concerned with the consciousness of the concept of freedom and the way in which it expresses itself in individuals. There is not only a classical form, but also a classical content; and besides, form and content are so intimately connected in works of art that the former can only be classical in so far as the latter is also classical. If the content is fantastic and not self-contained – and it is reason alone which supplies both measure and goal – the form becomes unbalanced and amorphous, or awkward and trivial.

In the same way, it is equally possible to draw parallels between Chinese and Indian philosophy, and between Eleatic, Pythagorean, and Spinozistic metaphysics – or even modern metaphysics in general – for all of them do indeed base themselves on the One or on unity, the wholly abstract universal; but to compare or even to identify them in this way is a highly superficial procedure. For it overlooks the one essential factor, i.e. the determinate characteristics of the unity in question; and this involves an essential distinction, for the unity may be understood either in an abstract or in a concrete sense (concrete to the point of being a unity in itself, which is the same thing as spirit). Those who treat them as identical merely prove that they have recognised only the abstract kind of unity; and although they pass judgements on philosophy, they are ignorant of the very factor from which philosophy derives its interest.

On the other hand, there are also areas which remain the same despite all differences in the substantial content of the cultures in question. These differences concern the thinking reason; and freedom, whose self-consciousness consists in this reason, has one and the same root as thought. Since man alone – as distinct from the animals – is a thinking being, he alone possesses freedom, and he possesses it solely by virtue of his ability to think. Consciousness of freedom consists in the fact that the individual comprehends himself as a person, i.e. that he sees himself in his distinct existence as inherently universal, as capable of abstraction from and renunciation of everything particular, and therefore as inherently infinite. Consequently, the areas which lie outside this variety of comprehension are a common denominator amidst the substantial differences referred to above. Even morality, which is so closely connected with the consciousness of freedom, can attain a high degree of purity before any such consciousness is present; for it may simply enunciate universal duties and rights as objective commandments, or even remain purely negative in character, prescribing a formal elevation of the mind and a renunciation of the sensual and of all sensual motives. Chinese morality, since the Europeans have become acquainted with it and with the writings of Confucius, has received the highest praise and the most flattering tributes to its merits even from those who are familiar with Christian morality; in the same way, men have acknowledged the sublimity with which the religion and poetry of India (or at least the higher kinds of these), and in particular the Indian philosophy, express and enjoin the removal and sacrifice of all sensual things. Yet these two nations are lacking – indeed completely lacking – in the essential self-consciousness of the concept of freedom. The Chinese look on their moral rules as if they were laws of nature, positive external command-ments, coercive rights and duties, or rules of mutual courtesy. Freedom, through which the substantial determinations of reason can alone be translated into ethical attitudes, is absent; morality is a political matter which is administered by government officials and courts of law. Their writings on the subject are not, however, collections of legal statutes, but are addressed to the subjective will and disposition of the reader. Like the moral writings of the Stoics, they read like a series of commands which purport to be necessary for the attainment of happiness, so that it is left to the individual to adopt and follow such commands or not; in the same way, the idea of an abstract subject, the wise man, is the culmination of such doctrines with both the Chinese and the Stoic moralists.[52] *And in the **Indian** doctrine of the renunciation of sensuality, desires, and all earthly interests, positive ethical freedom is not the goal and end, but rather the extinction of consciousness and the suspension of spiritual and even physical life.*

A nation is only world-historical in so far as its fundamental element and basic aim have embodied a universal principle; only then is its spirit capable of producing an ethical and political organisation. If nations are impelled merely by desires, their deeds are lost without trace (as with all fanaticism), and no enduring achievement remains. Or the only traces they leave are ruin and destruction. In this way, the Greeks speak of the rule of Chronos or Time, who devours his own children (i.e. the deeds he has himself produced); this was the Golden Age, which produced no ethical works. Only Zeus, the political god from whose head Pallas Athene sprang and to whose circle Apollo and the Muses belong, was able to check the power of time; he did so by creating a conscious ethical institution, i.e. by producing the state.

An achievement is only objective in so far as it is an object of knowledge. It contains the determination of universality or thought in its very element; without thought, it has no objectivity, for thought is its basis. The nation must know the universal on which its ethical life is based and before which the particular vanishes away, and it must therefore know the deter-minations which underlie its justice and religion. The spirit cannot rest content with the mere existence of an order or cult; its will is rather to attain this knowledge of its own determinations. Only in this way can it succeed in uniting its subjectivity with the universal of its objectivity. Admittedly, its world is also composed of distinct elements to which it responds through the medium of external intuition, etc., but the unity of its innermost nature with this external world must also be present to it. This is its supreme liberation, since thought is its innermost nature. The highest point in the development of the nation is reached when it has understood its life and condition by means of thought, and acquired a systematic knowledge of its laws, justice, and ethical life; for in this achievement lies the closest possible unity which the spirit can attain with itself. The aim of its endeavours is for it to have itself as its own object; but it cannot have itself as its object in its true essentiality unless it thinks itself. At this point, then, the spirit knows its own principles, the universal aspect of its real world. Thus, if we wish to know what Greece really was, we find the answer in Sophocles and Aristophanes, Thucydides and Plato; in them, we find the historical expression of what Greek life actually was. For in these individuals, the Greek spirit comprehended itself through representation and thought.

This spiritual self-consciousness is the nation's supreme achievement; but we must remember in the first place that it is also only ideal. In this achievement of thought lies the profounder kind of satisfaction which the nation can attain; but since it is of a universal nature, it is also ideal, and accordingly different in form from the real activity, the real work and life which made such an achievement possible. The nation now has both a real and an ideal existence. At such a time, we shall therefore find that the nation derives satisfaction from the idea of virtue and from discussion of it – discussion which may either coexist with virtue itself or become a substitute for it. All this is the work of the spirit, which knows how to bring the unreflected – i.e. the merely factual – to the point of reflecting upon itself. It thereby becomes conscious to some degree of the limitation of such determinate things as belief, trust, and custom, so that the consciousness now has reasons for renouncing the latter and the laws which they impose. This is indeed the inevitable result of any search for reasons; and when no such reasons – i.e. no completely abstract universal principles – can be found as the basis of the laws in question, men's ideas of virtue begin to waver, and the absolute is no longer regarded as valid in its own right, but only in so far as it has reasons to justify it. At the same time, individuals gradually became isolated from one another and from the whole, selfishness and vanity intervene, and men seek to obtain their own advantage and satisfaction at the expense of the whole. For the consciousness is subjective in nature, and subjectivity carries with it the need to particularise itself. Vanity and selfishness accordingly make their appearance, and passions and personal interests emerge unchecked and in a destructive form. This is not, however, the natural death of the national spirit, but merely a state of internal division.

And thus Zeus, who set limits to the depredations of time and suspended its constant flux, had no sooner established something inherently enduring than he was himself devoured along with his whole empire. He was devoured by the principle of thought itself, the progenitor of knowledge, of reasoning, of insight based on rational grounds, and of the search for such grounds. Time is the negative element in the world of the senses; thought is equally negative, but it is at the same time that innermost and infinite form into which all existence – and in the first place finite being or determinate form – is dissolved. Time, then, is indeed the corrosive aspect of negativity; but spirit likewise has the property of dissolving every determinate content it encounters. For it is the universal, unlimited, innermost and infinite form itself, and it overcomes all that is limited. Even if the objective element does not appear finite and limited in content, it does at least appear as something given, immediate, and authoritative in nature, so that it is not in a position to impose restrictions on thought or to set itself up as a permanent obstacle to the thinking subject and to infinite internal reflection.

This dissolving activity of thought also inevitably gives rise to a new principle. Thought, in so far as it is universal in character, has the effect of dissolving every determinate content; but in this very dissolution, the preceding principle is in fact preserved, with the sole difference that it no longer possesses its original determination. The universal essence is preserved, but its universality as such has been brought out into relief. The preceding principle has been transfigured by universality; its present mode must be considered as different from the preceding one, for in the latter, the present mode existed only implicitly and had an external existence only through a complex series of manifold relationships. What formerly existed only in concrete particulars now has the form of universality conferred upon it; but a new element, another further determination, is also present. The spirit, in its new inward determination, has new interests and ends beyond those which it formerly possessed. This change in the principle's form also brings with it new and additional determinations of content. Everyone knows that a cultured* man has quite different expectations from those of his uncultured fellow-countryman, although the latter lives within the same religion and ethical community and his substantial condition is precisely the same. Culture would at first seem

* *gebildet.*

147

to be purely formal in character, but it does also give rise to differences in content. The cultured and the uncultured Christian appear completely identical in one respect, but their needs are nevertheless completely different. And it is precisely the same with property relations. Even the serf has property, but it is coupled with obligations which render another person the joint owner of it. If, however, we define property in terms of **thought**, it of course follows that only one man can be the owner. For thought brings out the universal aspect, thereby creating a different interest and different needs.

The determinate nature of the transition which takes place in all such changes is therefore as follows: what at present exists becomes an object of thought, and it is thereby elevated into universality. The nature of the spirit is to comprehend the universal, i.e. that which is essential. Universality, in its truest sense, is the substance, the essence, that which truly exists. In the case of the slave, for example, the appropriate universal is that of the human being; for it is at this point that particularity passes over into universality. If, therefore, particularity is transcended in a given nation – for example, in that of Athens – by means of thought, and if thought develops to the point where the particular principle of the nation in question is no longer essential, that nation cannot continue to exist; for another principle has meanwhile emerged. World history then passes over to another nation. Such principles are present in world history in the shape of national spirits; but the latter also have a natural existence. The particular stage which the spirit has reached is present as the **natural principle** of the people in question or as the **nation**. According to the different ways in which it manifests itself in this determinate natural element, the spirit appears in various forms. Thus, although its new and higher determination within a particular national spirit does appear as the negation or destruction of the preceding one, its positive side also emerges in the shape of a new nation. A nation cannot pass through several successive stages in world history or make its mark in it more than once. If it were possible for genuinely new interests to arise within a nation, the national spirit would have to be in a position to will something new – but where could this new element come from? It could only take the shape of a higher and more universal conception of itself, a progression beyond its own principle, or a quest for a more universal principle – but this would mean that a further determinate principle, i.e. a new spirit, was already present. In world history, a nation can be dominant only once, because it can only have one task to perform within the spiritual process.

This advance or progression appears to be a process of infinite duration, in keeping with the notion of perfectibility – a constant progress which must always remain distant from its goal. But even if, in the advance towards a new principle, the content of the preceding one is comprehended in a more universal sense than before, it is at least certain that the new form which emerges will again be a determinate one. Furthermore, history has to do with reality, in which the universal must in any case assume a determinate form. And no limited form can establish itself permanently in face of thought or the concept. If there were something which the concept could not digest or resolve, it would certainly represent the highest degree of fragmentation and unhappiness. But if something of the kind did exist, it could be nothing other than thought itself in its function of self-comprehension. For thought alone is inherently unlimited, and all reality is determined within it. In consequence, the fragmentation would cease to exist, and thought would be satisfied within itself. This, then, would be the ultimate purpose of the world. Reason recognises that which is truthful, that which exists in and for itself, and which is not subject to any limitations. The concept of the spirit involves a return upon itself, whereby it makes itself its own object; progress, therefore, is not an indeterminate advance ad infinitum, for it has a definite aim – namely that of returning upon itself. Thus, it also involves a kind of cyclic movement as the spirit attempts to discover itself.

It is sometimes said that goodness is the ultimate end. But in the first place, this is an indefinite kind of expression. One might well be reminded – and should be reminded – of the equivalent form in religion. For in philosophy, we must on no account adopt the attitude of ignoring other venerable insights out of a misplaced sense of awe. From the point of view of religion, the ultimate aim is that man should attain a state of holiness. This, in religious terms, is indeed the proper aim so far as individuals are concerned. The subject gains itself as such and fulfils its end within the institution of religion. But seen in this light, the end already presupposes a content of a universal kind, i.e. a state in which souls may find their salvation. One might well object that this conception of salvation is no concern of ours, since salvation is a future end whose fulfilment lies in another world. But then we would still be left with existence in this world as a preparation for that future state. This whole distinction, however, is only subjectively valid; it would leave individuals with no choice but to regard whatever leads them to salvation as nothing more than a means. But this is not at all the case, for the latter must undoubtedly be understood in an absolute sense. From the point of view of religion, the aim of both natural existence and spiritual activity is the glorification of God. Indeed, this is the worthiest end of the spirit and of history. The nature of the spirit is to make itself its own object and to comprehend itself. Only then is it really present as the product and result of its own activity. 'To comprehend itself' means, of course, to comprehend itself by means of thought. But this implies not merely a knowledge of arbitrary, casual, and ephemeral determinations, but a comprehension of the absolute itself. The aim of the spirit is therefore to make itself conscious of the absolute, and in such a way that this consciousness is given to it as the sole and exclusive truth, so that everything must be – and actually is – brought into conformity with it, and world history is ruled by it in reality as it was all along. To become actively aware of this means to do honour to God or to glorify the truth. This is the absolute and ultimate end, and truth is itself the power which produces its own glorification. In honouring God, the individual spirit is itself honoured – not, however, in a particular sense, but through the knowledge that the activity it performs in honour of God is of an absolute nature. Here, the individual spirit exists in truth, and participates in the absolute; it is therefore self-sufficient. Here also, the dichotomy which besets the limited spirit (which knows its own being only as a restriction, and raises itself above it by means of thought) is removed. And here again, not even natural death can intervene.

In our understanding of world history, we are concerned with history primarily as a record of the past. But we are just as fully concerned with the present. Whatever is true exists eternally in and for itself – not yesterday or tomorrow, but entirely in the present, 'now', in the sense of an absolute present. Within the Idea, even that which appears to be past is never lost. The Idea is of the present, and the spirit is immortal; there is no past or future time at which it did not exist or would not exist; it is not over and done with, nor does it not yet exist – on the contrary, it exists absolutely now. This in fact means that the present world and the present form and self-consciousness of the spirit contain within them all the stages which appear to have occurred earlier in history. These did admittedly take shape independently and in succession; but what the spirit is now, it has always been implicitly, and the difference is merely in the degree to which this implicit character has been developed. The spirit of the present world is the concept which the spirit forms of its own nature. It is this which sustains and rules the world, and it is the result of 6000 years of effort; it is all that the spirit has created for itself through the labours of world history, and all that was destined to emerge from these labours. This, then, is how we should understand world history, which presents us with the work of the spirit in its progressive recognition of its own nature and in its application of this knowledge to all the various spheres which are affected by it.

In this connection, it should be remembered that every individual, in his cultural development, must pass through various spheres which together form the basis of his concept of the spirit and each of which has taken shape and developed independently at some time in the past. But what the spirit is now, it has always been; the only difference is that it now possesses a richer consciousness and a more fully elaborated concept of its own nature. The spirit has all the stages of the past still adhering to it, and the life of the spirit in history consists of a cycle of different stages, of which some belong to the present and others have appeared in forms of the past. Since we are concerned with the Idea of the spirit and look upon everything in world history merely as a manifestation of it, we are invariably occupied with the present whenever we review the past, no matter how considerable that past may be. For philosophy is concerned with what is present and real. Those moments which the spirit appears to have outgrown still belong to it in the depths of its present. Just as it has passed through all its moments in history, so also must it pass through them again in the present – in the concept it has formed of itself.

Appendix

1. The natural context or the geographical basis of world history

---

a. *General determinations*

The universal premise of this investigation is that world history represents the Idea of the spirit as it displays itself in reality as a series of external forms. The stage of self-consciousness which the spirit has reached manifests itself in world history as the existing national spirit, as a nation which exists in the present. Consequently, this stage of self-consciousness exists within time and space, and its mode is that of natural existence. The particular spirits which we have to consider in their simultaneous and successive existence are particular, because each of them has its own determinate principle; and each world-historical nation has the functions of a distinct principle allotted to it. It must admittedly pass through various principles in its own right in order that its distinct principle may attain maturity; but in world history, it always retains a single form. It may well occupy several positions in the course of its historical existence; but it can never command the first place in world history in more than one of these. On the contrary, it is eventually assimilated into another principle which, since it is itself original, is incompatible with the former one. But every particular national principle is also subject to natural determinants, so that it also appears as a natural principle. The various national spirits are separated in time and space; and in this respect, the influence of the natural context, the relationship between the spiritual and the natural (i.e. the national temperament, etc.) makes itself felt. Seen against the universality of the ethical whole and its own active individuality, this relationship is a purely external one; but as the ground on which the spirit moves, it is nevertheless an essential and necessary basis.

When the spirit first enters existence, it takes on the mode of finitude and hence of natural existence in general. Its particular forms diverge from one another; for the form of natural existence is that of disparity, in that its particular determinate characteristics appear as *separate units*. It follows as a necessary consequence of this abstract determination that whatever appears as a particular stage in the development of the spirit will also appear as a particular natural *form*, existing independently and to the exclusion of all others. This particularity, since it manifests itself in the natural world, is a natural particularity; in other words, it exists as a natural principle or as a particular natural determination. It follows from this that every people which represents a particular stage in the development of the spirit constitutes a *nation*; its natural characteristics correspond to the nature of the spiritual principle within the series of spiritual forms.

This natural dimension leads us to consider the influence of geography; for the latter includes all that belongs to the purely natural phase. But in natural existence, we can immediately distinguish two aspects of determinate reality: on the one hand, it includes the nation's natural will or subjective disposition; but on the other, it is also present in the shape of a particular external nature. In so far as man is unfree and natural, he can be described as a creature of the senses. The world of the senses, however, consists of two distinct aspects: that of subjectivity and that of external nature. The latter is the geographical aspect, which can be recognised at first glance as part of external nature in general. What we have to consider, therefore, are differences which are grounded in nature. They must also be seen first and foremost as particular possibilities from which the spirit germinates, and they accordingly lend it its geographical basis. It is not our business to acquaint ourselves with the nation's environment as an external locality, but merely with the natural type to which the latter belongs; for this is intimately connected with the type and character of whatever nation is rooted in this particular soil. The nation's character consists simply in the form and manner in which it appears in world history and takes up its position and stance within it. But this connection between nature and the character of men would seem to be incompatible with the freedom of the human will. We call it the realm of the senses, and one might well argue that man possesses truth within himself independently of nature. But we must not assume that the relationship of dependence between man and nature implies that the character of a nation is formed exclusively by the natural characteristics of its environment. The spirit should not be thought of as something abstract which only later acquires its content from nature. On the contrary, the spirits which emerge in history are already particular and determinate; the speculative Idea shows how the particular is contained within the universal without in any way obscuring it. Since nations are spirits whose form is of a particular nature, their determinateness is spiritual in character, although it is also matched by a corresponding natural determinateness.

That which still exists within itself exists only on the level of nature; thus the child is a human being in itself, and, as a child, it remains a purely natural being which has only a latent capacity for existing in and for itself as a free human being.

This consideration would seem to tally with what is usually said concerning the influence of *climate* on human affairs. It is a general and widely held opinion that the particular national spirit is linked with the climate of the nation in question, and that the nation is by birth a single people. This is a very commonly expressed sentiment. But however necessary the connection between the spiritual and the natural principle may be, we must not rest content with everyday opinions and ascribe over-specific effects and influences to climate. For example, a great deal is often said about the mild Ionic sky which supposedly produced Homer, and it did undoubtedly contribute much to the charm of the Homeric poems. But the coast of Asia Minor has always been the same, and is still the same today; nevertheless, only *one* Homer has arisen among the Ionic people. It is not the nation which sings; a poem is composed only by one person, by a single individual – and even if several persons were involved in the composition of the Homeric songs, they were still only a group of individuals. Despite the mild sky, no further Homers emerged, particularly under the Turkish rule. The effect of climate is limited to minor particulars; but we are not concerned with these, and they have no real influence in any case.

Climate does have a certain influence, however, in that neither the *torrid* nor the *cold region* can provide a basis for human freedom or for world-historical nations. At his first awakening, man possesses an immediately natural consciousness in relation to nature in general. Since this is so, there is necessarily a relationship between the two: all development involves a reflection of the spirit within itself in opposition to nature, or an internal particularisation of the spirit as against its immediate existence, i.e. the natural world. The moment of naturalness is itself part of this particularisation, because it is itself of a particular nature; and in this way, an opposition arises between the spirit and the external world. Nature is therefore the original basis from which man can achieve inward freedom. For in so far as man is primarily a creature of the senses, it is imperative that, in his sensuous connection with nature, he should be able to attain freedom by means of internal reflection. But where nature is too powerful, his liberation becomes more difficult. His sensuous existence and his withdrawal from it are themselves his natural mode of existence, and the latter, as such, embodies the determination of quantity.

It is therefore essential that man's connection with nature should not be too powerful in the first place.

Nature, in contrast to the spirit, is a quantitative element whose power must not be so great as to render it omnipotent in its own right. Extreme conditions are not conducive to spiritual development. *Aristotle* has long since observed that man turns to universal and more exalted things only after his basic needs have been satisfied.[1] But neither the torrid nor the frigid zone permits him to move freely, or to acquire sufficient resources to allow him to participate in higher spiritual interests. He is kept in too insensible a state; he is oppressed by nature, and consequently cannot divorce himself from it, although this is the primary condition of all higher spiritual culture. The power of the elements is too great for man to escape from his struggle with them, or to become strong enough to assert his spiritual freedom against the power of nature. The frost which grips the inhabitants of Lappland and the fiery heat of Africa are forces of too powerful a nature for man to resist, or for the spirit to achieve free movement and to reach that degree of richness which is the precondition and source of a fully developed mastery of reality. In regions such as these, dire necessity can never be escaped or overcome; man is continually forced to direct his attention to nature. Man uses nature for his own ends; but where nature is too powerful, it does not allow itself to be used as a means. The torrid and frigid regions, as such, are not the theatre on which world history is enacted. In this respect, such extremes are incompatible with spiritual freedom.

All in all, it is therefore the *temperate zone* which must furnish the theatre of world history. And more specifically, the northern part of the temperate regions is particularly suited to this purpose, because at this point, the earth has a broad breast (as the Greeks put it), i.e. the continents are closely connected. This formation calls to mind the distinction which is commonly made between north and south; for the earth is widest in the north and divided in the south, where it separates out into many distinct points as in America, Asia, and Africa. The same peculiarity shows itself in natural products. All the interconnected northern countries, as we know from natural history, have many natural products in common; but in the widely separated promontories of the south, they diverge much more widely. In terms of botany and zoology, the northern zone is therefore the most important one; the largest number of animal and vegetable species is found in it, whereas in the south, where the land is broken up into separate points, the natural forms also diverge widely from one another.

If we now consider those determinate differences which have a bearing on the distinct characteristics of national spirits, it should be remembered that we must confine ourselves to such essential and universal distinctions as are necessary to thought and at the same time founded in empirical reality. For determinateness must be distinguished from mere diversity, which is in some measure contingent. To isolate these determining differences is the task of philosophical enquiry, and we must take care not to lose ourselves in formless diversity. The latter comes into play as soon as we consider what is usually understood by the indefinite word 'climate', which we have already dealt with above. Our next step will be to discuss in more detail the universal distinctions which occur in the natural world.

In the sphere of natural determinateness, the universal relation which is of most importance to history is that of *land and sea*. As far as land is concerned, three fundamental distinctions can be made. Firstly, there are the waterless uplands; secondly, valley formations which are watered by rivers; and thirdly, the coastal regions. These three moments are the most essential of those which admit of conceptual differentiation, and to which all other determinations can be reduced.

The first moment is that solid, metallic element which remains indifferent, enclosed, and amorphous – the *uplands* with their great steppes and plains. They may well furnish impulses to activity, but such impulses are of a wild and mechanical nature. These waterless plains are primarily the abode of *nomads*, as of the Mongol and Arab nations in the Old World. The nomads are in themselves of a mild disposition, but their principle is an unstable and volatile one. They are not tied to the soil, and they know nothing of those rights which, in an agricultural society, oblige men to live together. This restless principle is associated with the patriarchal constitution, but it readily breaks out into mutual wars and depredations, or even into assaults upon other peoples; the latter are first subjugated, and then the invaders become amalgamated with them. The wanderings of the nomads are purely formal, because they are confined within uniform and circumscribed paths. But this limitation is merely factual; the possibility exists for them to sever their ties. The soil is not cultivated, and it can be found wherever they go; consequently, any external or internal impulse can lead such nations to migrate. But the spirit of restlessness does not really lie in the nations themselves. In the lower regions of the upland plains which border on settled countries, such nations are driven to plundering, whereas the higher regions are bounded by high mountains in which powerful nations have their home. But the tribes of the lower regions will clash with hostile inhabitants and come into conflict with them, so that these particular nomads are destined to live in a state of war with those around them, with the result that they become fragmented. This fosters the individual personality and an unruly and fearless independence, but also the abstract quality of fragmentation. The mountains are the seat of pastoral existence; but their varied soil also makes agriculture possible. Their extremely variable climate with its harsh winters and hot summers, along with the many dangers they contain, is conducive to bravery. But mountain life remains isolated by the very nature of the environment. If such a nation finds the locality too restricting, it only needs a leader for it to swoop down on the fertile valleys and plains. But such incursions are not just symptoms of unsettledness, for they are prompted by a definite aim. The natural conflicts which occur in Asia are invariably based on antitheses of this kind.

The context here is accordingly one of highland regions surrounded by mountain chains. The second characteristic of such regions is that the mountain massif is broken up by rivers which, from their source in the highlands, flow downwards and burst through the chain of mountains. For as a rule, an upland region is surrounded by mountains which are penetrated by rivers; these may subsequently form valleys with gentler slopes if the distance to the sea is sufficiently great. They then flow through an area of greater or less breadth before debouching into the sea. The decisive factor here is whether their precipitous reaches lie close to the sea or not, i.e. whether only a narrow strip lies before them or rather a broad obstacle which compels them to develop a long course, whether they flow into a moderately hilly region or into a wide river basin. Although the mountain chains of Africa are penetrated by rivers, these quickly flow into the sea, and the coastal strip is for the most part extremely narrow. The same applies to parts of South America, such as Chile and Peru, and likewise to Ceylon. Chile and Peru are narrow coastal territories, and they have no culture of their own. Brazil is quite different in this respect. But, apart from this, another factor may be involved; for the highlands themselves may consist entirely of mountain ranges with very few level areas among them.

Uplands such as these are to be found in Central Asia, the home of the Mongols (in the general sense of the word); steppes of this kind extend northwards from the Caspian Sea and across towards the Black Sea. Other similar regions which call for mention are the deserts of Arabia, those in Barbary in North Africa, and those around the Orinoco and in Paraguay in South America. The main peculiarity of the inhabitants of these upland regions, which are watered only by occasional rain or by the overflowing of a river (as in the plains of the Orinoco), is their patriarchal way of life, for they are split up into separate family units. The soil on which they live is either completely infertile or fertile only for short periods; consequently, their wealth lies not in their land, from which they derive only a meagre harvest, but in the animals which accompany them in their wanderings. The animals find pasture for a time on the plains, and when these cease to support them, the community moves on to other regions. They lead a carefree life and do not store provisions for the winter, so that half of their herds must frequently perish. No legal system exists among these highland peoples, and their life is therefore marked by the extremes of hospitality and marauding – the latter occurring more frequently if they are surrounded by civilised countries, as in the case of the Arabs, who are aided in their attacks by their horses and camels. The Mongols live on mare's milk, so that their horses are both a means of sustenance and instruments of war. Although their patriarchal existence usually assumes the form outlined above, it also frequently happens that they congregate together in large numbers and are led by some impulse to move outwards from their homeland. Although formerly of a peaceful disposition, they now fall like a raging torrent upon the civilised countries, and the ensuing revolution produces only destruction and devastation. National upheavals of this kind occurred under Genghis Khan and Tamerlane; the invaders trampled down everything before them and then finally disappeared, just as an overflowing forest stream must eventually subside, since it has no inner principle of vitality. The next level below the highlands is that of the narrow mountain valleys. These are inhabited by peaceful mountain nations – pastoral peoples who also practise agriculture, like the Swiss. Such nations are also to be found in Asia, but they are on the whole of less importance.

The second major division is the transitional region, that of the *broad river valleys*. Such valleys are formed by the major rivers, which are surrounded by peaceful dales. The gradual accumulation of silt has made the soil fertile, and the land owes its entire fertility to the rivers which have shaped it. It is here that centres of civilisation, which brings with it internal independence, first arise. It is not, however, that unenlightened independence of the previous region, but a differentiated state – although this differentiation does not extend beyond the confines of the society in question, but leads instead to a process of internal development. The river plains are the most fertile lands; agriculture becomes established there, and with it, the rights of communal existence are introduced. The fertile soil automatically brings about the transition to *agriculture*, and this in turn gives rise to understanding and foresight. Agriculture has to adapt itself to the changing seasons; it is not a question of gaining immediate satisfaction for individual needs, for these are now satisfied in a universal manner. The cares of man are no longer confined to a single day, but extend far into the future. Tools have to be invented, and practical ingenuity and art develop. Fixed possessions, property, and justice are instituted, and this in turn gives rise to distinct social classes. The demand for manufactured implements and the need to conserve provisions lead to a settled existence, confined to a specific locality. As the land in question is cultivated, the determinations of property and justice come into being. Natural isolation is overcome by this mutually determined and exclusive (but at the same time universal) independence; a condition of universality prevails, and the purely particular is excluded from it. This opens up the possibility of a universal sovereign – and, what is more important, of the rule of law. Great empires grow up in such countries, and the foundations of powerful states are laid. This process of finite development, therefore, is not one of aimless expansion, but of adherence to the universal. In Oriental history, we shall encounter states which have only just attained this condition, i.e. the empires on the banks of the rivers of China, and of the Ganges, the Indus, and the Nile.

In more recent times, in which it has been argued that states must necessarily be separated by natural elements, we have become accustomed to look on water as a creator of divisions. The main objection to this is that nothing unites so effectively as water, for the civilised countries are invariably river territories. Water is in fact the uniting element, and it is the mountains which create divisions. If countries are separated by mountains, they are separated far more effectively than they would be by a river or even by the sea. France and Spain, for example, are separated by the Pyrenees; and Cadiz used to have closer links with America than with Madrid. Mountains create divisions between nations, customs, and characters. But a country is constituted by the river which flows through it, and both banks of the river properly belong to one and the same country. Silesia is the basin of the Oder, Bohemia and Saxony are the valley of the Elbe, and Egypt is the valley of the Nile. During the Wars of the Revolution, the French used to maintain that rivers are the natural frontiers between countries, but this is mistaken. And it is precisely the same with the sea. Communications between America and Europe are much easier than in the interior of Asia or America. Since the discovery of America and the East Indies, the Europeans have constantly maintained contact with these countries; yet they have scarcely penetrated the interior of Africa and Asia, because it is far more difficult to communicate by land than it is by water. Similarly, history tells us that Brittany and Britain were united for centuries under English rule, and it took many wars to sever the links between them. Sweden formerly possessed Finland, as well as Courland, Livonia, and Estonia. Norway, however, did not belong to Sweden, but had a far more cordial relationship with Denmark.

We can therefore appreciate that the third class of countries will contrast just as pronouncedly with the second class as the second did with the first. The third division is that of *coastal countries*, and the relationship here is that between land and sea. The countries in question are linked with the sea, and have expressly developed this relationship. Traces of such distinctions can still be seen in Europe; for example, Holland, the country in which the Rhine flows into the sea, cultivates its maritime associations, whereas Germany has not expanded along the line of its principal river. Similarly, Prussia forms the coastal strip which dominates the mouth of the Vistula to the seaward side of Poland, whereas the Polish interior is quite different in character, having a different culture and different needs from those of the coastal strip which has developed its links with the sea. The rivers of Spain flow into the sea in Portugal. One might well think that Spain, since it has rivers, must also have links with the sea; but in this particular case, it is Portugal which has developed the latter more fully.

The *sea* in fact always gives rise to a particular way of life. Its indeterminate element gives us an impression of limitlessness and infinity, and when man feels himself part of this infinity, he is emboldened to step beyond his narrow existence. The sea itself is limitless, and it is not conducive to the peaceful and restricted life of cities as the inland regions are. Land – in the sense of the broad river valleys – binds man to the soil; consequently a whole series of ties attaches him to the locality he lives in. But the sea lifts him out of these narrow confines. The sea awakens his courage; it lures him on to conquest and piracy, but also to profit and acquisition. Any work performed with a view to gain will be associated with the particular nature of the ends it serves, i.e. with what we refer to as needs. The work which men undertake in order to satisfy these needs will have the effect of compelling them to adopt a settled routine of earning their living. But if this leads them to go to sea, the relationship is changed. Those who sail the seas will and can profit and earn in the process; but the means they employ entail the direct opposite – i.e. danger – of the result they intend: the relationship is reversed, in that they thereby place their lives and property at risk. This invests their employment of such means with a courageous quality, and gives the individual a consciousness of greater freedom and independence. It is this which elevates acquisition and trade above their usual level and transforms them into a courageous and noble undertaking. The sea awakens men's courage; those who sail on it to earn their livelihood and wealth must earn them by hazardous means. They must be courageous, and they must put their lives and riches at stake and treat them with contempt. The quest for riches, as already remarked, is elevated into a courageous and noble activity in so far as it is directed towards the sea. At the same time, the sea awakens men's cunning, for they have to battle with an element which appears to submit itself peacefully to everything and to adapt itself to all possible forms, but which can nevertheless be extremely destructive. Courage is here inseparably linked with understanding, with the highest degree of cunning. For it is the very weakness of this element, i.e. its submissive and yielding quality, which holds the greatest danger. Thus, bravery in face of the sea must be coupled with cunning; for the element which confronts such bravery is itself cunning, and the most unstable and treacherous of all the elements. The sea's infinite surface is absolutely yielding, for it does not resist the slightest pressure – not even of a breath of air; it appears infinitely innocent, compliant, benevolent, and ingratiating, yet it is this very compliance which transforms the sea into the most dangerous and power-ful of the elements. And man, *aes triplex circa pectus,** opposes its power and deceit with nothing more than a simple piece of wood, and embarks on this, relying only on his courage and presence of mind; he thereby abandons the stable shore for the unstable depths, taking his artificial land along with him. The ship, this swan of the seas which cuts through the expanse of the waves in quick and graceful movements or describes circles on its surface, is an instrument whose invention does the highest credit both to man's boldness and to his understanding. The Oriental states, splendid edifices though they are, lack this maritime outlet from their limited landbound existence, even if – as in the case of China – they are themselves situated on the sea. The sea, for them, is merely the termi-nation of the land, and they have no positive relationship with it. The activity which the sea inspires is of a wholly peculiar nature, and it breeds a wholly peculiar character.

In these three departments of the natural world, we can perceive

---

* The quotation is from Horace, *Odes*, I. iii: 'illi robur et aes triplex / circa pectus erat, qui fragilem truci / commisit pelago ratem / primus...' ('Oak and triple bronze must have girt the breast of him who first committed his frail bark to the angry sea...'); *Horace. The Odes and Epodes*, translated by C. E. Bennett (Loeb Classical Library), Cambridge, Mass., and London, 1914, revised edition, 1946, pp. 12-13.

the essential influence of nature upon the life of nations. The greatest contrast is that between the inland principle and that of the coastal regions. More highly developed states combine the distinct attributes of both: the stability of the inland regions and the roving character of coastal life with all its contingencies.

b. *The New World*

The world is divided into the Old and the New – the latter taking its name from the fact that America and Australia only became known to the Europeans at a later stage of history. But the difference between them is not merely an external one, for the two are in fact essentially distinct: the New World is not just relatively new, but absolutely so, by virtue of its wholly peculiar character in both physical and political respects. Its geological age does not concern us here. I will not deny it the honour of also having risen from the sea at the time of the world's creation (or however we wish to describe it). Nevertheless, the archipelago between South America and Asia displays a physical immaturity even in respect of its origin; for most of the islands are based on coral, and are so constituted as to be, so to speak, merely a superficial covering for rocks which rise up out of the bottomless depths and bear the marks of relatively recent origin. *New Holland* appears geographically no less immature; for if we proceed further inland from the English settlements, we encounter vast rivers which have not yet reached the stage of cutting channels for themselves, but lose themselves instead in marshy plains. *America*, as everyone knows, is divided into two parts; and although these are connected by an isthmus, it does not facilitate communications between them. On the contrary, they remain quite definitely separate. In *North America*, we first of all encounter a broad coastal strip along the eastern seaboard, beyond which a mountain range – the Blue Mountains or Appalachians, with the Allegheny Mountains to the north – extends. The rivers which flow from these water the coastal regions, which are admirably suited to the needs of the free North American states which first grew up in this area. Beyond this mountain range, the St Lawrence River, which is connected with the Great Lakes, flows from south to north, with the northern colonies of Canada along its banks. Further west, we meet the basin of the great Mississippi, with the other territories of the Missouri and Ohio Rivers which flow into it before it empties itself into the Gulf of Mexico. To the west of this region lies another long mountain range which runs on through Mexico and the Isthmus of Panama; under the name of the Andes or Cordilleras, it cuts off the entire western side of

South America. The coastal strip formed by these mountains is narrower and less hospitable than that of North America. Peru and Chile are situated on it. To the east of the mountains, the vast Orinoco and Amazon Rivers flow eastwards; they have formed wide valleys, which are not, however, a suitable setting for civilisation, for they are really no more than vast steppelands. To the south flows the Rio de la Plata, some of whose tributaries rise in the Cordilleras, and others in the northern mountain ridge which separates it from the basin of the Amazon. The basin of the Rio de la Plata includes Brazil and the Spanish republics. Columbia is the northern coastal region of South America, and in its western half the Magdalena River flows along the Andes and into the Caribbean.

The New World may even have been connected with Europe and Africa at one time. But the recent history of the transatlantic continent indicates that, although it did possess an indigenous culture when it was first discovered by the Europeans, this culture was destroyed through contact with them; the subjugation of the country amounted, in fact, to its downfall. We do have information concerning America and its culture, especially as it had developed in Mexico and Peru, but only to the effect that it was a purely natural culture which had to perish as soon as the spirit approached it. America has always shown itself physically and spiritually impotent, and it does so to this day. For after the Europeans had landed there, the natives were gradually destroyed by the breath of European activity. Even the animals show the same inferiority as the human beings. The fauna of America includes lions, tigers, and crocodiles, but although they are otherwise similar to their equivalents in the Old World, they are in every respect smaller, weaker, and less powerful. We are even assured that the animals are not as nourishing as the food which the Old World provides. And although America has huge herds of cattle, European beef is still regarded as a delicacy.

As for the human population, few descendants of the original inhabitants survive, for nearly seven million people have been wiped out. The natives of the West Indian islands have died out altogether. Indeed, the whole North American world has been destroyed and suppressed by the Europeans. The tribes of North America have in part disappeared, and in part withdrawn from contact with the Europeans. Their degeneration indicates that they do not have the strength to join the independent North American states. Culturally inferior nations such as these are gradually eroded through contact with more advanced nations which have gone through a more intensive cultural development. For the citizens of the independent states of North America are all of European descent, and the original inhabitants were unable to amalgamate with them.

The natives have certainly learnt various arts from the Europeans, including that of brandy drinking, whose effect upon them has been disastrous. The only inhabitants of South America and Mexico who feel the need for independence are the *Creoles*, who are descended from a mixture of native and Spanish or Portuguese ancestors. They alone have attained a higher degree of self-awareness, and felt the urge for autonomy and independence. It is they who set the tone in their country. But it would appear that only a few native tribes share their attitude. Admittedly, we do hear reports of native peoples who have identified themselves with the recent efforts of the Americans to create independent states, but it is probable that very few of their members are of pure native origin. For this reason, the English have also adopted the policy in India of preventing the rise of a native Creole population, i.e. a people of mixed European and native blood.

We should also note that a larger native populace has survived in South America, despite the fact that the natives there have been subjected to far greater violence, and employed in gruelling labours to which their strength was scarcely equal. The local populace is subjected to every kind of degradation. One must read the accounts of travellers to appreciate their mildness and passivity, their humility and obsequious submissiveness towards a Creole, and even more towards a European; and it will be a long time before the Europeans can succeed in instilling any feelings of independence into them. Some of them have visited Europe, but they are obviously unintelligent individuals with little capacity for education. Their inferiority in all respects, even in stature, can be seen in every particular; the southern tribes of Patagonia are alone more powerfully constituted, although they still live in a natural state of lawlessness and savagery. The religious brotherhoods have treated them in the correct manner, first impressing them by their spiritual authority and then allotting them tasks calculated to awaken and satisfy their needs. When the Jesuits and Catholic clergy first set out to acquaint the Indians with European culture and manners (for, as everyone knows, they founded a state in Paraguay and established monasteries in Mexico and California), they went into their midst and prescribed their daily duties for them as if they were minors; and, however idle the natives otherwise were, they duly carried them out in compliance with the authority of the fathers. The clergy also built storehouses for them and instructed them in their use, so that they might provide for their future needs. They chose the most appropriate means of bettering them, treating them much as one would treat children. I even recollect having read that a clergyman used to ring a bell at midnight to remind them to perform their matrimonial duties, for it would otherwise never have occurred to them to do so. These precepts at first served – quite rightly – to awaken their needs, which are the springs of all human activity.

The Americans, then, are like unenlightened children, living from one day to the next, and untouched by higher thoughts or aspirations. The weakness of their physique was one of the main reasons why the negroes were brought to America as a labour force; for the negroes are far more susceptible to European culture than the Indians. The Portuguese were more humane than the Dutch, Spanish, and English. For this reason, it was easier on the coast of Brazil than elsewhere for slaves to gain their freedom, and large numbers of free negroes were to be found in this region. Among them was the black physician Dr *Kingera*, who first acquainted the Europeans with quinine. An English writer reports that, among the wide circle of his acquaintances, he had encountered instances of negroes becoming skilled workers and tradesmen, and even clergymen and doctors, etc. But of all the free native Americans he knew, he could think of only one who had proved capable of study and who eventually became a clergyman; but he had died soon afterwards as a result of excessive drinking. The weakness of the human physique in America is further aggravated by the lack of those absolute instruments which can alone establish a firmly based authority – namely horses and iron, the principal means by which the natives were subdued. And if at any time we speak of free citizens in South America, this applies only to peoples of mixed European, Asiatic, and American blood. The true Americans are only now beginning to adapt themselves to European culture. And where they do take steps to achieve independence, it is foreign means which have enabled them to do so: the cavalry of the Llanos, for example, is excellent; but it employs the European horse. But all of these native states are still in the process of formation, and their position is not commensurate with that of the Europeans. In Spanish and Portuguese America, the natives still have to liberate themselves from slavery, and in North America, they lack a focus of communal existence without which no state can exist.

Since the original American nation has vanished – or as good as vanished – the effective population comes for the most part from Europe, and everything that happens in America has its origin there. The surplus population of Europe has emigrated to America, by a process not unlike that which occurred in former times in the Imperial German Cities. For these cities had many commercial privileges, and numerous emigrants fled to them in order to settle nearby so that they might enjoy the same rights as they did. In this way, Altona grew up near Hamburg, Offenbach near Frankfurt, Fürth near Nürnberg, and Carouge near Geneva. Similarly, citizens who had suffered bankruptcy, and who could no longer enjoy the privileges of their trade in the city itself or attend its institutions without disgrace, would settle in the adjoining territory; they would have there all the advantages which such a town can offer – exemption from the dues which the older cities exacted from them, and from all obligation to belong to a guild. Thus, in the vicinity of the enclosed cities, new settlements arose in which the same trades were practised, but without the controls which the cities imposed upon them. The relationship between North America and Europe is similar. Many Englishmen have settled there, for the burdens and levies which are imposed on trade and commerce in Europe no longer apply in America. They bring with them all the advantages of civilisation, and are able to practise their skills without interference. The accumulation of European methods and skills has enabled them to reap some benefit from the vast areas of hitherto virgin soil. America has also become a place of refuge for the dregs of European society. Indeed, emigration to America offers many advantages, for the emigrants have cast off much that might restrict them at home, and they bring with them the benefits of European self-reliance and European culture without the accompanying disadvantages; and to those who are willing to work hard and who have not found an opportunity to do so in Europe, America certainly offers ample scope.

With the exception of Brazil, the states of South America are generally republics, as in North America. But if we compare South America (including Mexico) with North America, we discover an astonishing contrast.

North America owes its prosperity to the growth of its industry and population and to civil order and firmly established freedom; the whole federation constitutes a single state with various political centres. In South America, however, the republics are based solely on military force; their whole history is one of continuous revolution: federations of states are dissolved and new ones are formed, and all these changes are the product of military revolutions. The more specific differences between the two parts of America reveal two opposing tendencies – the one in politics, and the other in religion. South America, in which the Spanish settled and asserted their supremacy, is Catholic, whereas North America, although a land of innumerable sects, is fundamentally Protestant. A further incongruity is that South America was conquered, while North America was colonised. The Spanish took possession of South America in order to dominate it and to enrich themselves both through political office and by exacting tributes from the natives. Living far away from the mother country on which they depended, they had more scope to indulge their arbitrary inclinations; and by force, adroitness, and self-confidence they gained a great preponderance over the Indians. The noble and magnanimous aspects of the Spanish character did not accompany them to America. The Creoles, who are descended from the Spanish immigrants, lived on in the presumptuous ways they had inherited, and behaved in an arrogant manner towards the natives. The Creoles were themselves subject to the influence of the European Spaniards, and were fired by base ambitions for rank and titles. The people lived under the influence of a strict hierarchy and the dissolute rule of the secular and regular clergy. These peoples have still to extricate themselves from the spirit of hollow interests before they can attain the spirit of rationality and freedom.

The North American states, however, were entirely *colonised* by the Europeans. Since Puritans, Episcopalians, and Catholics were constantly at loggerheads in England, with each party gaining the upper hand in turn, many of them emigrated to another continent in search of religious freedom. These were industrious Europeans who applied themselves to agriculture, tobacco and cotton planting, etc. Soon, their whole concern was with their work; and the substance which held the whole together lay in the needs of the populace, the desire for peace, the establishment of civil justice, security, and freedom, and a commonwealth framed in the interests of the individuals as discrete entities, so that the state was merely an external device for the protection of property. The mutual confidence of individuals and their trust in the goodwill of their fellows had their source in the Protestant religion; for in the eyes of the Protestant Church, religious works constitute the whole of life and human activity. Among the Catholics, however, there can be no grounds for any such confidence. For in worldly affairs, force and voluntary subservience rule supreme, and the forms which go under the name of constitutions are in this case merely a necessary expedient, offering no protection against mistrust. Thus, the population which has settled in North America is of a completely different order from that of South America. They had no united church to bind the states together and impose restrictions upon them. The industrial principle was imported from England, and industry itself contains the principle of individuality: for in industry, the individual understanding is developed and becomes the dominant power. In North

America, therefore, the various states were shaped in conformity with the various religions of the citizens.

If we next compare North America with Europe, we find that the former affords a perennial example of a republican constitution. It has a subjective unity; for the head of state is a president who, as a guarantee against any monarchic ambitions, is elected for only four years. Universal protection of property and the almost complete absence of taxes are facts which are constantly held up for praise. This indeed sums up the basic character of the community: the private citizen is concerned above all with industry and profit, and particular interests, which look to the universal only in order to obtain private satisfaction, are dominant. A state of justice and a formal code of laws are certainly present; but this formal justice is devoid of genuine integrity, and the American traders have the bad reputation of practising deceit under the protection of the law. If, on the one hand, the Protestant Church evokes the essential element of confidence (as we earlier noted), it thereby entails on the other hand a recognition of the moment of feeling, which can readily open the way to every kind of caprice. Those who adopt this point of view maintain that everyone is entitled to his own personal beliefs, and hence also to his own peculiar religion. This explains why their religion has split up into so many sects, culminating in the extremes of insanity; many of them practise forms of worship characterised by transports of enthusiasm, and sometimes by the most sensual forms of self-abandonment. This anarchy of worship has reached such proportions that the various congregations employ and dismiss their ministers as they see fit; for the church is not something which exists in and for itself, possessing a substantial spirituality and a corresponding external framework, because religious affairs are simply regulated in accordance with the desires of the moment. In North America, the most unbridled licence prevails in all matters of the imagination, and there is no religious unity of the kind which has survived in the European states, where deviations are limited to a few confessions.

As to the politics of North America, the universal purpose of the state is not yet firmly established, and there is as yet no need for a closely knit alliance; for a real state and a real government only arise when class distinctions are already present, when wealth and poverty are far advanced, and when a situation has arisen in which a large number of people can no longer satisfy their needs in the way to which they have been accustomed. But America has a long way to go before it experiences tensions of this kind; for the outlet of colonisation is fully adequate and permanently open, and masses of people are constantly streaming out into the plains of the Mississippi. By this means, the principal source of discontent has been removed, and the continued existence of the present state of civil society is guaranteed.

The example of the United States of America is frequently cited as an objection to the proposition that it is impossible in our times for a large state to have a liberal constitution; for it supposedly proves that republican states are possible on a large scale. But this argument is inadmissible; North America cannot yet be regarded as a fully developed and mature state, but merely as one which is still in the process of becoming; it has not yet progressed far enough to feel the need for a monarchy. It is a federal state, but such states are in the worst possible position as regards external relations. Its peculiar geographical situation has alone prevented this circumstance from bringing about its complete destruction. This was already obvious in the last war against England. The Americans could not conquer Canada and the English were able to bombard Washington simply because the strained relations between the provinces prevented them from mounting a vigorous campaign. Besides, there is no neighbouring state in America with which the United States could have the kind of relationship which prevails among the European nations, a state which they would have to view with distrust and against which they would have to maintain a standing army. Canada and Mexico present no serious threat, and England has found over the last fifty years that a free America is more useful to it than a dependent one. In the War of Independence, the American militia certainly proved themselves just as brave as the Dutch under Philip II; but when they do not have to fight for their independence, they display less vigour, so that their militia acquitted itself badly against the English in 1814. Furthermore, America is a coastal country. The main principle in its states is that of *trade*, which is an extremely one-sided one; in particular, they practise intermediate trade, which has not yet attained the stability of the English system. It has neither credit nor security of capital, and still lacks a solid basis. Besides, it still deals only in raw materials, but not yet in factory goods or industrial products. The hinterland – i.e. the interior of North America – has devoted itself to agriculture, and has made far greater progress in cultivating the land, although it is still not sufficiently developed either. Land can be obtained easily and cheaply, and no direct taxes are paid; but these advantages are counterbalanced by considerable inconveniences. The agricultural class has not yet become self-contained; it does not feel itself under pressure, and when this feeling does arise, it will easily find an outlet in cultivating new tracts of land. On this side of the Allegheny

Mountains, wave upon wave of farmers rolls on every year to occupy new areas. A state cannot truly exist as such until it has ceased to direct its energies into constant emigration; the agricultural class must no longer be able to spread outwards, but must rather turn in upon itself and join together to establish towns and town-based industries. Only then can a system of civil society arise, and this in turn is a prerequisite for the existence of an organised state. North America is still at the stage of cultivating new territories. Only when, as in Europe, it has ceased merely to augment its farming population will the inhabitants press in upon each other to create town-based industries and communications instead of moving outwards in search of new land; only then will they set up a compact system of civil society and feel the need for an organic state. A comparison between the free states of North America and the countries of Europe is therefore impossible; for Europe, despite all its emigrations, has no natural outlet for its population such as America possesses: if the ancient forests of Germany still existed, the French Revolution would never have occurred. North America will be comparable with Europe only after the measureless space which this country affords is filled and its civil society begins to press in upon itself.

In physical terms, America is not yet fully developed, and it is even less advanced in terms of political organisation. It is certainly an independent and powerful state, but it is still engaged in developing its purely physical assets. Only when the country is completely occupied will a firmly established order be introduced. Such rudiments as already exist are of a European character. For the moment, the surplus population of the European states can continue to settle there; but when this comes to an end, the whole will turn in upon itself and become consolidated. It is therefore not yet possible to draw any lessons from America as regards republican constitutions. Consequently, this state does not really concern us, any more than do the other American states which are still struggling for independence. Only its external relations with Europe come into consideration, inasmuch as America is an annex which has accommodated the surplus population of Europe. The American continent had in some respects outlived itself when we first came into contact with it, and in other respects, it is still not yet fully developed.

America is therefore the country of the future, and its world-historical importance has yet to be revealed in the ages which lie ahead – perhaps in a conflict between North and South America. It is a land of desire for all those who are weary of the historical arsenal of old Europe. Napoleon is said to have remarked: *Cette vieille Europe m'ennuie.* It is up to America to abandon the ground on which world history has hitherto been enacted. What has taken place there up to now is but an echo of the Old World and the expression of an alien life; and as a country of the future, it is of no interest to us here, for prophecy is not the business of the philosopher. In history, we are concerned with what has been and what is; in philosophy, however, we are concerned not with what belongs exclusively to the past or to the future, but with that which *is*, both now and eternally – in short, with reason. And that is quite enough to occupy our attention.

c. *The Old World*

Putting aside the New World and whatever dreams we might build upon it, we now pass on to the *Old World*. It is essentially the setting of those events which we have to consider here, i.e. the setting of world history. Here again, we must first direct our attention to the moments and determinations of nature. America is split up into two parts, and although these are connected by an isthmus, the connection is only a superficial one. The Old World consists of three parts, as the Ancients, with their eye for nature, correctly discerned. These divisions are not fortuitous, but the expression of a higher necessity which accords with the underlying concept. The whole character of its territories is composed of three distinct elements, and this tripartite division is not arbitrary but spiritual, for it is essentially based on determinations of nature. The three continents of the Old World are therefore essentially related, and they combine to form a totality. Their distinguishing feature is that they all lie around a sea which provides them with a focus and a means of communication. This is an extremely important factor. For the connecting link between these three continents, the *Mediterranean*, is the focus of the whole of world history. With its many inlets, it is not an ocean which stretches out indefinitely and to which man has a purely negative relationship; on the contrary, it positively invites him to venture out upon it. The Mediterranean Sea is the axis of world history. All the great states of ancient history lie around it, and it is the navel of the earth. Greece, that resplendent light of history, lies there. Then in Syria, Jerusalem is the centre of Judaism and Christianity; south-east of it lie Mecca and Medina, the fountainhead of the Moslem faith; to the west lie Delphi and Athens, with Rome and Carthage further west still; and to the south lies Alexandria, an even greater centre than Constantinople in which the spiritual fusion of east and west took place. The Mediterranean is therefore the heart of the Old World, its conditioning and vitalising principle. It is the centre of world history, in so far as the latter possesses any internal coherence. World history would be inconceivable without it; it would be like ancient Rome or Athens without the forum or street where all the life of the city converged. The whole eastern part of Asia is remote from the current of world history and plays no part in it; the same applies to the north of Europe, which appeared in world history only at a later date and had no share in it in ancient times; for ancient history was strictly confined to the countries around the Mediterranean. Julius Caesar's crossing of the Alps, the conquest of Gaul, and the resultant contact between the Germanic peoples and the Roman Empire, were epoch-making events in world history; for world history crossed the Alps along with them. The eastern part of Asia is one extreme and the lands to the north of the Alps are the other. The eastern portion lives on in its mono-lithic unity; it does not enter into the movement of world history, which takes place rather at the other extreme, at the western end. The lands which lie beyond Syria constitute the beginning of world history, and this beginning itself lies suspended, as it were, outside the historical process; the occidental portion marks the end of this process, and its agitated centre lies around the Mediterranean. The latter is a major natural feature, and its influence is truly considerable; we cannot conceive of the historical process without the central and unifying element of the sea.

We have already specified the geographical distinctions which can be observed within each continent as a whole – the upland regions, the broad river valleys, and the coastal lands. They occur in all three continents of the Old World, so that we can classify these according to which of the three principles is dominant within them. Africa, generally speaking, is the continent in which the upland principle, the principle of cultural backwardness, predominates. Asia, on the other hand, is the continent in which the great antitheses come into conflict, although its distinguishing feature is the second principle, that of the broad river valleys; these support a culture which broods for ever within itself. The totality consists in the union of all three principles, and this is to be found in Europe, the continent in which the spirit is united with itself, and which, while retaining its own solid substance, has embarked upon that infinite process whereby culture is realised in practice. (The only principle left over for America would be that of incompleteness or constant non-fulfilment.) The spiritual character of the three continents varies in accordance with these natural differences. In Africa proper, man has not progressed beyond a merely sensuous existence, and has found it absolutely impossible to develop any further. Physically, he exhibits great muscular strength, which enables him to perform arduous labours; and his temperament is characterised by good-naturedness, which is coupled, however, with completely unfeeling cruelty. Asia is the land of antithesis, division, and expansion, just as Africa is the land of concentration. One pole of the antithesis is that of ethical life, the universal rational essence which remains solid and substantial; the other is the exact spiritual opposite, that of egotism, infinite desires, and boundless expansion of freedom. Europe is the land of spiritual unity, of retreat from this boundless freedom into the particular, of control of the immoderate and elevation of the particular to the universal, and of the descent of the spirit into itself. It was *Ritter*[2] who formulated these distinctions between the continents and expressed them in a direct and tangible form. His works offer interesting sidelights on the historical implications of geography.

a. Africa

Generally speaking, Africa is a continent enclosed within itself, and this enclosedness has remained its chief characteristic. It consists of three parts, which are essentially distinct from one another. The divisions in its geographical configuration are so pronounced that even the differences in its spiritual character remain tied to these physical peculiarities. One might almost say that Africa consists of three continents which are entirely separate from one another, and between which there is no contact whatsoever. The first of these is Africa proper, the land to the south of the Sahara desert; it consists of almost entirely unexplored highlands with narrow coastal strips along its shores. The second is the land to the north of the desert, a coastal region which might be described as European Africa. And the third is the region of the Nile, the only valley land of Africa, which is closely connected with Asia.

North Africa lies on the Mediterranean Sea and extends westwards along the Atlantic; it is separated from southern Africa by the great desert – a waterless sea – and by the River Niger. The desert is a more effective division than the sea, and the character of the people who live immediately on the Niger reveals the difference between the two regions particularly clearly. The northern region stretches across to Egypt, interspersed with numerous sandy wastes to the north and traversed by ranges of mountains; between the mountains lie fertile valleys, which make it one of the most fruitful and attractive of territories. It includes the countries of Morocco, Fas (not Fez), Algeria, Tunis, and Tripoli. It could be said that this whole region does not really belong to Africa but forms a single unit with Spain, for both are part of one and the same basin. With this in mind, the prolific French writer and politician *de Pradt*[3] has said that, in Spain, one is already in Africa. This northern region is the non-independent portion of Africa, for it has always been subject to foreign influences; it is not itself a theatre of world-historical events, and has always been dependent on revolutions of a wider scope. It was originally colonised by the Phoenicians, who established themselves as an independent power in Carthage, then by the Romans, the Vandals, the Romans of the Byzantine Empire, the Arabs, and finally by the Turks, under whom it dissolved into various piratical states. It is a country which merely shares the fortunes of great events enacted elsewhere, but which has no determinate character of its own. This portion of Africa, like the Near East, is orientated towards Europe; it should and must be brought into the European sphere of influence, as the French have successfully attempted in recent times.

Egypt, the land of the Nile, depends on this river for its entire existence and life. Unlike North Africa, it is one of those regions which we have described as constituting a focus, as destined to become the centre of a great and independent culture. It does have an association with the Mediterranean, an association which was at first interrupted but then intensively cultivated at a later date.

Africa proper is the characteristic part of the whole continent as such. We have chosen to examine this continent first, because it can well be taken as antecedent to our main enquiry. It has no historical interest of its own, for we find its inhabitants living in barbarism and savagery in a land which has not furnished them with any integral ingredient of culture. From the earliest historical times, Africa has remained cut off from all contacts with the rest of the world; it is the land of gold, for ever pressing in upon itself, and the land of childhood, removed from the light of self-conscious history and wrapped in the dark mantle of night. Its isolation is not just a result of its tropical nature, but an essential consequence of its geographical character. It is still unexplored, and has no connections whatsoever with Europe. For occupation of its coasts has not led the Europeans to penetrate its interior. Its shape is that of a triangle: to the west lies the Atlantic coast, which forms a deep indentation in the Gulf of Guinea, to the east lies the coast of the Indian Ocean from the Cape of Good Hope to Cape Guardafui, and to the north, the desert and the Niger. The northern part is in the process of acquiring a new character through contact with the Europeans. The main characteristic of Africa proper is that it appears to be predominantly an upland region, and in particular, that it has a very narrow coastal strip, habitable only in a few isolated spots. The next region towards the interior, in almost every case, is a belt of swampland; it lies at the foot of a circle of high mountains which are broken only at rare intervals by rivers, and even these do not afford a means of access to the interior: for the gaps they form are never far from the tops of the mountain ranges, creating only a few narrow openings which are often blocked by impassable waterfalls and raging cross-currents. The north of Africa proper also appears to be cut off by a belt of mountains – the Mountains of the Moon to the south of the Niger. The coastal strip of Africa has been occupied for centuries by Europeans; but they did not succeed in reaching the interior until approximately fifteen years ago.[4] At the Cape of Good Hope, the missionaries have recently crossed the mountains into the interior. Europeans have settled on the coastal strip in several places: on the east coast in Mozambique, and on the west coast in the Congo and Loango regions, on the Senegal, which flows through sandy deserts and mountains, and on the Gambia; but throughout the three to three-and-a-half centuries that they have known the coastal strip and occupied parts of it, they have only crossed the mountains at a few isolated places and for brief periods of time, and have nowhere gained a permanent footing beyond them. The coastal strip is sandy in parts and inhospitable, but further inland it is nevertheless fertile. Beyond it, however, lies the belt of swampland, full of the most luxuriant vegetation; it is also the home of all manner of rapacious animals, and its atmosphere is pestilential and almost poisonous to breathe. This, as in Ceylon, has made it virtually impossible to reach the interior. The English and Portuguese have often sent sufficient troops for such expeditions; but most of them have died in the swamplands, and the rest have invariably been overcome by the natives. Since so many rivers run through the mountains, one might well imagine that these would allow access by ship to the interior. The Congo (which is thought to be a branch of the Niger) and the Orange River have indeed proved navigable for short stretches, but then they are interrupted by frequent and impassable waterfalls. Given these natural conditions, the Europeans have gained little knowledge of the African interior; but from time to time, upland tribes have descended from the mountains, and displayed such barbarous ferocity that it proved impossible to establish any contact with them. Such outbreaks occur from time to time, and they are among the oldest traditions of the African continent. In the fifteenth and sixteenth centuries in particular, it is reported that the most assorted hosts of natives, terrible hordes, descended at several widely separated points upon the peaceful inhabitants of the slopes and the nations of the coasts, driving them down to the edge of the sea. A similar attempt was made at the Cape of Good Hope, but the assault was repulsed before it had passed the mountains. Several nations on the west coast appear to be remnants of such incursions; they have eventually been subjugated by later invaders, and reduced to the most wretched condition. Negro hordes have poured down across Abyssinia, and on the other side of the continent too. When their fury has abated, and when they have lived for a time on the slopes or in the coastal region and become pacified, they prove mild and industrious, although they seemed completely intractable at the time of their initial onslaught. It is uncertain whether these upheavals are occasioned by internal unrest, and what the nature of this unrest may have been. What we do know of these hordes is the contrast in their behaviour before and after their incursions: during their wars and forays, they behaved with the most unthinking inhumanity and revolting barbarity, yet subsequently, when their rage had died down and peace was restored, they behaved with mildness towards the Europeans when they became acquainted with them. This was the case with the Fula and Mandingo peoples who inhabit the mountain terraces of Senegal and Gambia.

In this main portion of Africa, history is in fact out of the question. Life there consists of a succession of contingent happenings and surprises. No aim or state exists whose development could be followed; and there is no subjectivity, but merely a series of subjects who destroy one another. In the past, little attention has been paid to this peculiar mode of self-consciousness which the spirit exhibits in Africa. Numerous reports have come in from the most diverse regions, but most people regard them as incredible; they provide us rather with a collection of fearful details than with a determinate image or principle such as we shall now attempt to extract from them. The literature on a subject of this kind is somewhat indefinite in scope, and anyone who wishes to go into it in detail must avail himself of such information as is available in the useful works of reference. The best general account of Africa is that provided in *Ritter's* geography.

We shall now attempt to define the universal spirit and form of the African character in the light of the particular traits which such accounts enumerate. This character, however, is difficult to comprehend, because it is so totally different from our own culture, and so remote and alien in relation to our own mode of consciousness. We must forget all the categories which are fundamental to our own spiritual life, i.e. the forms under which we normally subsume the data which confront us; the difficulty here is that our customary preconceptions will still inevitably intrude in all our deliberations.

It must be said in general that, in the interior of Africa, the consciousness of the inhabitants has not yet reached an awareness of any substantial and objective existence. Under the heading of substantial objectivity, we must include God, the eternal, justice, nature, and all natural things. When the spirit enters into relations with substantial things such as these, it knows that it is dependent upon them; but it realises at the same time that it is a value in itself in so far as it is capable of such relationships. But the Africans have not yet attained this recognition of the universal; their nature is as yet compressed within itself: and what we call religion, the state, that which exists in and for itself and possesses absolute validity – all this is not yet present to them. The circumstantial reports of the missionaries fully bear this out, and Mohammedanism seems to be the only thing which has brought the negroes at all nearer to culture. The Mohammedans also know better than the Europeans how to penetrate the interior of the country.

The characteristic feature of the negroes is that their consciousness has not yet reached an awareness of any substantial objectivity – for example, of God or the law – in which the will of man could participate and in which he could become aware of his own being. The African, in his undifferentiated and concentrated unity, has not yet succeeded in making this distinction between himself as an individual and his essential universality, so that he knows nothing of an absolute being which is other and higher than his own self. Thus, man as we find him in Africa has not progressed beyond his immediate existence. As soon as man emerges as a human being, he stands in opposition to nature, and it is this alone which makes him a human being. But if he has merely made a distinction between himself and nature, he is still at the first stage of his development: he is dominated by passion, and is nothing more than a savage. All our observations of African man show him as living in a state of savagery and barbarism, and he remains in this state to the present day. The negro is an example of animal man in all his savagery and lawlessness, and if we wish to understand him at all, we must put aside all our European attitudes. We must not think of a spiritual God or of moral laws; to comprehend him correctly, we must abstract from all reverence and morality, and from everything which we call feeling. All this is foreign to man in his immediate existence, and nothing consonant with humanity is to be found in his character. For this very reason, we cannot properly feel ourselves into his nature, no more than into that of a dog, or of a Greek as he kneels before the statue of Zeus. Only by means of thought can we achieve this understanding of his nature; for we can only feel that which is akin to our own feelings.

Thus, in Africa as a whole, we encounter what has been called the *state of innocence*, in which man supposedly lives in unity with God and nature. For in this state, man is as yet unconscious of himself. The spirit should not remain permanently in such a state, however, but must abandon this primitive condition. This primitive state of nature is in fact a state of animality. Paradise was that zoological garden in which man lived in an animal condition of innocence – but this is not his true destiny. Man is not truly a human being until he knows what goodness is, has experienced opposition, and become divided within himself. For he can only know what is good if he also has knowledge of evil. For this reason, the state of paradise is not a perfect one. That early state of perfection of which the myths of all nations speak means simply that the abstract destiny of man was already potentially present; but whether it also existed in reality is quite another matter. Its potential presence has been confused with its real existence. For the concept of the spirit is only potentially present, and it has wrongly been assumed that it already existed in reality. It is still only potentially present for us; but the purpose of the spirit is to ensure that it is also realised in practice. In real existence, this represents the final stage in history, although in terms of mere potentiality, it is equivalent to the first stage. We hear much about the higher intelligence of mankind in the earlier stages of history, of which – as Schlegel has claimed – the wisdom of the Indians in astronomy etc. allegedly still shows vestiges. But as far as this Indian wisdom is concerned, we have already pointed out that such traditions have proved extremely unreliable, and that the numbers they specify are empty fabrications [cf. p. 133 above].

As we now proceed to review the principal moments within the African spirit, we shall have occasion to examine in detail certain particular features which illuminate its nature more fully; but our main concern must be with the general conception. Thus, if we turn first of all to the *religion* of the Africans, our own conception of religion tells us that it requires that man should recognise a supreme being which exists in and for itself as a completely objective and absolute being or higher power; this supreme being determines the course of everything, and, in contrast to it, man appears as a weaker and humbler creature. It can be conceived of either as a spirit, or as a natural power which governs the course of nature (although this is not its true form). Alternatively, the fantastic attitude has prevailed whereby men have worshipped the moon, the sun, and the rivers; they have animated these natural forms in their own imagination, at the same time treating them as completely independent agents. Religion begins with the awareness that there is something higher than man. But this kind of religion is unknown to the negroes. The character of the Africans shows the antithesis between man and nature in its earliest form. In this condition, man sees himself and nature as opposed to one another, but with himself in the commanding position; this is the basic situation in Africa, as *Herodotus* was the first to testify. We can sum up the principle of African religion in his declaration that all men in Africa are sorcerers.[5] That is, as a spiritual being, the African arrogates to himself a power over nature, and this is the meaning of his sorcery. Even today, the reports of the missionaries carry the same implication. *Sorcery* does not entail the idea of a God or of a moral faith, but implies that man is the highest power and that he alone occupies a position of authority over the power of nature. There is therefore no question of a spiritual adoration of God, nor of a realm of justice. God thunders, but he is not recognised as God. For the human spirit, God must be more than a thunderer, but this is not the case among the negroes. The Africans see nature as opposed to them; they are dependent upon it, and its powers fill them with fear. The river may swallow them up, and the earthquake may destroy their abodes. The success of the harvest and of the fruits on the trees is dependent upon the weather. At times they have too much rain, and at others too little; they need the storm, the rainy season, and the end of the rains, for neither the rains nor the dry season must last for too long. But although these natural forces, as well as sun, moon, trees, and animals, are recognised as powers in their own right, they are not seen as having an eternal law or providence behind them, or as forming part of a universal and permanent natural order. The African sees them ruling over him, but he also sees them as powers over which man can in some way gain mastery in turn. Man, then, is master of these natural forces. This has nothing whatsoever to do with veneration of God or the recognition of a universal spirit as opposed to the spirit of the individual. Man knows only himself and his opposition to nature, and this is the sole rational element which the African peoples recognise. They acknowledge the power of nature, and attempt to raise themselves above it. They therefore also believe that man never dies from natural causes, and that it is not nature but the will of an enemy which has killed him by means of sorcery; they then resort to sorcery in turn, as they would against all natural agencies.

Not everyone possesses this magical power; on the contrary, the Africans believe that it is concentrated in certain individuals. These individuals issue commands to the elements, and it is this activity which they call sorcery. Many devote themselves exclusively to regulating, predicting, and producing such effects for the benefit of mankind or of their peoples. The kings have ministers and priests – and sometimes a fully organised hierarchy of officials – whose task is to practise sorcery, to command the powers of nature, and to determine the weather. When their commands have proved persistently ineffectual, they are given a sound thrashing. Every place possesses such sorcerers, who conduct special ceremonies with all kinds of movements, dances, din, and clamour; and amidst this deafening noise they make their dispositions. If thunderstorms – and these are truly formidable – should break when the army is in the field, the sorcerers must perform their duty by threatening and commanding the clouds to be still. In the same way, they have to make rain in times of drought. They do not invoke God in their ceremonies; they do not turn to any higher power, for they believe that they can accomplish their aims by their own efforts. To prepare themselves for their task, they work themselves into a state of frenzy; by means of singing, convulsive dancing, and intoxicating roots or potions, they reach a state of extreme delirium in which they proceed to issue their commands. If they do not succeed after prolonged efforts, they decree that some of the onlookers – who are their own dearest relations – should be slaughtered, and these are then devoured by their fellows. In short, man considers himself the highest commanding authority. The priest will often spend several days in this frenzied condition, slaughtering human beings, drinking their blood, and giving it to the onlookers to drink. In practice, therefore, only some individuals have power over nature, and these only when they are beside themselves in a state of dreadful enthusiasm. All this applies to the African nations at large, although there are some modifications in individual cases. The missionary *Cavazzi*,[6] for example, enumerates many such instances among the negroes. Among the Jagas or Jakas, there were priests known as Chitomen who had the reputation of being able to protect men against animals and water by means of amulets and the like.

The second feature of their religion is that they give this power of theirs a visible form, projecting it out of their own consciousness and making images of it. The first object they encounter which they imagine has power over them – whether it be an animal, a tree, a stone, or a wooden image – is given the status of a genius. Each individual will fetch himself some such object from the priest. It is a *fetish*, a word to which the Portuguese first gave currency, and which is derived from *feitiço* or magic. Here, in the fetish, the arbitrary will of the individual does seem to be faced with an independent entity, but since the object in question is nothing more than the will of the individual projected into a visible form, this will in fact remains master of the image it has adopted. What they regard as their ruling power is therefore not an objective entity with an independent existence distinct from their own. The fetish remains in their power, and they reject it when it does not do their will. They then adopt something else as their higher authority and imagine that it exercises power over them, but keep it in their own power for this very reason. If something unpleasant occurs which the fetish has failed to avert, the oracles which they have consulted are deemed to be false and become discredited. If the rain does not come or the crops do badly, they bind and beat the fetish or destroy and discard it, and at once create another to take its place. In other words, their god remains in their power, to be acknowledged and rejected at will, so that they do not progress beyond a condition of arbitrariness. A fetish of this kind has no independent existence as an object of religion, and even less as a work of art. It is merely an artifact which expresses the arbitrary will of its creator, and which always remains in his hands. In short, this religion does not involve any relationship of dependence. And it is the same with the spirits of the dead, to whom they attribute a mediating function like that of the sorcerers. These spirits are also men, but what does suggest the presence of a higher authority here is that they are men who have cast off their immediate existence. This is the source of the Africans' *cult of the dead*, in which their deceased ancestors and forefathers are regarded as a power capable of acting against the living. They resort to these spirits in the same way as to fetishes, offering them sacrifices and conjuring them up; but where this proves unsuccessful, they punish the departed ancestor himself, casting his bones away and desecrating his remains. On the other hand, they believe that the dead avenge themselves if their needs are not satisfied, and misfortunes in particular are ascribed to their agency. We have already referred to the negroes' conviction that it is not nature or natural agencies which cause human sickness, and that men do not die by natural means; they believe that all this is the work of some sorcerer or enemy, or the vengeance of one of the dead. This is simply the superstition of witchcraft, whose terrible rule once prevailed in Europe too. The natives combat such sorcery by other more powerful magic. It sometimes happens that the keeper of the fetish is disinclined to make it perform its task; he is accordingly beaten and forced to work his magic. One of the main kinds of magic practised by the Chitomen consists in propitiating the dead or exacting their services by the most fearful abominations. At the command of the dead, reincarnated in the priests, human sacrifices etc. are offered. Thus, the object of their religion always remains subject to their own arbitrary will. The power of the dead over the living is indeed recognised, but held in no great respect; for the negroes issue commands to their dead and cast spells upon them. In this way, the substance always remains in the power of the subject. Such is the religion of the Africans, and it does not extend beyond these limits.

It does admittedly presuppose that man is superior to nature, but only in an arbitrary sense. For it is only his contingent will which stands above the natural world, and he regards this as no more than a means. He does not do it the honour of treating it in accordance with its own nature, but simply commands it to do his will. This nevertheless embodies a more correct principle than does nature-worship, which is often considered an act of piety; for people frequently maintain that natural phenomena are works of God, thereby implying that the works of man, i.e. the works of reason, are not likewise divine. The negroes' consciousness of nature is not a consciousness of its objective existence; still less is it a consciousness of God as a spirit, as something higher in and for itself than nature. Nor do they possess that understanding which uses nature as a means – by sailing on the sea, for example, and generally exercising control over nature. The negroes' power over nature is only an imaginary power, an illusory authority.

As for the relationship between men themselves, it follows, firstly, that man is posited as the highest instance, and secondly, that he has no respect for himself or for others; for such a respect would touch on a higher or absolute value peculiar to man. Only when he attains a consciousness of a higher being does man become capable of true reverence. For if the arbitrary will is the absolute, and the only solid and objective reality recognised by man, the spirit cannot have reached the stage of knowing anything universal. For this reason, the Africans know nothing of what we call the immortality of the soul. They do recognise what we call ghosts, but this is not the same thing as immortality: for immortality implies that man is a spiritual being in and for himself, and that his nature is unchanging and eternal. The negroes have, therefore, a complete *contempt* for man, and it is this above all which determines their attitude towards justice and morality. Their belief in the worthlessness of man goes to almost incredible lengths; their political order can be regarded as tyranny, but this is considered perfectly legitimate and is not felt to constitute an injustice. Along with this goes the belief that it is quite normal and permissible to eat human flesh. This is certainly the case among the Ashanti, and among the tribes further south on the River Congo and on the eastern side of Africa. Cannibalism at once strikes us as utterly barbarous and revolting, and we instinctively reject it. But we cannot speak of instinct in the case of human beings, for such reactions have a spiritual quality about them. All men who have progressed even to a limited extent in consciousness have respect for human beings as such. In an abstract sense, we may well say that flesh is flesh, and that what we eat is simply a matter of taste; but our powers of representation* tell us that this is human flesh, identical with that of our own bodies. The human body is of an animal nature, but it is essentially the body of a being capable of representation; in short, it has psychological associations. But this is not the case with the negroes, and the eating of human flesh is quite compatible with the African principle; to the sensuous negro, human flesh is purely an object of the senses, like all other flesh. It is not used primarily as food; but at festivals, for example, many hundreds of prisoners are tortured and beheaded, and their bodies are returned to those who took them prisoner so that they may distribute the parts. In some places, it is true, human flesh has even been seen on sale in the markets. At the death of a rich man, hundreds may well be slaughtered and devoured. Prisoners are murdered and slaughtered, and as a rule the victor consumes the heart of his slain enemy. And at magical ceremonies, it very often happens that the sorcerer murders the first person he encounters and divides his body among the crowd.

Since human beings are valued so cheaply, it is easily explained why *slavery* is the basic legal relationship in Africa. The only significant relationship between the negroes and the Europeans has been – and still is – that of slavery. The negroes see nothing improper about it, and the English, although they have done most to abolish slavery and the slave trade, are treated as enemies by the negroes themselves. For one of the main ambitions of the kings is to sell their captured enemies or even their own subjects, and, to this extent at least, slavery has awakened more humanity among the negroes. The negroes are enslaved by the Europeans and sold to America. Nevertheless, their lot in their own country, where slavery is equally absolute, is almost worse than this; for the basic principle of all slavery is that man is not yet conscious of his freedom, and consequently sinks to the level of a mere object or worthless article. In all the African kingdoms known to the Europeans, this slavery is endemic and accepted as natural. But the distinction between masters and slaves is a purely arbitrary one. The lesson we can draw from this condition of slavery among the negroes – and the only aspect of it which concerns

* *Vorstellung.*

183

us here – is the same as that which we have already learnt in the realm of ideas: namely that the state of nature is itself a state of absolute and consistent injustice. Every intermediate stage between it and the reality of the rational state admittedly does retain certain elements and aspects of injustice, so that we encounter slavery even in the Greek and Roman states, and serfdom has survived until the most recent times. But when it occurs within an organised state, it is itself a stage in the progress away from purely fragmented sensuous existence, a phase in man's education, and an aspect of the process whereby he gradually attains a higher ethical existence and a corresponding degree of culture. Slavery is unjust in and for itself, for the essence of man is freedom; but he must first become mature before he can be free. Thus, it is more fitting and correct that slavery should be eliminated gradually than that it should be done away with all at once.

Slavery ought not to exist, as it is by definition unjust in and for itself. This 'ought' expresses a subjective attitude, and as such, it has no historical justification. For it is not yet backed up by the substantial ethical life of a rational state. In rational states, slavery no longer exists; but before such states have come into being, the authentic Idea is present in some areas of life only as an unfulfilled obligation, in which case slavery is still necessary: for it is a moment in the transition towards a higher stage of development. We cannot yet expect that man will be regarded as essentially free simply because he is a human being. This was not the case among the Greeks and Romans either; the Athenian was free only as a citizen of Athens, and so on. It is now generally accepted that man, as a human being, is free; but where this is not the case, man has value only in one or other of his particular capacities: for example, partners in marriage, relatives, neighbours, and fellow citizens are of value to one another. Among the negroes, however, even these values are scarcely present; their moral sentiments are extremely weak, or, to be more precise, they are altogether deficient. The first ethical relationship of all, that of the family, is a matter of total indifference to the negroes. Men sell their wives, parents sell their children, and children sell their parents whenever they have it in their power to do so. Since slavery is so prevalent, all those bonds of moral esteem which we cherish towards one another have disappeared, and it never occurs to the negroes to expect of others what we are entitled to demand of our fellows. They devote no attention to their sick parents, apart from seeking occasional advice from the Chitomen. Philanthropic sentiments of love etc. entail a consciousness of the self which is no longer confined to the individual person. For when

I love someone, I am conscious of myself in the other person; or, as Goethe puts it, my heart is open. Love, then, is an enlargement of the self. The polygamy of the negroes often has the sole object of producing many children, so that they can all be sold as slaves; and they are quite oblivious to the injustice of this situation. Indeed, they carry this anomaly to unbounded lengths. The king of Dahomey, for example, has 3333 wives; every rich man has numerous wives, and his many children provide him with a new source of revenue. Missionaries[7] tell us how a negro once came to church and announced to the Franciscans with fearful lamentations that he was now completely destitute, as he had already sold all his relatives, including his father and mother.

The distinguishing feature of the negroes' contempt for humanity is not so much their contempt for death as their lack of respect for life. They set as little value on life as they do on human beings as such, for life is only valuable in so far as there is a higher value in man. Their contempt for life does not mean that they are weary of it, or that some fortuitous irritation has overtaken them; on the contrary, life in general has no value for them. The negroes often kill themselves if their honour is violated or if they have been punished by the king. If someone in this position fails to do so, he is regarded as a coward. They give no thought to the preservation of life, or to death itself. The great courage of the negroes, reinforced by their enormous physical strength, must also be ascribed to this lack of respect for life; for they allow themselves to be shot down in thousands in their wars with the Europeans. In the war between the Ashanti and the English, the natives persisted in running straight up to the mouths of the cannon, although they were invariably shot down fifty at a time. In fact, life is of no value unless it has a worthy object.

If we now turn to the elements of the *political constitution*, we must realise that the whole nature of Africa is such that there can be no such thing as a constitution. The government must necessarily be patriarchal in character. The main characteristic of this patriarchal phase is the arbitrary rule of the senses, the energy of the sensuous will; in this arbitrary state, ethical relationships of an essentially universal content – i.e. those which take no account of the consciousness in its individual aspects, but see its value as residing in its inner universality (whether in legal, religious, or ethical contexts) – are as yet completely undeveloped. Where this universal quality is weak or remote, the political union cannot be that of a state governed by free rational laws. For, as we have seen, even the family ethos is lacking in strength. In marriage and domestic life, polygamy predominates; as a result, the parents are indifferent towards each other and towards their children, and the children themselves are indifferent towards their parents and their fellows. Thus, the arbitrary will has no bond whatsoever to restrain it. Under these conditions, that larger union of individuals which we call the state cannot possibly come into being; for the state is based on rational universality, which is a law of freedom. Where the arbitrary will prevails, there can be no union except that created by external force; for the arbitrary will itself offers no incentive for men to unite, but merely allows them to follow their own individual inclinations. Consequently, the African regime is one of despotism; the external authority is itself arbitrary, for there is no rational and communal spirit of which the government could be the representative and executor. A ruler stands at the head, for sensuous barbarism can only be restrained by despotic power. This despotism does have an imposing quality, because it places restraints on the arbitrary will, which, for all its arrogance, has no intrinsic value. From the formal point of view, the arbitrariness of the autocrat deserves respect, for it is the basis of the whole political union; it therefore represents a higher principle than that of individual arbitrariness. Arbitrariness, whether sensuous or reflective in character, requires a unifying principle which only an external authority can supply. If it has no power in its own right and is subject to a higher authority, it adopts a cringing demeanour; but when it itself comes to power, it behaves arrogantly towards the same authority before which it had previously humbled itself. Consequently, it can manifest itself in many different ways. And wherever we encounter despotism ruling in a particularly savage manner, we find that its arbitrary power is itself cancelled out by counteracting forces. In the negro states, the king is always accompanied by the executioner, whose office is regarded as extremely important; he is used by the king to eliminate all suspect persons, just as the king himself may be killed by him if the nobles of the country demand it. For, since the subjects are men of equally savage temper, they impose restrictions on their master in turn. Elsewhere, the power of despots is mediated, and on the whole they have to yield to the arbitrary will of the mighty. The form which despotism then assumes is that, although a chieftain – whom we may call the king – is the supreme ruler, he has under him a group of grandees, chiefs, or captains, whom he must consult on all matters and whose consent he must obtain if he wishes in particular to declare war, conclude peace, or levy a tribute. This is the case among the Ashanti; the king is served by a multitude of subordinate princes, and even the English pay him a tribute which he shares with his various chiefs.

In this way, the African despot can acquire more or less authority, and dispose of this or that chief by means of force or stratagem as the occasion presents itself. Besides, the kings enjoy certain additional privileges. Among the Ashanti, the king inherits all the property left by his deceased subjects; in other places, all unmarried girls belong to the king, and anyone who seeks a wife must buy her from him. But if the negroes are dissatisfied with their king, they depose and execute him. There is a little-known kingdom in the vicinity of Dahomey which has something approaching a history of its own – that ruled by the king of Eyio. It lies deep in the interior of Africa, which does not consist entirely of great arid deserts. In fact, all the expeditions which have succeeded in reaching the interior have discovered large empires, and the Portuguese of earlier times report that armies of around 200,000 men have done battle there. The king of Eyio also has several hundred thousand cavalrymen. Like the ruler of the Ashanti, he is surrounded by grandees who are not wholly subject to his arbitrary power. If he does not rule justly, they send him a deputation which presents him with three parrot's eggs. The delegates then put forward certain proposals; they thank him for the efforts he has made to rule them justly, and then tell him that his exertions have probably over-taxed his energy and that he is doubtless in need of sleep and rest. The king thanks them for their understanding and advice, acknowledges their goodwill, and retires to his apartments; he does not lie down to sleep, however, but has himself strangled by his women. A king of the Ashanti who allowed himself to be detained in the kingdom of his father-in-law by the blandishments of his wife was similarly deposed twenty years ago. His lieutenants invited him to return for the annual festival; but when he did not arrive, they placed his brother on the throne instead.

Thus, even such despotism as this is not completely blind; the peoples of Africa are not just slaves, but assert their own will too. In East Africa, *Bruce*[8] travelled through a state in which the prime minister was the executioner, although the only person he was permitted to decapitate was the king: thus, the sword really hangs above the despot's head day and night. On the other hand, the monarch has absolute power over the lives of his subjects. Where life has no value, it is recklessly squandered. The African nations engage in bloody battles which often last for a week on end and in which hundreds of thousands perish. The issue is usually decided by chance, and then the victors massacre everyone within their reach. Under many princes, the executioner is the prime minister. It is much the same in all the negro states, which are very numerous. The office of head of state is usually inherited, but the successor rarely comes to power in a peaceful manner. The prince is held in very high esteem, but he must share his power with his generals. The negroes also have courts of law and trials. In the north, where the Moors have propagated the Moslem faith, their customs have become less barbarous. And the negroes with whom the English first had dealings were Mohammedans.

Their character being as it is, the Africans are extremely prone to fanaticism. The realm of the spirit is so poor among them, and yet the spirit in itself is so intensive that any idea which is disseminated among them may drive them to respect nothing and destroy everything. We find them living a peaceful and good-natured existence over long periods of time. But, for all their good nature, they are also capable of transports of frenzy. They are conscious of so few things which deserve respect in and for themselves that whatever idea takes hold of them becomes their sole motive force, spurring them on to annihilate everything they encounter. They seize upon and realise every idea which is thrown into their minds with all the energy of their will, and destroy everything in the process. Such nations live peacefully over long periods, and then suddenly surge up into a complete state of frenzy. The destruction which results from this sudden ferment and upheaval has no real content or thought behind it, for it is rather a physical than a spiritual fanaticism. Thus, we often see such nations rushing down to the coast in a wild fury, killing everyone they meet, with no other motive than that of madness and rage; their bravery is solely a product of their fanaticism. In the negro states, every decision takes on a quality of fanaticism, a fanaticism which surpasses all belief. An English traveller[9] reports that, when the Ashanti have resolved to go to war, solemn ceremonies are first enacted; these include the washing of the bones of the king's mother with human blood. As a preliminary to war, the king decrees an attack on his own capital, as if to drive himself into a fury. When a punitive war was about to be launched against a nation which had refused to pay tribute, the king despatched a note to the English resident *Hutchinson*[10] with the following message: 'Christian, take heed and watch over your family. The messenger of death has drawn his sword and will smite the necks of many of the Ashanti; when the drum is sounded, it will be the signal of death for multitudes. Come to the king if you can, and fear not for yourself.' The drum was sounded; the warriors of the king, armed with short swords, went out on their murderous mission, and a terrible bloodbath ensued: all who encountered the frenzied negroes as they rushed through the streets were struck down. Nevertheless, no great numbers were murdered on this occasion; for the people had learnt in advance of the attack and taken appropriate precautions. On such occasions, the king has all whom he regards as suspect killed, and the deed then takes on the character of a sacred act. And it is much the same at funerals, where everything bears the mark of frenzy and dementedness. The slaves of the deceased man are slaughtered, and it is decreed that their heads belong to the fetish and their bodies to the relatives, who duly devour them. When the king dies in Dahomey, a general tumult breaks loose in his palace, whose dimensions are enormous; all utensils are destroyed, and universal carnage begins. The wives of the king prepare for death (and, as already mentioned, there are 3333 of them); they look upon their death as necessary, adorn themselves in preparation for it, and order their slaves to kill them. All the bonds of society are loosed in the town and throughout the kingdom; murder and theft break out everywhere, and private revenge is given free rein. On one such occasion, 500 women died in the palace in the space of six minutes. The officers of state proceed with all possible speed to appoint the successor to the throne, in order to put an end to the riot and slaughter.

The most fearful instance is that of a woman who ruled over the Jagas in the depths of the Congo.[11] She was converted to Christianity, became apostate, and was converted once again. She lived an extremely dissolute life, and was constantly in conflict with her mother, whom she removed from the throne. She established a state of women, which made itself famous by its conquests, and renounced all love towards her mother and towards her son. She pounded the latter, who was still a young child, in a mortar before a public assembly, besmeared herself with his blood, and made sure that the blood of such pounded children was always in supply. Her laws were indeed terrible. She had all the men expelled or murdered, and all the women were compelled to kill their male offspring. Pregnant women had to leave the encampment and give birth in the scrubland. And at the head of this nation of women, she proceeded to wreak the most terrible havoc. Like furies, they destroyed everything in the neighbourhood, and lived on human flesh; and, since they did not cultivate the soil, they were compelled to support themselves by plundering. Subsequently, the women were permitted to use their prisoners of war as husbands, who duly became their slaves, and even to give them their freedom. This way of life continued for many years. That women go to war is one of the peculiarities of African existence. In Ashanti-Dahomey, there is a corps of women who go on expeditions with the king. And in Dahomey, one might imagine that Plato's republic had been partially realised, for the children do not belong to the family, but are brought up publicly and distributed among the villages soon after birth. The king has a large number of them around him; and anyone who wishes to marry must pay a few dollars at the royal palace, whereupon he is presented with a wife. Each must take the woman he is given, be she young or old. The wives of the king receive these candidates for marriage, and first give each of them a mother, whom they are required to maintain. They must then return for a second time before they are given a wife.

From all these various traits we have enumerated, it can be seen that intractability is the distinguishing feature of the negro character. The condition in which they live is incapable of any development or culture, and their present existence is the same as it has always been. In face of the enormous energy of sensuous arbitrariness which dominates their lives, morality has no determinate influence upon them. Anyone who wishes to study the most terrible manifestations of human nature will find them in Africa. The earliest reports concerning this continent tell us precisely the same, and it has no history in the true sense of the word. We shall therefore leave Africa at this point, and it need not be mentioned again. For it is an unhistorical continent, with no movement or development of its own. And such events as have occurred in it – i.e. in its northern region – belong to the Asiatic and European worlds. Carthage, while it lasted, represented an important phase; but as a Phoenician colony, it belongs to Asia. Egypt will be considered as a stage in the movement of the human spirit from east to west, but it has no part in the spirit of Africa. What we understand as Africa proper is that unhistorical and undeveloped land which is still enmeshed in the natural spirit, and which had to be mentioned here before we cross the threshold of world history itself.

β. Asia

Having disposed of these preliminary matters, we now at last find ourselves on the real theatre of world history. Among the negroes, the natural will of the individual is not yet negated; but it is only through its negation that a consciousness of being in and for itself can arise. This consciousness first emerges in the Oriental world. We find here a power which exists in and for itself, and man only exists in and for himself in so far as he is related to this universal substance. It is this relationship to the substantial power which unites the individuals with one another. Thus, it is in Asia that the ethical world of political consciousness first arose. Asia is the continent of sunrise and of origins in general. Admittedly, every country is both east and west in relation to others, so that Asia is the western continent from the point of view of America; but just as Europe is the centre and end of the Old World – i.e. absolutely the west – so also is Asia absolutely the east. It is there that the light of the spirit, the consciousness of a universal, first emerged, and with it the process of world history.

We must first of all outline the geographical nature and formation of Asia. In terms of world history, the natural conditions in Africa are on the whole negative; but in Asia, they are positive. This also explains why the Asians have so great an appreciation of nature. Just as nature is the basis of history itself, so also must it be the basis of our study of history. The natural world and the spiritual world together form the living totality of *history*. The physical constitution of Asia presents absolute antitheses and the essential relationship between these antitheses. Its various geographical principles are in themselves fully developed and perfected forms. The two types of locality in question, the uplands and the valley plains, are in Asia the theatre of completely contrasting ways of life; but their relationship is essentially one of interaction, and they are not isolated in the same way as Egypt, for example. On the contrary, this very relationship between the two completely opposite dispositions is a characteristic feature of Asia.

We must first of all eliminate Siberia, the northern slope of Asia. For it lies outside the scope of our enquiry. The whole character of Siberia rules it out as a setting for historical culture and prevents it from attaining a distinct form in the world-historical process. It does have certain advantages, in that it contains great rivers which flow down from the Altai Mountains to the northern ocean; but these advantages are nullified by the effects of climate. The rest of Asia, like Africa, contains in the first place a massive upland region, surrounded by a ring of mountains which include the highest peaks in the world. This ring of mountains forms a continuous range, with steep escarpments on its outward edges. The uplands of Asia are bounded to the south and south-east by the Mustag or Imaus Mountains, with the Himalayas running parallel to them further south. Towards the east, the basin of the Amur is bounded by a mountain chain which runs from south to north. Most of this region belongs to the Manchus, who are also the rulers of China; their original way of life, which even the Emperor of China adopts in the summer season, is nomadic. To the north lie the Altai and Dzungarian Mountains; the latter are linked in the north-west with the Mussart and in the west with the Belurtag, which are in turn linked with the Mustag by way of the Hindu Kush.

This high chain of mountains is pierced by great rivers which subsequently form broad valley plains of immense fertility and luxuriant growth, each the centre of its own peculiar culture. They are alluvial plains which cannot properly be described as valleys; they are quite different in structure from the river territories of Europe, which have more true valleys with endless branches on either side. Such plains include that of China, formed by the Huang-Ho and Yangtze-Kiang (the Yellow and Blue Rivers), which flow from west to east; next, there is that of India, formed by the Ganges; the Indus, which also supports a culture in the north (in the Punjab region), is of less importance, for the region it flows through to the south consists largely of sandy plains; and then there are the countries of the Tigris and Euphrates, which rise in Armenia and flow down to the west of the Persian mountains. Similar river valleys occur to the east and west of the Caspian Sea – those to the east are formed by the Oxus and Yaxartes (Gihon and Sihon), which flow into the Aral Sea. The first of these, the Gihon, formerly flowed into the Caspian Sea, but subsequently changed its course. The vast region between the Belurtag and the Caspian Sea is a broad plain with the foothills of the neighbouring mountains, and is of particular importance for world history. To the west, the Cyrus and Araxes (Kura and Araks) form a narrower but equally fertile plain. The central Asian highlands, in which Arabia (as the higher part of the plains) may be included, resemble both the plains and the highlands in character. Here, the opposite principles receive their freest expression; they are the home of light and darkness, of outward splendour and the abstraction of pure contemplation – in short, of what we call Orientalism. This is particularly true of Persia.

The plains and uplands form a complete contrast to one another; the third type of country is a combination of these two principles, such as is found in the Near East. This includes Arabia, the land of deserts and high plateaux, the empire of unrestricted freedom from which the most extreme fanaticism has sprung; it also includes Syria and Asia Minor, which are connected with the sea and form a link with Europe. Their culture is drawn towards Europe, with which they are constantly in contact.

After these remarks on the geographical peculiarities of Asia, something must be said about the effects these have had on the character of its peoples and history. The most important feature is the relationship between the uplands and the river plains. Or, to be more precise, it is not so much the upland plateau itself which is of great world-historical importance, as the mountain ravines which lie at the conjunction of the mountains and the plains. The relationship between the nations who live in such areas with the kind of culture which is found on the river plains calls for particular emphasis in Asian history. Among the mountain nations, the basic principle is that of stock-rearing, whereas the principle of the river plains is that of agriculture and the development of trade. The third principle, which is peculiar to the Near East, is that of foreign commerce and navigation. These principles have been presented here in abstract terms, but they also enter into essential relations with one another; they thereby appear in various distinct determinations, and form the common principles which underlie the way of life and historical character of the nations in question.

For example, the stock-rearing of the mountain peoples leads to three different kinds of existence. On the one hand, we see the peaceful life of the nomads running its uniform cycle with few needs to be satisfied. On the other hand, unrest may give rise to a life of plundering, which is also found among the nomadic peoples. And thirdly, they may actually embark on a career of conquest. Such nations, without developing a historical status of their own, do have a powerful impulse towards internal change; and even if they do not yet possess a historical content, they nevertheless contain the beginnings of history. In their immediate activity – the rearing of horses, camels, and sheep (and to a lesser extent cattle) – they pursue their own wandering and unstable life; this can either remain in its usual peaceful course, or give way to a life of plundering, or lead to a situation in which great masses congregate together and swoop down upon the river plains. Such nomadic hordes never attain any degree of internal development; they become civilised only when they have lost their original character through living on the river plains, where they first appeared in the role of conquerors. But incursions of this kind provide enormous historical impulses, creating havoc and transforming the external configuration of the world.

The second principle, that of the river plains with their agricultural existence, is the most interesting one for our present purposes. Agriculture, by its very nature, requires that the nomadic existence should come to an end. It necessarily entails a settled way of life, and demands foresight and provision for the future. Reflection on a universal object is thereby awakened, for the family must be provided for in a universal manner; and this in itself involves the principle of property and of private industry. China, India, and Babylon have become great civilised countries in this way. But they have remained enclosed within themselves and have not developed their links with the maritime principle – at least not after their own peculiar principle had come to fruition; and if they do subsequently take to the sea, it plays no real part in their culture and civilisation. Thus, the only connection they could have with later developments in history was through being visited and explored by other nations. But it is the intermediate principle which properly characterises Asia; the antithesis of day and night – or in geographical terms, that of river plains and a ring of mountains – is the determining factor in Asian history. The ring of mountains round the upland region, the uplands themselves, and the river plains, determine the physical and spiritual character of Asia. But these are not themselves the concrete elements of history, for the poles of the antithesis are absolutely related to one another: the settled existence of those who inhabit the fertile plains is the goal to which the unstable, restless, and nomadic inhabitants of the mountains and upland regions constantly aspire. Regions which are naturally distinct from one another become essentially related in the course of history.

In the *Near East*, both of these elements are united: it is the country of varied forms, and its main peculiarity is its relationship with Europe. It has not retained its own productions, but has passed them on to Europe. It has given birth to principles which were not developed in their country of origin but were brought to fruition in Europe. It has witnessed the rise of all religious and political principles, but their development took place in Europe. This region is associated with the Mediterranean Sea. Arabia and Syria – and particularly the Syrian coast with Judaea, Tyre, and Sidon – have adopted the principle of commerce from its earliest beginnings, and developed it in the direction of Europe. In Asia Minor, Troas and Ionia, as well as Colchis on the Black Sea with Armenia beyond it, have been major points of contact between Asia and Europe. But the broad plain of the Volga is also noteworthy as the route along which the vast hordes of Asia poured across into Europe.

γ. Europe

In Europe, we do not find the same physical differences which we encountered in Africa and even more pronouncedly in Asia. It lacks that solid nucleus of highlands which these continents possess, for the uplands of Europe occupy a subordinate position. The principle of the plains is likewise secondary; the south and west in particular display a greater assortment of valleys, surrounded by mountains and hills. The character of Europe is such that the differences in its physical structure do not form abrupt contrasts as they do in Asia; they are more closely intermingled, so that the antitheses of Asia disappear or are at least modified, and each natural division merges into the next. Even in the structure of Europe, however, three separate parts can be distinguished. But since there is no abrupt contrast between uplands and river plains, we must employ another method of classification.

The first part is *Southern Europe*, i.e. the country south of the Pyrenees, the south of France and Italy (which are cut off by the Alps from the rest of France and from Switzerland and Germany), and the series of eastern countries towards the Balkan Peninsula, south of the Danube basin, including Greece. This region, which was long the theatre of world history, does not have a clearly defined nucleus of its own, but is orientated outwards, looking towards the Mediterranean. While the middle and north of Europe were still uncultivated, the world spirit had its residence here. The land to the north of the Alps must be subdivided into two further parts: the western part, which includes Germany, France, Denmark, and Scandinavia, is the *heart of Europe*, the world which was first opened up by Julius Caesar. Caesar's world-historical action in opening this new terrain was a deed of manhood, just as Alexander the Great's plan to impose an occidental character on the Near East was a deed of youth. But Alexander was less successful in his attempts to raise the east to the Greek way of life than Caesar was in his undertaking. Nevertheless, although Alexander's achievement was transient, it established a link between east and west from which the first great world-historical events of the west could subsequently arise. In its implications, his deed appeals strongly to the imagination on account of its greatness and splendour, but, in its results, it soon vanished away like a mere ideal.

The third region is the *north-east of Europe*. It contains the northern plains, which have a peculiar character of their own; they once belonged to the Slavonic nations, and form a link with Asia, particularly with Russia and Poland. These countries are late arrivals in the series of historical states, and they maintain a constant connection between Europe and Asia.

Since no one particular type of environment predominates in Europe as it does in the other continents, man too is more universal in character. Those particular ways of life which are tied to different physical contexts do not assume such distinct and peculiar forms as they do in Asia, on whose history they have had so great an effect; for the geographical differences within Europe are not sharply defined. Natural life is also the realm of contingency, however, and only in its universal attributes does it exercise a determining influence commensurate with the principle of the spirit. The character of the Greek spirit, for example, grew out of the soil of Greece, a coastal territory which encourages individual autonomy. Similarly, the Roman Empire could not have arisen in the heart of the continent. Man can exist in all climates; but the climates are of a limited character, so that the power they exercise is the external counterpart to man's inner nature. Consequently, European man also appears naturally freer than the inhabitants of other continents, because no one natural principle is dominant in Europe. Those distinct ways of life which appear in Asia in a state of mutual conflict appear in Europe rather as separate social classes within the concrete state. The main distinction in geography is that between the interior and the coast. In Asia, the sea is without significance, and the Asiatic nations have in fact shut themselves off from it. In India, going to sea is positively forbidden by religion. In Europe, however, this maritime relationship is of vital importance, and it creates an enduring difference between the two continents. The European state is truly European only in so far as it has links with the sea. The sea provides that wholly peculiar outlet which Asiatic life lacks, the outlet which enables life to step beyond itself. It is this which has invested European political life with the principle of individual freedom.

2. The phases of world history

The following scheme of historical phases contains a general survey of world history. Its aim is also to make the historical process intelligible in the light of the Idea and its underlying necessity.

In the course of our geographical survey, we have already indicated the general direction of world history. The sun rises in the Orient. The sun is light, and light is universal and simple self-relatedness, i.e. universality in itself. This light, though universal in itself, exists in the sun as an individual or subject. We often imagine someone watching the moment of daybreak, the spreading of the light, and the rise of the sun in all its majesty. Descriptions of this kind tend to emphasise the rapture, astonishment, and infinite self-oblivion which accompany this moment of clarity. But when the sun has ascended further, the astonishment diminishes, and the eye is constrained to turn instead to nature and to the self; it will see by its own light, become conscious of itself, and progress from its original state of astonishment and passive contemplation to activity, to independent creation. And by evening, man has constructed a building, an inner sun, the sun of his own consciousness, which he has produced by his own efforts; and he will value it more highly than the actual sun outside him. As a result of his activity, he now stands in the same relationship to the spirit as he originally stood to the external sun, except that this new relationship is a free one: for his second object is his own spirit. Here, in a nutshell, is the course of the whole historical process, the great day of the spirit and the day's work it accomplishes in world history.

World history travels from east to west; for Europe is the absolute end of history, just as Asia is the beginning. World history has an absolute east, although the term east in itself is wholly relative; for although the earth is a sphere, history does not move in a circle around it, but has a definite eastern extremity, i.e. Asia. It is here that the external and physical sun rises, and it sets in the west: but it is in the west that the inner sun of self-consciousness, which emits a higher radiance, makes its further ascent. World history imposes a discipline on the unrestrained natural will, guiding it towards universality and subjective freedom.

Among all the phenomena of history, our true object is the *state*. As the state is the universal Idea and universal spiritual life to which individuals react from birth with trust and habit, in which they have their being and reality, their knowledge and volition, and through which they acquire and preserve their worth, two basic determinations are involved. Firstly, there is the universal substance of the state, the one inherently valuable spirit, the absolute power, the independent spirit of the nation; and secondly, there is individuality as such, the realm of subjective freedom. The question is whether the real life of individuals is one of unreflecting habit and custom in relation to the basic unity, or whether these individuals are reflecting personalities and subjects who exist for themselves. In this connection, we must distinguish between *substantial* freedom and *subjective* freedom. Substantial freedom is the implicit rationality of the will which is subsequently developed in the state. But in this determination of reason, individual insight and volition are not yet present; in other words, subjective freedom, which can only determine itself in the individual and which constitutes the reflection of the individual in his own conscience, has not yet come into being. Where there is merely substantial freedom, commandments and laws are regarded as firmly established in and for themselves, and the individual subject adopts an attitude of complete subservience towards them. Besides, these laws need not accord with the will of the individual, and the subjects are therefore like children, who obey their parents without will or insight of their own. But as subjective freedom arises and man descends from the realm of external reality into his own spirit, reflection creates an antithesis which contains the negation of reality. For withdrawal from the present world necessarily gives rise to an antithesis, one pole of which is God and the divine, and the other the individual subject. The sole purpose of world history is to create a situation in which these two poles are absolutely united and truly reconciled. They are reconciled in such a way that the free subject is not submerged in the objective existence of the spirit, but is accorded its independent rights; and at the same time the absolute spirit, the realm of pure objective unity, realises its absolute right. In the immediate consciousness of the Orient, the two are not yet distinct. The substantial world is distinct from the individual, but the object has not yet been located in the spirit itself.

Thus, the first form which the spirit assumes is that of the *Orient*. This world is based on the immediate consciousness, on substantial spirituality; its knowledge is no longer a matter of individual arbitrariness – for the sun has now risen – but of an essential will which exists independently and autonomously for itself and to which the will of the individual subject responds primarily with an attitude of faith, trust, and obedience. In more concrete terms, it is a *patriarchal relationship*. Within the family, the individual is a totality in his own right, but he is also a moment within the whole; he partakes of a common purpose which, since it is common to all, has its own separate existence whereby it also becomes an object of the individual consciousness. This consciousness is embodied in the head of the family, who is the will of the whole; he acts in the interests of the common purpose, cares for the individuals, directs their activity towards the common end, educates them, and ensures that they remain in harmony with the universal end. Their knowledge and desires do not go beyond this end and its embodiment in the head of state. This is necessarily the first mode of national consciousness.

At this stage, the state is already present, but the subject has not yet come into its rights. Ethical life has an immediate and lawless character, for this is the childhood of history. This early phase has two distinct aspects. The first is the state, which is based on the family relationship: it is a state of paternal guardianship, for the whole is held together by admonitions and punishments, and its character is prosaic, for it is still devoid of opposition and ideality. But it is also an enduring state, for it cannot change itself by its own efforts. Such is the character of the *Far East*, and of the Chinese empire in particular. As to the second aspect, this spatial continuity is matched by continuity in time. The states in question, without any change in themselves or in their underlying principle, are constantly changing in relation to one another, for they are engaged in an interminable conflict which rapidly leads to their downfall. Since the state is outwards-orientated, an awareness of the principle of individuality begins to dawn, for struggle and conflict require self-collectedness and self-comprehension. But this dawning awareness is still relatively weak, unconscious, and rooted in nature; it is a light, but not yet the light of self-conscious personality. History is still predominantly unhistorical, for it is merely a repetition of the same majestic process of decline. The innovations with which courage, strength, and magnanimity replace the splendours of the past go through the same cycle of decline and fall. But it is not a true downfall, for no progress results from all this restless change. Whatever innovation replaces what has been destroyed must sink and be destroyed in turn; no progress is made: and all this restless movement results in an unhistorical history. At this point, history passes over to central Asia – but the transition is only an external one, for the second phase has no connection with the first. If we continue the comparison with the ages of man, this would be the boyhood of history, which no longer displays the calm and trusting qualities of the child, but behaves in a boisterous and turbulent manner.

The Oriental spirit is closer in its determination to the sphere of *intuition*, for its relationship to its object is an immediate one. But the subject is still immersed in substantial existence, and has not yet extricated or liberated itself from its original state of unmixed unity to attain subjective freedom. Thus, the subject has not yet produced the universal object from within itself, and the object has not yet been reborn from within the subject. Its spiritual mode is not yet that of representation; on the contrary, it still exists in a condition of immediacy, and its mode is that of immediate existence. The object is therefore an individual subject, and is determined in an immediate way. Its mode is that of a natural sun, for, like it, it is an image of the sensuous rather than the spiritual imagination; and for this reason, it takes the form of a natural and individual human being. Thus, the spirit and substance of the nation are objectively present to its individual members in the shape of a single individual. For humanity is always the highest and worthiest means of representation. The subject, then, is primarily a human being, who is known by his people as the spiritual unity and form of subjectivity in which the one totality has its existence. Such is the principle of the Oriental world: the individuals have not yet attained subjective freedom within themselves, but appear as accidental properties of the underlying substance. This substance is not purely abstract, however, like that of

Spinoza, but is present to the natural consciousness in the shape of a head of state, and everything is seen as belonging exclusively to him.

The substantial power contains two distinct aspects: the spirit, which is dominant, and the natural world, which stands in opposition to it. These two moments are united within the substantial power. There is a master who gives expression to the substance, and who stands in the relation of a lawgiver towards the world of particular things. But this ruling power is not exclusively confined to what we know as secular government, for spiritual government has not yet assumed a distinct existence. The government of the Oriental world can be described as a theocracy. God is the secular ruler, and the secular ruler is God; the ruler is both of these simultaneously, and the state is ruled by a God incarnate. But we must now consider the three distinct forms which this principle assumes.

The *Chinese and Mongolian empire* is the realm of *theocratic despotism*. The state is fundamentally patriarchal; it is ruled by a father who also presides over what we would regard as matters of conscience. In China, this patriarchal principle is organised so as to form a state, but among the Mongols it is not so systematically developed. The head of state in China is a despot, and he leads a systematically constructed government with a numerous hierarchy of subordinate members. Even religious matters and family affairs are regulated by laws of state, and the individual has no moral selfhood.

In *India*, the difference lies in those firmly established divisions which necessarily arise within a highly developed national culture. In this case, it is the castes which determine the rights and duties of each individual. This system of government can be described as a *theocratic aristocracy*. These fixed distinctions are transcended by an ideality of the imagination, an ideal realm which has not yet become divorced from the world of the senses. The spirit does indeed ascend to the unity of God, but it cannot remain for long at this level. The transcendence of particularity is merely a wild and aimless movement which always sinks back to the point at which it began.

In *Persia*, the substantial unity has attained a purer form. Its natural manifestation is light, and the spiritual is the good. This form can be described as *theocratic monarchy*. The monarch's function is to implement the good. The Persians have ruled over many nations, but all of these have been allowed to retain their own peculiar character; their kingdom can therefore be likened to an empire. While China and India remained fixed in their principles, the Persians form the true transition from the Orient to the west. And just as Persia is the outward transition, so also is *Egypt* the inner transition to the free life of Greece. In Egypt, we encounter that contradiction of principles which it is the mission of the west to resolve.

The splendour of the Oriental way of life lies before us – its view of the One and of the substance in which everything inheres and from which nothing has yet become detached. Its basic view is of a firmly coordinated power to which all the riches of the imagination and of nature belong. Within this system, subjective freedom has not yet come into its rights; it does not yet derive its honour from itself, but only from the absolute object. The splendid edifices of the Oriental states are substantial forms which contain all the determinations of reason, but in such a way that the individual subjects remain purely accidental. These revolve around a centre, round the ruler, who, as a patriarch (but not as a despot in the sense of the Roman Empire), stands at the head of the state. For his task is to implement the claims of morality and of the substance: he has to uphold those essential commandments which are already established; and what for our purposes belongs entirely to the province of subjective freedom proceeds in this case from the universal totality itself. But this determination of the substance at once breaks up into two distinct moments, simply because it has not assimilated and overcome its antithesis. The antithesis has not yet developed within it and consequently falls outside it. On the one hand, therefore, we find permanence and stability, and on the other, a self-destructive arbitrariness. All that is contained within the Idea is essentially present and existent; but everything depends on the *manner* in which it is present, and whether its moments have been realised in their authentic form. And since subjectivity is an essential moment within the spirit, it must necessarily be present too. But in the Oriental state, it is not yet reconciled or unified, and it still awaits satisfaction. Consequently, this splendid edifice with its unified power, which nothing can escape and within which nothing can attain an independent existence, is coupled with unrestrained arbitrariness. On the one hand, this terrible unappeased arbitrariness is present within the political edifice itself, in the worldly aspect of the substantial power; and on the other hand, it also pursues its unwholesome and restless career outside it. In terms of the Idea, it has no place within the political edifice; but it is inevitably present, for all its inconsistency, as an extraneous factor outside the substantial unity. We accordingly find that the political structures of Oriental substantiality are accompanied by wild hordes who descend from the verge of the uplands into the peaceful states. They lay them waste and destroy them, razing everything to the ground, although they subsequently amalgamate with them and abandon their savagery; but since they are inherently intractable, they invariably disperse, leaving no lasting result behind them.

The Oriental world does possess what we would call states; but within these states, we do not find a purpose of the kind which we would describe as political. Their political life does contain substantial (i.e. realised and rational) freedom; but although this develops, it does not attain the inward conditions of subjective freedom. The state is that which is thought substantially for itself in the form of a universal substantial end for everyone. But in the Orient the state is an abstraction which has no universal existence for itself; it is not the universal end but the sovereign who constitutes the state. As already remarked, this phase can be likened to that of childhood in general.

The second phase, which comprehends the *world of Greece*, may be likened to the period of adolescence. It is characteristic of the Greek world that it witnesses the rise of numerous states. It is the realm of beautiful freedom, and it is in the context of immediate ethical existence that individuality develops within it. The principle of individuality, of subjective freedom, has its origin here, although it is still embedded in the substantial unity. As in Asia, morality is a principle, but it is also associated with individuality, so that it is identical with the free will of individuals. The two extremes of the Oriental world – subjective freedom and substantiality – are now combined; the kingdom of freedom – not that of unrestrained and natural freedom but of ethical freedom – is now realised. Its end is not arbitrary or particular but universal, for it takes the universal end of the nation as the object of its will and its knowledge. But it is merely the realm of beautiful freedom, and its union with the substantial end is natural and unreflecting. It is the union of the ethical with the subjective will, in which the Idea is united with a plastic form: it does not exist abstractly for itself, but is immediately bound up with the real, just as the sensuous bears the stamp and expression of the spiritual in a beautiful work of art. It is not yet morality, but merely unreflecting ethical existence; for the individual will of the subject intuitively adopts the customs and habits laid down by justice and the laws. The individual is therefore unconsciously united with the universal end. Accordingly, this kingdom is truly harmonious; like a lovely but ephemeral and quickly passing flower, the Greek world is a most serene yet inherently unstable structure, in that it is destined to forfeit its purity under the influence of reflection; and since the unity between its two principles is merely an immediate one, it constitutes the greatest of contradictions within itself. The two principles of the Oriental world – those of substantiality and of subjective freedom – are here united. But their unity is purely immediate, so that they are in the highest degree self-contradictory. In the Orient, the contradiction lies in two opposite extremes which come into conflict with one another. In Greece, however, these are united, but their union cannot survive in the form it assumes in Greece. For the aesthetic existence of Greece cannot be equated with true ethical life. It has not been reborn from the struggle through which subjective freedom is itself reborn, but remains at the earliest stage of subjective freedom; as such, it still bears the mark of natural ethicality instead of being born anew to the higher and purer form of universal ethical life. The ethical life of Greece will therefore be an unstable one which works towards its own dissolution; and the reflection of its extremes within themselves must bring about the downfall of the entire realm. In this way, a new and higher form is developed, bringing with it the third phase in history. Inwardness and reflection, in their incipient stages, are indeed present as a moment within the Greek world; and the next step is taken when this inner reflection, i.e. thought and the activity of thought, liberates itself and presses forward, so preparing the way for a new universal end.

Thus, the principle of the third phase is that of universality, of an end which exists as such, but as yet in abstract universality; this is the era of the Roman Empire. The end with which the individuals are confronted and to which all their actions are directed is the state as such. This phase can be regarded as the manhood of history. For manhood follows neither the arbitrary will of a master, nor its own aesthetic arbitrariness; its life is one of arduous labour and service, not of the free and happy pursuit of its own end. But although the end to which man must dedicate himself is universal, it is also an inflexible one. A state, laws, and constitutions are ends, and it is these which the individual must serve: the individual is immersed in them and achieves his own end only in the universal one. (Such an empire seems destined to last for ever, especially if it also embodies the principle of subjective satisfaction, even in its religion, as was the case in the Holy Roman Empire. Nevertheless, the Holy Roman Empire came to an end two decades ago.)

The state begins to take on an abstract existence and to develop itself towards an end in which its individual members participate, although this end is not yet an exhaustive and concrete one. For the free individuals are sacrificed to its rigorous demands, and they must dedicate themselves to it in the service of the abstract universal. The Roman Empire is no longer a commonwealth of individuals such as the city of Athens was. It is no longer a world of gladness and joy, but of hard and arduous toil. The interest of the state becomes detached from the individual citizens, although the latter gain abstract formal universality in themselves. The universal subjugates the individuals, who must surrender themselves to it; but in return, their own universality, i.e. their personality, is recognised: they are treated as persons with rights of their own in their capacity as private individuals. And just as individuals are assimilated into the abstract concept of personality, so also must individual nations undergo the same fate; their concrete forms are crushed beneath this universal existence, and incorporated into it as part of an indifferent mass. Rome becomes a pantheon embracing all gods and all spiritual existence, but these gods and this spirit no longer retain their own distinct vitality.

The transition to the next historical principle should be seen as a struggle between abstract universality and individuality. Since it is abstract, this law-governed state must come to an end in complete subjectivity. The subject, the principle of infinite form, has not acquired a substantial existence, and must therefore appear as an arbitrary rule: and the reconciliation of the antithesis is thereby posited in the secular world. But the spiritual reconciliation can only be effected when the individual personality has been purified and transfigured as personal subjectivity in and for itself, thereby attaining a universal existence in and for itself. This is the divine personality; it must manifest itself in the world, but as something universal in and for itself.

If we consider the two aspects of this development more closely, we perceive that the kingdom of the universal end, based as it is on reflection and abstract universality, contains the express and explicit antithesis within itself: it is therefore the essential embodiment of the struggle which the antithesis presupposes, with the necessary result that arbitrary individuality, the completely contingent and purely worldly power of an autocrat, gains ascendancy over abstract universality. At the beginning of this phase, an antithesis exists between the end of the state as abstract universality on the one hand and abstract personality on the other. As the principle of abstract universality is developed and realised, the individual is absorbed into it; and from this process, the subject emerges as a distinct personality. As a result, the individual subjects become isolated from one another. The universality (or rather the abstract universality) which they thereby acquire gives them the status of legal personalities with an independent and essential existence of their own. On the other hand, this at the same time gives rise to a world of formal abstract right, the right of property. But since this process of fragmentation into numerous individual personalities takes place within the state, the state no longer confronts the individuals as an abstract entity, but as the power of an autocrat over the individual citizens. Within an abstract political framework whose highest value is no longer the universal end but the right of the individual personality, the power and cohesive force which are required to counteract the process of fragmentation can only be of an arbitrary nature, as distinct from a rational political power. Thus, as the individual personality gains the ascendant with the progress of history and the disintegration of the whole into atoms can only be restrained by external force, the subjective power of autocracy comes forward as if summoned to perform this task. For abstract legality has no concrete existence or internal organisation of its own, and when it has gained predominance its motive and ruling power is purely arbitrary in the sense of contingent subjectivity; and the individual then seeks consolation for his lost freedom by cultivating his private rights. Thus, an arbitrary power comes into play, reconciling the antithesis and establishing order and peace. But this peace is accompanied by absolute internal disunion; the reconciliation of the antithesis is purely worldly and external in character, and it is accordingly counterbalanced by internal insurgency as the pains of despotism make themselves felt. But secondly, the true reconciliation, which is of a higher and spiritual nature, must be effected before the antithesis can be removed; a condition must arise in which the individual personality is contemplated, known, and willed as inwardly purified and elevated to universality. The spirit, driven back into its innermost depths, abandons the godless world, seeks the reconciliation within itself, and embarks on a life of inwardness – a fulfilled and concrete inwardness, endowed with a substantiality which is based not merely on external existence. On the contrary, the purely worldly empire referred to above is now matched by the spiritual empire of subjectivity which knows itself and its own essential being, i.e. of the spirit made real. The principle of the spirit has become manifest, in that subjectivity has acquired a universal character.

The empire of self-knowing subjectivity marks the rise of the real spirit; this is the beginning of the fourth phase in history, which, in natural terms, would correspond to the old age of the spirit. In the natural world, old age is equivalent to weakness; but the old age of the spirit is the age of its complete maturity, in which it returns to a condition of unity while retaining its spiritual nature. The spirit as infinite power contains within itself the moments of its earlier development and thereby attains its totality.

We have now reached the stage of spirituality and spiritual reconciliation; and this spiritual reconciliation is the principle of the fourth phase in history. The spirit has become conscious that the spirit itself is the truth, and it now exists as an object of thought. This fourth phase necessarily consists of two parts: on the one hand, the spirit as consciousness of an inner world – i.e. the spirit which is known as the essential being, as thinking consciousness of the highest things, or the will of the spirit – is again of an abstract nature, for it remains tied to spiritual abstraction. So long as consciousness remains at this stage, worldly existence is at odds with itself, and is given over to savagery and barbarism; it is accompanied by a total indifference towards worldly things, for the latter have no connection with the spiritual world and have not attained a rational organisation within the consciousness. Such is the nature of the *Mohammedan world*, in which the Oriental world reaches its highest transfiguration and its highest perception of the One. Its origin is admittedly later than that of Christianity; but it took many centuries for Christianity to achieve world importance, a process which was finally completed by Charlemagne. Mohammedanism, however, because of the abstract nature of its principle, was able to become a world empire within a short space of time; but it is a more primitive system than that of Christianity.

The second stage in the development of this spiritual world begins when the spiritual principle has translated itself into a concrete world. This principle is the consciousness and volition of subjectivity as a divine personality, and it manifests itself initially in a single subject. But it subsequently develops into an empire of the real spirit. This phase can be described as the *Germanic world*, and those nations on which the world spirit has conferred its true principle may be called the Germanic nations. The realm of the real spirit has as its principle the absolute reconciliation of subjectivity which exists for itself with the diversity which exists in and for itself, i.e. with that true and substantial condition in which the subject is free for itself in so far as it accords with the universal and has an essential existence: in short, the realm of concrete freedom.

From now on, the *worldly* empire and the *spiritual* empire are opposed to one another. On the one hand, the principle of the spirit which exists for itself is freedom, in its own peculiar form, and subjectivity. The individual mind seeks to be united with that which it is bound to respect.

It must not be contingent, however, but rather the mind in its essential being and spiritual truth. This is what Christ has revealed to us in his religion; his own truth, which is that of the mind, is that we should posit ourselves as united with the divinity. At this point, the reconciliation in and for itself is accomplished. But since it has only been accomplished in itself, this phase of history, by virtue of its immediacy, begins with an antithesis.

Admittedly, its historical origin lies in that reconciliation which Christianity brought with it; but since this itself has only begun, and exists only implicitly for the consciousness, we find initially the greatest possible antithesis (although it is subsequently regarded as an injustice which ought to be removed). It is the antithesis between the spiritual and religious principle on the one hand and the secular realm on the other. Yet the secular realm is no longer what it formerly was, for it has now been converted to Christianity and ought therefore to accord with the truth. But the spiritual realm must also come to recognise that spirituality is realised in the secular world. But in so far as both worlds are still immediate, the secular realm has not yet cast off its arbitrary subjectivity, and the spiritual realm has not yet recognised the secular world; consequently, the two are in conflict. The course of history is therefore not one of peaceful and unopposed development, for the spirit does not approach its realisation in a peaceful manner. In the course of history, both sides must renounce their one-sidedness, i.e. their inauthentic form. On the one hand, we find a hollow reality which ought to accord with the spirit but does not yet do so; and for this reason, it must be destroyed. And on the other hand, the spiritual realm is primarily an ecclesiastical one which has become immersed in outward secularity; and while the secular authority is suppressed by external influences, the ecclesiastical authority falls into decay. The situation to which this gives rise is one of barbarism.

As already remarked, the reconciliation is at first implicit (i.e. in itself), but it still has to become explicit (i.e. for itself). Consequently, the principle must begin with the greatest possible antithesis; and it must also be the most abstract of antitheses, for the reconciliation is absolute. As we have seen, this antithesis consists on the one hand of the spiritual principle in its ecclesiastical form, and on the other of wild and barbarous secularity. The first stage in this historical development is one of hostility between the two, although they are allied to one another inasmuch as the ecclesiastical principle is recognised by the secular realm; yet the latter does not accord with the former, although it ought, by its own admission, to do so. The secular realm, which is now forsaken by the spirit, is oppressed by the ecclesiastical authority; and the primary form of ecclesiastical authority is such that it itself lapses into secularity, thereby losing its spiritual determination and subsequently also its power. The decline of both worlds culminates in the disappearance of barbarism, and the spirit then discovers a higher form which is in general worthy of it, i.e. the form of rationality, of free and rational thought. The spirit, driven back upon itself, comprehends its own principle and produces it within itself in its free form, in the form of thought, in an intellectual shape. It is now able to coexist in harmony with external reality at large, to insinuate itself into it, and to realise the principle of rationality through the secular world itself.

Only after it has gained its objective (i.e. intellectual) form can the spiritual principle become truly congruent with external reality; only then can the spiritual aim be realised in the secular world. It is the form of thought which brings about the fundamental reconciliation: the profundity of thought is the agent by which the reconciliation is effected. This profundity of thought will then manifest itself in the world of appearance, and this subjectivity is the source of knowledge and the point at which appearance and existence coincide. Thus, the principle of reconciliation between Church and state has emerged, and the ecclesiastical world thereby discovers and possesses its concept and rationality in the secular world. In this way, the antithesis between the Church and the so-called state vanishes; the state is no longer inferior and subordinate to the Church, and the Church retains no special prerogative; the spiritual world is no longer alien to the state. Freedom has found the means of realising its concept and its truth. Thus it has happened that, through the activity of thought – i.e. universal determinations of thought whose substance is this concrete principle or the nature of the spirit itself – the realm of reality or concrete thought has come into conformity with substantial truth. Freedom discovers its concept in reality, and has developed the secular world into the objective system of a specific and internally organised state. It is this triumphant progress which gives history its interest, and the point at which reconciliation and existence for itself are reached is now an object of knowledge: reality is transformed and reconstructed. This is the goal of world history: the spirit must create for itself a nature and world to conform with its own nature, so that the subject may discover its own concept of the spirit in this *second nature*, in this reality which the concept of the spirit has produced; and in this objective reality, it becomes conscious of its subjective freedom and rationality. Such is the progress of the Idea in general; and this must be our ultimate point of view in history. The more detailed process whereby the Idea is realised is history proper; and that work still remains to be done in it is a purely empirical matter. In our study of world history, we have to cover more circumstantially that long route which we have just surveyed in outline, the path which history follows in realising its aim. But temporal duration is something entirely relative, and the spirit belongs to eternity. Duration, strictly speaking, does not exist for it. The further labour of history is that this principle should develop and unfold, and that the spirit should attain its reality and become conscious of itself in the real world.

3. Additions from the winter semester of 1826-7

[to p. 28:]
The rational is (1) the *logically* rational, with which we cannot concern ourselves here; there is, however, (2) the form of *nature*, which is a reflection or embodiment of reason; but natural reason is not our present concern either, for our object is rather (3) reason in its manifestation as *self-conscious spirit* (not, however, in a general sense, but as it unfolds itself in deeds and actions in the world in which its essence is realised).

The spirit in general is the basis of history, in which it unfolds itself in the various forms which we call nations. It is in this capacity that we shall consider it here.

Reason in and for itself is eternal and at rest, but it is likewise activity, and its actions are exclusively rational. It produces itself from within itself and is consequently a product or end in which it realises its own nature. It is not our business to demonstrate this concept here; in the present context, we can only postulate it and lend it plausibility. The earlier stages of philosophy contain its actual proof. The prior assumptions which must be made here need only be mentioned in order to remind us of the conceptions which underlie our remarks and which tally with those which are also present in our ordinary consciousness.

[to pp. 29f.:]
The antitheses which present themselves on a closer examination of world history are, in general terms, (1) the antithesis between subjective reason

and its object, i.e. history itself (this may be called the *theoretical* anti-thesis), and (2) the relationship between freedom and necessity, or the *practical* antithesis.

The two prior assumptions with which we approached this study of history were (1) that the world is ruled by a providence, and (2) that it is possible to discern the plan by which this providence operates. But how are we to recognise the rationality of history and the ultimate end of the world in its historical application? The Idea has two distinct components: (*a*) the Idea as such, and (*b*) the existence of the nation in history, i.e. the empirical side of existence. The universal Idea is the unity of these two aspects, although they are basically distinct. The first is the *theoretical* aspect; our aim is to recognise the Idea, and the question is: how are we to do so? It seems as if we shall have to consider history in itself and that its ultimate end will reveal itself to us in the process. That is, we take the empirical element of ordinary history as our point of departure, and hope that it will reveal to us the nature of the divine will. But if we are to know the latter, we must come to the study of history equipped with reason, just as we need eyes before we can perceive blue. A rational man observes the data before him, and thoughts come into his mind. They do not come from outside, however, for he has them within himself; the objects before him are merely the impulse or incentive which causes him to reflect. If we approach the world with subjective and one-sided views, we shall be inclined to criticise everything; we know how it ought to be, and find that it is not so. But anything which deserves such censure will inevitably be finite in content; for the substance, i.e. the content which matters, must be of a rational nature.

Our God is not an Epicurean one who lives in total aloofness in the empty regions of the universe.

Before we can recognise the substance, we must already be conscious of its existence. The nature of the substance remains concealed from the senses, just as the hand cannot perceive the nature of colour; and the understanding, which comprehends the finite world, cannot perceive it either. The motley confusion of all the shapes and phenomena of existence contains the truth within itself, and it is the eye of the concept which penetrates the exterior and recognises the truth. And it is philosophy which purges the understanding of such subjective conceits.

[to p. 31:]
Even in ordinary history, we have to select from the deeds and events with which we are confronted and arrange them in a certain way; for

our aim is not to depict the entire happenings of the past. This applies even more so to the philosophical study of history. Given so great a mass of material, a *summary* procedure is required. But we must not summarise in such a way that numerous events are left out altogether; on the contrary, those events which form an extensive series in reality must be reduced to a single *unity* and included within a universal representation* which will contain everything which occurs in the individual instances. If, for example, we speak of battles, victories, and the like, these are universal representations which embrace a multitude of deeds, etc. – the deeds of all the individuals concerned. To make the battle immediately present, these would have to be depicted here and now, and in each of their successive moments. In the sentence: 'The army was victorious', the whole collection of intermediate steps is fully expressed in a single general representation.

This character of *universality* is derived from the nature of thought, and our study of history uses thought as its instrument. Those who reject the thinking approach to history in favour of an intuitive one do not know their own mind; for intuition† is also universal, and it also involves thought.

It is the understanding which makes this distinction between the essential and the inessential; and on closer investigation, we find that what is essential in one instance is inessential in another. The understanding must place the emphasis on thought, relate everything to the basic unity, and pass over all that is irrelevant. Herein lies the difference between the historian and the chronicler. The latter admittedly recounts all the events, but he will overlook numerous changes which quietly take place beneath the surface.

Those ends – such as the state, the nation, learning, and art – to which the historian relates the events he describes may be highly relative, and a distinction at once arises between specific or particular ends and those which are dear to the heart and to reason. Everything which we regard as important, such as the destiny of nations, of religion, of learning, etc., will only appear important in so far as it is related to those ends which exist in and for themselves. But what are these ends? If we approach history from the point of view of thought and philosophy, we must have a determinate consciousness of that which interests us, i.e. of the ends which underlie our study of history.

* *Vorstellung.* † *Anschauung.*

[to p. 32:]

In the history of the world, we see before us the concrete image of *evil* in its most fully developed form. If we consider the mass of individual happenings, history appears as an *altar* on which individuals and entire nations are immolated; we see all that is noblest and finest destroyed. No real gain appears to have been made, and only this or that ephemeral work lingers on, already bearing the mark of decay on its brow and soon to be supplanted by another as ephemeral as itself.

[to p. 40:]

Above all, one must know the nature of God, who has revealed himself in the Christian religion. The Bible refers to those who know nothing of God as heathens. The Christian God is the God who has revealed himself to men. The most exalted attribute of Christianity is not its moral content, for the heathens also had a very high morality. We ought to have knowledge of God's actions; otherwise we are like the Athenians who built an altar to the unknown god.

[to p. 43:]

Reason, however, rejects the category of the purely negative and assumes that this negative element, this universal activity of mankind, has produced a lasting achievement, and that our present reality is the result of the whole of human history. The finite and momentary ends are moments within a universal end; the perishable contains an imperishable element which these ends have helped to create. This affirmative element exists not merely in memories of the past, but is itself a product which belongs to reality, or rather a product to which we ourselves belong.

[to p. 46:]

This ultimate end is firmly fixed in and for itself. It may also be described as the *good* which is destined to be realised in the world. World history is rooted in the soil of the spirit, not in that of nature, so that its ultimate end can only be deduced from the nature of the spirit.

[to p. 48:]

Justice and the ethical world are nothing more than the concept which the spirit has formed of itself. The ancients did not know that man as such is free.

[to pp. 52f.:]

This universal spirit or world spirit is not the same thing as God. It is the rationality of the spirit in its worldly existence. Its movement is such that it makes itself what it is, i.e. what its concept is. This movement is rational, and in accord with the divine spirit. God is the spirit in his community; he lives and really exists in it. The world spirit is the system of this process whereby the spirit produces for itself the true concept of its own nature.

[to pp. 61f.:]
The concept of the spirit is a turning in of the spirit upon itself; as it turns in upon itself, the spirit discovers itself in its externalised form and possesses a definite goal and absolute ultimate end. In so far as its principle is a particular one, its limits become evident in the life of the nation in question. The nation then degenerates, but at the same time knowledge and philosophy flourish. As the nation degenerates, reflection, knowledge, and the conscience make their appearance. When a nation has satisfied itself in relation to its principle, its further development is marked by the sudden emergence of thought and reflection. The times of instinctive behaviour in a nation are also those in which its virtues are apparent, but it does not remain permanently at this instinctive level. Its withdrawal into itself involves abstract thought. As it withdraws into thought, the spirit asks itself whether reality is in accord with it. For free thought in itself may not remain at variance with the spirit of reality.

The Greeks had no conscience. Justice and duty were defined by the law of the state, and it was never considered whether they were indeed justice and duty. But no one is a free man unless he *understands* that what the state demands is also good. If this is not so, the individual is divorced from the ethical world around him; a division arises between the inward and formal dimension and the unity which is already present. Personal interests must be accorded their rights and the claims of the substance must also be fulfilled.

[to p. 71:]
The second antithesis is the *practical* and objective antithesis of necessity and freedom. Freedom in the subjective sense is the activity with which men respond to the outward vicissitudes of fate, sometimes triumphing over them and sometimes succumbing to them. The more precise significance of this antithesis is that we should recognise the necessity as divine. The divine will manifests itself on the one hand, but it is opposed on the other by man with his freedom and the interests of his reason and passion. How then are we to resolve this antithesis?

(3. xi. 1826) Necessity is not to be confused with mere external pressure; on the contrary, it is that irresistible and divine element which is an end in and for itself in relation to freedom. The difficulties involved in the resolution of this contradiction can only be made intelligible by means of conceptions drawn from ordinary life. The realm of law and justice is concerned with the protection of wealth etc., and it exists here and now. A lawful condition of this kind is an authority against arbitrariness. It is a common ground which no individuals can violate. And it is the same in technical matters. A house, for example, is the product of man's arbitrary will; it is opposed by the free power of the elements, although these are themselves employed in its construction. In this way, purposive activity is combined with necessity.

[to pp. 72f.:]
Individuality is the province of deeds and actions; the end is always a personal one. The end which exists in and for itself is produced by the individuals, and it is they who are active. Their ends must also be particular ones, related to them as particular beings. The species contains the entire nature of the genus, and it is not opposed to the universal, no more than gold is opposed to metal. Only the substantial can be truly fulfilled as such; all that is negative and evil is ephemeral. The universal must always be realised through the particular. Particular things compete with one another; but they also destroy themselves.

[to p. 92:]
The ultimate end of the will of the world spirit can be defined as follows: the subject as such possesses personal freedom and conscience, and its particular interest is to obtain satisfaction from its ethical state. The subject as such has infinite value; it should be considered as free, so that subjectivity may become conscious of its ultimate end. Subjectivity creates the one substantial end, which is produced by the infinite independence of all individuals. This substance is the foundation and basis on which the individual can attain formal freedom in the realm of subjectivity. The unity of the absolute antithesis is the end which exists in the depths of the spirit.

[to pp. 108f.:]
Nations which do not yet constitute states need not be considered here. The word 'state' is often applied exclusively to the political and legal framework; in another sense, it can also be taken to include religion. The

constitution is the relationship of the individual to the many, of individuals among themselves (i.e. legal relationships in general), and the means whereby different functions are assigned to different social classes.

[to pp. 110f.:]
The principle is expressed in religion; but it should also be translated into reality; the principle of the national spirit is meant to be realised. Religion is the inner and abstract relationship of the self-consciousness to the supreme being. In its concentrated form, religion remains indifferent towards the secular world as the latter declares itself, expresses itself, and develops. But once the inner realm is consolidated, its external counterpart and application make their appearance in turn.

[to p. 152:]
We must take notice of the influence of nature, for it is the immediate reality.

[to p. 162:]
(14. xi. 1826) The New World is still a new and young world. In this respect, we may exclude America from our investigation, and need only add a few comments on its relationship with Europe.

[to p. 170:]
America is in fact the world of the future, for it is still in the process of growth. The Old World can be said to lie around a central point, the Mediterranean Sea; the New World, however, is quite different in character: its two parts, North and South America, have quite different origins as regards the way[12] in which they have developed.

The South American states are still growing and developing; the peoples of Spanish and Portuguese America have still to emancipate themselves from slavery. They do not yet possess the spirit of rationality. The peoples of the northern part have still to overcome their isolation and to gather around a central focus; none of the provinces is autonomous, for they are all dependent upon their mother countries. The emigrants have brought with them the assets of European culture, so that they began life in America with advantages which, in Europe, were the fruit of thousands of years of development.

[to p. 172:]
Africa is characterised by concentrated sensuality, immediacy of the will, absolute inflexibility, and an inability to develop.

[to p. 173:]

Asia is the land of sunrise, of antithesis, and of unbounded expansion, whereas Europe is the land in which the spirit descends into itself and concentrates upon itself. The extravagance of the Orient gives way here to moderation, determinateness, and rationality, to control of the immoderate by the spiritual principle.

[to pp. 175f.:]

Africa is divided up amongst a multitude of peoples, so that it forms a loose conglomeration. It has often happened that a prince has subjugated many peoples, but has soon lost control of them again. They are united temporarily under a single sceptre; this has supplied us with sufficient information concerning Africa.

It is now regarded as almost certain that the Niger flows into the Bight of Benin; for 2000 years, no one has believed Herodotus' claim that it flows eastwards. But the remainder of its course is unknown.

[to p. 176:]

The interest of this study of Africa is that it shows us man living in a completely barbarous condition which nevertheless admits of a certain degree of development. In this primeval and completely natural state, man exists in his natural savagery; he lives outside the sphere of culture, which is not an integral part of his nature. Africa may be classed as belonging to the phase which precedes culture and development in the proper sense. China and India have a settled existence of their own, and they play no active part in historical progress; nevertheless, they are points of departure for the processes of history.

[to p. 178:]

God has created man in his own image; for man is a spiritual being. Man must therefore become what he is intended to be; that is, he must fulfil his destiny as a rational being. The spirit can only be what it makes itself; and its activity is that of producing and comprehending itself.

It is only by recreating itself that the spirit can realise its destiny. Thus, the primitive condition in which man has not yet entered that state of division from which he must create himself anew is an animal rather than a spiritual condition. Only the child or the animal is innocent; man is inevitably guilty. This does not mean that he ought to perpetrate evil. On the contrary, he ought to do good; but he is invariably responsible for his actions, in that he must have willed them and been implicated in them with his will. Guilt is not just the opposite of innocence, for guilt implies that the individual can be held responsible for his actions; and such responsibility is only possible in that state of division in which the consciousness is already differentiated. The state of perfection, if it exists at all, is a state of animality. Man is a spirit only in so far as he knows himself and has arrived at that state of division and opposition whose destiny contains both good and evil. The fact that the state of perfection – i.e. the state in which man is in accord with his concept – is described as man's earliest condition carries a further implication. It suggests that we must presuppose a correspondence between the individual and his concept as the true substance on which the concept rests. Whatever man is meant to aspire to must be in conformity with his concept and with the spirit. Mere potentiality, i.e. that state in which the end exists in itself, must be the original condition; the original condition is that which is present in and for itself in the concept and in the Idea, and which at first exists only inwardly. The inward realm which posits itself as an end, the motive impulse which relates all outward expressions to this primary factor, is the original condition. Innocence, i.e. the unity of the spirit with its determination (i.e. with nature) is absolutely primary, the prior condition of its determination, but not in a chronological sense. To represent it as actually existing is, however, an altogether different matter. For the rational takes on a new aspect if it is interpreted as existing in the present. What is in fact the goal of history is represented as the original existence of man from which he has subsequently lapsed.

This underlying basis is the unmoved mover of everything; what in itself is merely an inner basis or ultimate end which the spirit has yet to produce is represented by religion as something which has actually existed. For us, however, this Idea is the substance and the original condition.

As to the African character, it is still unknown to us, because the Europeans have not yet penetrated sufficiently far into the interior; Africa still remains cut off. The Europeans have not yet penetrated its interior, but they do have frequent commerce with the nations which have come down from the interior to the coastal belt. In particular, the Portuguese have occupied the coast of southern Guinea; they have tried to convert its peoples, but with little success. In Mozambique, they have penetrated somewhat further inland. The Dutch and the French have also established settlements on the coast of Senegambia; at one time, there was even a colony founded by Brandenburg at the mouth of the Gambia in Senegal, but it did not survive for long. In recent times, we have also learnt more about the Africans from the English. The nations which have come into contact with Europe have entered into relations with the Europeans, partly through war and partly through commercial associations; but their princes have refused to allow the Europeans to extend their territories further, and have acquired a monopoly of trade. They have indeed permitted certain commodities to be imported, particularly guns and gunpowder, but not by the Europeans.

[to p. 179:]
Natural man is at least sensible of the fact that his own existence is distinct from that of nature. Man occupies a higher and dominant position in relation to the natural world. The natural must subordinate itself to him, and nothing can stand up against him. He knows this, and we know it too. But we do not interpret man and the spiritual world in their immediate sense. The spiritual is what we call the divine; but in natural man, the finite spirit and the spirit which exists in and for itself have not yet been separated.

[to pp. 179f.:]
The next point to notice is that this power of sorcery which man is supposed to possess is not attributed to all human beings as such. The Africans see it as concentrated in certain individuals – in the priests, or in some nations in the rulers, or in those who are specially appointed by the king and who live in isolation from the rest.

   Their behaviour is at its most terrible among the Jagas or Jakas, who terrorised the Guinean kingdom of Congo in the sixteenth century, and also attacked Mozambique and Abyssinia. Such priests are known as Singilla or Chitomen. Many Portuguese Europeans have lived among them. They used to distribute amulets as a means of protection against wild beasts and the like, and Catholic priests, Capuchins and Franciscans would issue other amulets in turn to counteract the former...*Cavazzi* reports that many negroes were torn to pieces by wild beasts despite the fact that they wore amulets, but that those who had received them from him escaped unharmed.

[to pp. 180f.:]
Another kind of mediation involves the use of some external object which they set up as their god and ruling power. Such objects are called *fetishes*; any stone, butterfly, beetle, tree, or river they come across can be made into a fetish. They worship such fetishes and invest them with an

independent power, thereby projecting this power beyond their own spirit and giving it an external embodiment. The fetish of a given country may be an elephant, a tiger, or a river. The animal in question is shut up in a cage, worshipped, and credited with absolute power; this power is thus projected outside their own consciousness, and they do not see it as pertaining to their own minds. It is transferred to another object, but only to an object of the senses, and not to a universal spirit.

[to p. 181:]
One of their principal beliefs is that a deceased person may take possession of the Singilla and deliver his oracles and commands through the latter's mouth. If it is thought that a certain priest is tenanted by a departed spirit, that priest is invested with enormous power; he will constantly exact new services, offerings of food, and repeated human sacrifices.

[to p. 183:]
The negroes have no sentiments of regret at this condition of slavery. When the negro slaves have laboured all day, they are perfectly contented and will dance with the most violent convulsions throughout the night.

[to p. 185:]
The negroes wage numerous wars, and, on many occasions, their battles have lasted from five to eight days with more than half a million warriors engaged. They fight bravely, but their contests could more aptly be described as slaughters than as battles. 200,000 men have often perished on the field. The issue is decided by chance: one of the parties takes flight, and all who are caught by the pursuers are massacred.

[to pp. 185f.:]
As for the constitution – if one can speak of such a thing – it is determined by the factors already mentioned. There are numerous national groups, for the interior of Africa is densely populated. These nations are constantly at war, and their object is to acquire prisoners and slaves whom they subsequently devour. Sometimes a nation is subjugated by another, and sometimes provinces will rebel and make themselves independent; at the moment, the greatest empire is that of the Ashanti. The succession is hereditary, and it usually remains within the same family – although practice may vary according to whether the brother, the son, or some other relative is the heir. But the throne is rarely inherited in a peaceful manner, for it may be seized by other chiefs or relations. The violent overthrow of dynasties is a common occurrence.

[to p. 186:]
Some Englishmen recently penetrated a region which no Europeans had hitherto reached. One of them sat down in the shade in front of a house and came into conversation with a negro. Another approached him and begged for alms. The Englishman impatiently turned him away; the negro who sat beside him said that the other was a man who had access to all the leading citizens, for he was the executioner. He had come to office in the following way. He had been required to furnish an example of his art in order to demonstrate his abilities. He thereupon went home, beheaded his brother (who had been the executioner before him), and was granted the office. The executioner is often the prime minister, and his duty is to decapitate the king if the harvest turns out badly.

[to p. 188:]
Hutchinson describes various ceremonies, particularly the washing of the bones of the king's deceased mother and relatives during a solemn procession at which the king himself is present. The bones are washed in human blood; the rest of the blood of the victims who are slaughtered for this purpose is drunk by the king and his retinue. If the king sees fit, he will send a message to his deceased father by killing someone and ordering him to deliver it.

[to p. 189, l. 5 from below:]
The missionaries report that this law has existed for 120 years, and that they have known many women who have thrown their children into a river or exposed them to wild animals.

Cannibalism is still customary among the Ashanti. The English were shown many chiefs of whom it was said that they had torn their enemies' hearts from their bodies and eaten them while they were still warm and bleeding. They believe that devouring the hearts of their enemies will make them courageous. At public festivals, sheep are distributed among the people, and the king acts as host to his subjects. At the end, a human being is torn to pieces; his flesh is cast to the multitude and greedily eaten by all who can lay hands on it.

But enough of this primitive and savage condition of man.

NOTE ON THE COMPOSITION
OF THE TEXT

(by Georg Lasson)

In compiling the present edition, the editor had the following source
materials at his disposal:

1. A *manuscript in Hegel's hand*, prefixed by the date 8. xi. 30, and
accordingly composed for the last series of lectures on the philosophy of
history which Hegel ever delivered.[13] It is very carefully written on folded
folio sheets, but only in fragments between which Hegel himself has
left whole columns blank. Various supplementary passages and inter-
polations have been added in the margin for inclusion in the text, along
with brief notes and references to the sections into which the work is
divided.

In this edition, passages from Hegel's manuscript are printed in italics.
The reader can thereby distinguish exactly which parts of the text are
Hegel's own and which have been reconstructed from the lecture notes
of his students. The spelling has in the main been adapted to present-day
usage. But no alterations have been made to the actual wording without
some corresponding indication either in the text or in the footnotes. For
example, all additions – except where it was self-evident that words
accidentally omitted had to be restored – are enclosed in square brackets
in the text. In particular, in all cases where marginal notes consisting of
incomplete sentences had to be incorporated into the text, words supplied
to complete the sense are marked as editorial additions.

Hegel's manuscript breaks off in the middle of his discussion of those
points of view which enable us to make concrete distinctions between
the various cultural stages in history. In the second published edition of
the lecture course in Hegel's collected works, Karl Hegel appended to
this arbitrary conclusion a series of further passages from students'
lecture notes. In the notes themselves, these passages appeared much
earlier in the sequence of lectures, and we have accordingly restored them
to their original position. No wholly satisfactory conclusion can be
constructed from the available material; but what now appears at the

end of the discussion is at least clearly recognisable as a conclusion in the notes of those who attended the lectures.

A comparison between the text in Hegel's collected works and our present edition of Hegel's manuscript at once reveals that the two previous editors did not pay the least regard to those principles of philological accuracy which are nowadays taken for granted. A single example may serve to illustrate just how cursory their reading was. Hegel is fond of the comparative construction; but he is also inclined to omit the mute e in closed syllables at the ends of words. Consequently, his comparatives are usually distinguishable as such only by the single letter r; this has almost invariably been overlooked by the previous editors, so that Hegel's point has been blunted. And there is no lack of incorrect readings either; perhaps the most serious is the substitution of 'authorities' [*Autoritäten*] for 'a priori inventions' [*Apriolitäten*; p. 29, l. 26], although the word which Hegel wrote is perfectly legible. Furthermore, the editors have not always correctly interpreted the general headings in the margin; the most flagrant example occurs in the passage on the second half of page 35 in this edition, where the editors, having misunderstood Hegel's introductory words, were compelled simply to omit the greater part of the marginal note which can alone make Hegel's opinion clear.

The first editor, Eduard Gans, took somewhat more care to preserve Hegel's style, and did not alter the sequence in which the various sections occurred in Hegel's draft. But the second, Karl Hegel, not only made many additional changes to Hegel's mode of expression, but also, to facilitate the inclusion of new sections from students' notes, altered the order of certain sections in Hegel's manuscript, thereby obscuring and violating the thought-progression which Hegel intended. Both editors alike simply left out whole sentences of the manuscript and altered Hegel's diction in ways for which there was no justification and which often detract from the sense.

The way in which the first editors dealt with Hegel's own manuscript inspires little confidence in their treatment of the students' lecture notes which formed the main source on which their edition was based. And indeed, a comparison of one set of notes which was available both to them and to the present editor with the printed version reveals that they aspired neither to textual accuracy nor to comprehensiveness of content. It is astonishing how much important material in the notes in question has simply been left out altogether by the editors. This made it all the more necessary for the present editor to refer back to the lecture notes wherever this was possible.

2. Of the *sets of notes* taken down at Hegel's lectures, the present editor was able to consult the following:

(*a*) Philosophy of universal world history, a course of lectures delivered by Hegel in the winter semester of 1822–3, from the notes of *von Griesheim*. The author is the well-known military writer Gustav von Griesheim, who was born in 1798 and died in 1854 as Major General and Commandant of Koblenz (cf. *Allgemeine deutsche Biographie*, vol. 9, pp. 665ff.). His notes, already used by the first editors, fill two volumes; they are a most painstakingly written, extremely neat and eminently legible fair copy, every line of which bears witness to the diligence of the copyist. It cannot, of course, be demonstrated with complete certainty that the original text of Hegel's lectures has been preserved in full throughout. It is therefore particularly fortunate that at least the beginning of this same series has survived in a second copy, which is as follows:

(*b*) The philosophical history of the world. (The heading supplies no further information.) The notes are by *Hauptmann von Kehler*. No year is specified, but a comparison with von Griesheim's notes leaves no doubt whatsoever that both sets were based on the same lectures delivered in the winter semester of 1822–3. The days of individual lectures are also noted.

This set of notes fills only 23 quarto pages. Since the disposition of Hegel's lectures in this first Berlin series differs sharply from that of his final draft of the Introduction, those matters which are discussed in our edition in Chapter II, sections 2 and 3, are not dealt with until after the first two sections of Chapter III. This explains why Kehler's manuscript breaks off with a passage which does not appear until p. 133 in our edition, although the manuscript contains only the beginning of what was then the Introduction.

Kehler's notes are very hastily written, and are obviously the original version as copied down during Hegel's lectures. At the same time, they tally remarkably closely with the text of von Griesheim's notes; it can at most be said that a few turns of phrase are more vividly preserved than in the latter. It was very easy to construct a unified whole from these two texts.

(*c*) Philosophy of world history, from Hegel's lectures. Winter semester 1824–5. From the notes of *Hauptmann von Kehler*. The writer of the previous notes has in this case followed the lectures of the winter semester 1824–5 up to the middle of February. His hand is even more hasty than on the previous occasion, and is for the most part extremely difficult to decipher; but, at the same time, the original character of Hegel's mode of expression is incomparably well preserved. The painful task of deciphering these indistinct characters was richly rewarded by the joy of discovering a completely untapped and freshly flowing source of Hegel's deliberations from the period at which the great thinker was at the height of his powers.

(*d*) Philosophy of world history. Copied from Professor Hegel's lectures by *Stieve*. Berlin 1826–7.

The writer of these notes later attained eminence as a Privy Councillor in the Prussian Ministry of Education. He has not recorded Hegel's observations as fully as he might have done, but he does give an impression of the form which the lectures had assumed by the time of their third delivery, and supplies whole sections which are missing in the earlier series.

It was therefore possible to draw on students' notes from three separate years of Hegel's lecture course in compiling the present edition. Hegel subsequently repeated the course on two further occasions, in the winter semesters of 1828–9 and 1830–1, limiting it on the latter occasion to 'Part One of the Philosophy of World History'. As Karl Hegel informs us in his preface to the second edition of the lectures in Hegel's collected works, Hegel reduced his basic argument in length in these last years in favour of a more detailed historical survey. We may therefore assume that the loss occasioned by the absence of notes from the last two courses is less serious in the case of the Introduction than in that of the historical survey which follows it.

Few modifications were necessary to the wording of the notes. They obviously give a faithful rendering of Hegel's personal idiom, and what they may lack in polish is compensated for by the vigour and conciseness of the language. When Gans first edited the lectures, he saw his task as one of transforming a series of 'lectures' into a 'book'. He consequently tried to impart a more elegant form to Hegel's discourse; but it is evident that Hegel's own peculiar style has been unnecessarily diluted in the process. Today, our main interest is of course to obtain as accurate an image of Hegel's lectures as possible. It was therefore the duty of the present editor to alter the wording of the lecture notes only in those instances where grammatical or stylistic errors had intruded. Although there are some repetitions, few readers of this edition will presume to dismiss any sections of it as superfluous.

The only occasion on which such doubts could arise is in the discussion of the geographical basis of world history. Even the editor had to ask himself here whether the whole corpus of ethnographical information contained in the lecture notes really ought to be included in a contemporary edition, for much of it must appear antiquated today. It was finally decided to include it, not just for the sake of textual accuracy, but also on the grounds that information which may have lost its value as practical knowledge may still be of considerable value for an understanding of the way in which Hegel worked and thought. Hegel's wide reading, even in remote areas of learning, and his determination to come to terms with problems such as the historical role of America or the spiritual character of the natives of Africa, surely merit the attention even of present-day readers.

3. *The edition of the lectures in 'The Works of Hegel'*, vol. 9. The first edition was published by Gans in 1837, and the second, greatly enlarged edition – the Introduction in particular was much expanded – by Karl Hegel in 1840; a less accurate reprint of the latter was issued in 1848 as the third edition. The second edition must be regarded as the authoritative one. In 1907, a very good reprint of it was prepared for the Reclams Bibliothek series by Fritz Brunstäd; it is particularly distinguished for its more accurate presentation of the Introduction. It goes without saying that, wherever the lecture notes at the present editor's disposal contained passages parallel to those in the printed text, the text was corrected in the light of the notes in question. The editor can vouch for the authenticity of all those portions of the text in which the printed version was supplemented by manuscript material. But some sections remained for which no parallels could be found in the manuscript, and these are accordingly reproduced here exactly as they appeared in Hegel's collected works.

One further circumstance calls for mention. Gans had already remarked in the preface to his edition that he had at his disposal manuscripts in Hegel's hand, and that he had taken some material from them. We can only conclude that these were Hegel's own lecture notes. Besides, Karl Hegel assures us that the extensive additions he made to Gans's edition were not taken from the students' notes but from his father's own manuscripts. If we could assume from this that Hegel's deliberations in these manuscripts were already laid out in a more or less finished form, and were expressed in complete sentences with a coherent argument, we could then conclude that the passages added to the second edition of Hegel's works are the most reliable parts of that text. But until such time as Hegel's manuscripts come to light again, this assumption will have to be treated with scepticism. For, in the first place, we know from surviving manuscripts of Hegel that he was in the habit of collecting brief references, scattered notes, etc., for his lectures, and constructing the spoken version out of these; and secondly, comparison of various passages from the students' notes with the corresponding sections in Karl Hegel's edition clearly indicates that, on this occasion too, Hegel only gave concrete and adequate shape to his draft when he came to deliver the lecture itself. Consequently, in the case of those sections which could only be reproduced from the earlier edition, we must continue to suppose that they owe their precise formulation less to Hegel than to his original editors. And we must content ourselves with the knowledge that such sections are relatively few in number.

NOTES TO THE FIRST DRAFT
(1822 and 1828)

1 Karl Hegel's edition: 'compendium'.

2 Karl Hegel's edition: 'There are three possible ways of looking at history.'

3 Karl Hegel adds: 'It is impossible for one man to have seen everything for himself.'

4 This entire sentence is incoherent in Hegel's MS. Karl Hegel's edition reads instead: 'The historians bind together fleeting events and lay them up in the temple of Mnemosyne for everlasting life.' In the MS, the following words were added and later scored out: 'for it is one thing to have certain emotions, and quite another to present them poetically, i.e. creatively, to the consciousness.'

5 Lasson adds: 'Poems do not have historical truth or determinate reality as their content.'

6 Karl Hegel and Lasson add: 'The realm of perceived or perceptible reality affords a firmer foundation than the realm of transience from which such legends and poetic creations sprang; the latter lose their historical value as soon as nations have attained secure independence and mature individuality.'

7 The MS reads: 'they possess'.

8 Karl Hegel and Lasson add: 'Consider, for example, Herodotus, Thucydides, and Guicciardini' [the author of an *Istoria d'Italia* (1561), on which the historian Leopold von Ranke wrote].

9 The MS reads: 'He'.

10 Instead of this awkward sentence, Karl Hegel's edition has the following: 'And if, like Caesar, he is a member of the class of generals or statesmen, it is his *own* ends which he presents as history.' And Lasson adds the further elucidation: 'All this can also be applied to later epochs in history. In ages in which a nation's culture is far advanced, there are cultural differences within it which result from distinctions of social class. The writer, if he is to qualify as an original historian, must then be a member of the same class as those whose deeds he intends to describe, that is, a statesman or general.' Lasson then continues, following Karl Hegel's version and failing to notice the direct transition from the Zurich sheet to the Marbach sheet of the MS (cf. note 11 below): 'Yet although it has just been maintained that such historians do not reflect on their material but simply depict individuals and

227

nations in their own right, this would seem to be contradicted by the speeches which we read in Thucydides, for example, and of which we can confidently say that they were never delivered in the way he reports them.'

11 After this word, the Marbach MS begins.

12 Lasson adds: 'Men must be moved to action by speeches; and such speeches are an essential part of history.'

13 In the MS, this entire paragraph has been added in the margin.

14 This sentence too is a marginal addition in the MS.

15 The preceding passage does not appear in the edition of Lasson, who continues from the last paragraph as follows: 'They give us an insight into the reflections and principles of their age, making it unnecessary for the historian to add his own reflections. And even if he makes up such speeches himself, they are nevertheless speeches of his age, since he is himself part of the culture of his age. Thus even if Thucydides did elaborate on the speeches of Pericles, for example, they are still in no way alien to Pericles.'

16 The MS continues: 'apart from what he otherwise', and breaks off.

17 Marginal addition: 'We must distinguish between these and the *bibles* of nations; every nation has a book of this kind – the Bible, Homer.'

18 MS emendation from: 'have reached a high level'.

19 The three preceding sentences (from 'But such works') are supplied from notes in the margin of the manuscript – Karl Hegel, followed by Lasson, reads instead: 'In antiquity, these historians were necessarily great captains and statesmen; in the Middle Ages – if we except the bishops, who were at the centre of the business of state – there were certainly monks who wrote naive chronicles, but they were as isolated from the rest of their society as the ancient writers were immersed in theirs.'

20 Marginal note in MS: 'political consideration – life of the state'.

21 Marginal note in MS: '*α* Original [history] can cover only a *short period of time*. The need to survey the whole leads *β* to reflective history. *αα* Compendia, *ββ Counterpart.* – Imitation of original history merely superficial addition.'

22 Karl Hegel adds: 'In short, for what we call *universal history*.'

23 The following passage is scored out in the MS, but restored (or reintroduced from notes made by students in one of the years before 1828) by Karl Hegel and Lasson: 'Compilations of this kind include world-historical compendia at large, and more specific works such as *Livy's Roman History*, Diodorus Siculus etc., and *Johannes von Müller's* History of the Swiss. If well executed, they are highly meritorious, and indeed quite indispensable. But it is impossible to lay down general rules or definitions of how they should be written.'

24 Johannes von Müller (1752–1809), *History of the Swiss Confederation [Die Geschichte der Schweizerischen Eidgenossenschaft]*, vol. 1, Leipzig, 1786; vols. 2 and 3, 1786–95; vol. 4 and § 1 of vol. 5, 1805–8. Complete revised edition, Leipzig, 1826.

25 Aegidius Tschudi (1505–72), *Swiss Chronicle* [*Schweizerchronik*], Basel, 1734–6, 2 vols. – This work by the politician Tschudi reproduces a large number of now vanished documents which J. von Müller uses.

26 Marginal note: 'not just quantitative reductions, i.e. to general representations, by means of reflection'.

27 *Not* 'Ränken', as in Lasson's edition – this, by the way, is the only occasion in Hegel's works where he mentions the name of the great historian (whose career was then only beginning); cf. note 8 above.

28 In the margin, referred by symbols to this point in the text, are the following words: 'In general, *rational* history, αα *a totality of interests* – as the totality of a *state*, an epoch-making event, a war, or even of an individual – is the *object*. ββ The object here is also a *present* interest, but the *immediacy of tone*, of feeling, of external vividness [*Anschaulichkeit*] in circumstantial details and the careers of single individuals as such [is] dispensed with.'

29–31 In the course of major revisions to the MS, these words have been unintentionally deleted or not restored.

32 Above this is written: 'At first *primitive*, enclosed *nation*, as such [not an object], but only in so far as it succeeds in constituting a state. What it undertakes as a state, a national whole in itself, is a universal end of reason.'

33 Below this is written: 'Other individuals like *Napoleon* only momentary. Essential dependence.'

34 Parenthetical addition: 'French [above: Germans] more satisfying, – *this is how it was* –.'

35 Karl Hegel's edition reads instead: 'reflected'.

36 The bracketed passages here and in the following pages occur only in Lasson's edition; the rest of the text is almost identical in Karl Hegel's and Lasson's versions. In doubtful cases, I have followed the text of Karl Hegel.

37 Johannes von Müller, *Twenty-four Books of General Histories, with Special Reference to European Man* [*Vierundzwanzig Bücher allgemeiner Geschichten, besonders der europäischen Menschheit*], Tübingen, 1810, 3 vols.

38 Johannes von Müller, *Letters to Bonstetten* [*Briefe an Bonstetten*], 1809; *Letters to Woltmann* [*Briefe an Woltmann*], 1811; *Müller's Letters to his Oldest Friend* [*Briefe Müllers an seinen ältesten Freund*], ed. Füssli, Zurich, 1812.

39 Montesquieu, *De l'esprit des lois*, Geneva, 1748, 2 vols.; German translation, Halle, 1829, 3 vols.

40 Barthold Georg Niebuhr, *Roman History* [*Römische Geschichte*], Berlin, 1811–32, 3 vols.

41 Lasson reads: 'of bringing *the* present into the past', and Karl Hegel reads 'of achieving a present in history'.

42 Instead of the preceding paragraph Karl Hegel has the following words: 'In our times, this variety of conceptual history has been more emphasised and become more highly developed.'

43 Gustav Hugo (1764–1844) produced a German edition of Gibbon's *Survey of Roman Law* [*Übersicht des römischen Rechts*], Göttingen, 1789.
44 Karl Friedrich Eichhorn (1781–1854), *Political and Legal History of Germany* [*Deutsche Staats- und Rechtsgeschichte*], Göttingen, 1808–23, 4 parts.

NOTES TO THE SECOND DRAFT (1830)

1 The MS reads: 'in the correct relationship'.
2 Marginal addition: 'The preface to every new work on history – and then again in the introductions to reviews of such works – [brings a] new theory.'
3 Marginal note:
'α general concept,
β determinate,
γ mode of development.'
4 Marginal note: 'α reason.'
5 Marginal note: 'β faith – survey, result.'
6 Marginal note: 'γ historical procedure.'
7 Marginal note: 'δ apprehend accurately.'
8 The MS reads: 'thinking and brings'.
9 As, for example, in Niebuhr's remarks on priestly rule in his *Roman History* [*Römische Geschichte*], or in [Karl Ottfried] Müller's *The Dorians* [*Die Dorier*; 2 vols., 1824].
10 MS: 'on'.
11 Marginal note: 'ε Two points – Anax.'
12 The MS reads: 'this exposition of the earliest'.
13 The MS reads: 'of the inadequacy'.
14 Marginal note: 'ζ providence.'
15 Marginal note: 'η transition: plan of providence.'
16 Marginal note: 'This – understanding of our time.'
17 Lasson adds here the following (obviously corrupt) sentence: 'This negative element is rejected by thinking reason, which looks instead for an affirmative end.'
18 The MS reads: 'it'.
19 Marginal note: 'spirit *higher* than nature'.
20 Marginal note: 'α general destiny, β visible *means* of fulfilling this destiny, γ complete realisation, the state.'
21 Marginal note: 'Education of the human race [Translator's note: Hegel here quotes the title of Lessing's famous sketch of history as the progress of human reason] – to what? – to freedom – man is educated to it – but not directly – the result.'
22 The MS reads: 'nature merely'.

23 Marginal note: 'combination of particularity and generality in which the former becomes the means.'

24 Marginal note: 'one-sided (philosophy).'

25 Marginal note: 'Individual will.'

26 Marginal note: 'Will and aims of the individual.'

27 Marginal note: '*Geg. Hon.* [Translator's note: I have not been able to decipher – and hence translate – this abbreviation of Hegel's] – satisfaction of my own spirit – stubbornly pursued.'

28 The MS reads: 'needs'.

29 Marginal note: 'Nowadays, private interests are linked with the general interest.'

30 Marginal note: 'Reality at first only as nature.'

31 The MS reads: 'a further'.

32 Cf. Hegel's *Phänomenologie des Geistes*, ed. Johannes Hoffmeister, 1952, p. 468.

33 Marginal note: 'see Kant.'

34 The MS reads: 'have'.

35 Marginal note: 'Ethicality in its true form – in the state.'

36 The MS reads: 'his'.

37 The MS reads: 'his'.

38 Marginal note: 'Deceive the people – Goethe – Homer – war waged.'

39 The MS reads: 'of what contradicts'.

40 1651–1715. Archbishop of Cambrai. He deals with the education of princes in *Les aventures de Télémaque* (1699).

41 1759–1834. The founder of the French National Guard (1789), leader of the Feuillants during the Revolution, in exile from 1792 to 1797, thereafter in Paris, supporter of Louis Philippe in 1830.

42 The MS reads: 'are'.

43 Lasson substitutes for this: 'after which'.

44 Hegel erroneously prefixed the letter 'b' to this paragraph.

45 The MS adds: 'from its fetters'.

46 F. von Schlegel, *Philosophy of History* [*Philosophie der Geschichte*], I, 44 (first edition).

47 We have this interest to thank for many valuable discoveries in Oriental literature, and for the renewed study of previously accumulated treasures relating to the life, mythology, religion, and history of ancient Asia. In those Catholic countries which enjoy an advanced degree of culture, governments have ceased to resist the demands of the intellect and the need to ally themselves with scholarship and philosophy. In an eloquent and impressive fashion, the Abbé Lamennais[1] has reckoned it among the criteria of the true religion that it must be universal, i.e. catholic, and the oldest in point of time, and the *Congrégation*[2] in France has laboured zealously and diligently to ensure that such assertions should no longer be regarded as mere pulpit tirades and proclamations of authority, as was generally accepted

in the past. The religion of **Buddha** – a god incarnate – which commands so widespread a following, has attracted particular attention. The Indian Trimūrti and the Chinese abstraction of the Trinity are clearer in content, however. The scholars **Abel Rémusat**[3] and **Saint Martin**[4] have conducted the most praiseworthy investigations into Chinese literature, and thence into that of Mongolia; and if it were possible, these would be pursued into Tibetan literature in turn. And Baron **von Eckstein**,[5] in his own peculiar way (i.e. with the help of superficial conceptions and mannerisms borrowed from German natural philosophy in the style of **Friedrich von Schlegel**, which, although employed with greater ingenuity than in Schlegel's case, nevertheless made not the slightest impression in France), has argued in support of this primitive Catholicism in his journal *Le Catholique*; in particular, he has gained the government's support for the scholarly projects of the *Congrégation*, with the result that it has even commissioned expeditions to the Orient to discover new treasures in the hope of obtaining further information regarding its more profound doctrines, especially on the remoter antiquity and sources of Buddhism, thereby furthering the cause of Catholicism by this circuitous but scientifically interesting method.

[1] Lamennais, 1782–1854, leader of the Catholic democrats in France and editor of the journal *L'Avenir*, 1830–2.

[2] Hegel refers to the *Congregatio de propaganda fide*, founded on 21 June 1622 by Pope Gregory XV, usually known simply as the Propaganda.

[3] Rémusat, Jean Pierre Abel, 1788–1832, Professor of Sinology at the Collège de France.

[4] Saint-Martin, Marquis de, 1743–1803, theosophist; author of *L'homme de désir* (1790) and *De l'esprit des choses* (1800).

[5] Eckstein, Ferdinand Baron von, 1790–1861, partisan of the Restoration and of Ultramontanism, historiographer to the French Foreign Ministry until 1830.

48 Bailly [*Histoire de l'astronomie ancienne*, 1775] has written with superficial knowledge on the astronomy of the Indians. In our own age, it has admittedly been shown, e.g. by Lambert [*Cosmological Letters on the Constitution of the Universe* (*Kosmologische Briefe über die Einrichtung des Weltbaues*), 1761], that the Indians did possess some knowledge of astronomy; for example, the Brahmans predicted eclipses of the sun by means of unreflectingly applied formulas. But the spirit which once inhabited these formulas (albeit in a purely mechanical fashion) has long ceased to tenant them. In fact, the methods they have inherited from tradition do not possess that excellence with which they were formerly credited.

49 The MS reads instead: 'b. Process of World History.'

50 The MS reads: 'it'.

51 Karl Hegel amends this to 'logic'.

52 Marginal note: 'Love.'

NOTES TO APPENDIX

1 *Metaphysics*, A, 2, 982b.
2 Ritter, Karl, 1779–1859, the founder of scientific geography.
3 Pradt, Dominique Dufour de, 1759–1837, Archbishop of Malines from 1808, politician of varying leanings, published his *Mémoires historiques sur la révolution d'Espagne* in 1816.
4 From the lecture course of 1824–5.
5 Herodotus II, c. 33; γόητας εἶναι ἅπαντας.
6 Giovanni Antonio Cavazzi, *Istorica descrizione dei tre regni Congo, Matamba, Angola*. Bologna, 1687 (quotations here are from the edition published in Milan in 1690).
7 Cavazzi, p. 55.
8 James Bruce, *Travels to Discover the Sources of the Nile*, 1768–73.
9 T. E. Bowdich, *Mission from Cape Coast Castle to Ashantee*. London, 1819. 2 vols.
10 Resident in Kumassi in 1817.
11 Cavazzi, pp. 149ff.
12 Lasson's edition reads 'results'.
13 On the previous holograph manuscript to the Introduction, cf. the present editor's preface.

SUGGESTIONS FOR FURTHER
READING

The following bibliography is limited as strictly as possible to works dealing with the text to which it is here appended: it contains only literature on Hegel's *Lectures on the Philosophy of World History*, even in cases where this is not immediately evident from the titles listed.

Relevant sections from comprehensive studies of Hegel and from other works of a wider scope have also been included. But works dealing with problems of the philosophical theory of history or historicity with reference to Hegel's other writings (particularly the *Logic* and the *Phenomenology of Spirit*) are omitted, as are all studies which discuss the philosophy of history in the light of the *Lectures on Aesthetics*, the *Lectures on the Philosophy of Religion*, and the *Lectures on the History of Philosophy*.

Inevitably, no absolutely clear distinction can be made in this bibliography between the *Philosophy of History* on the one hand, and the political theories of the *Philosophy of Right* and the doctrines of the *Encyclopaedia* concerning the objective spirit on the other. For in the latter work Hegel assigns the philosophy of world history its place within his system, and in the former he discusses it in outline (cf. *Elements of the Philosophy of Right*, §§ 341–60, and *Encyclopaedia of the Philosophical Sciences*, third edition, §§ 548–52).

The following list is intended as an aid to further study. As such, it does not claim to provide an exhaustive bibliography on the theme in question. Above all, a complete bibliography would have to include further references to works of non-German origin.

The titles are listed in chronological sequence. In general, this arrangement gives some impression of the history of interpretations of Hegel's philosophy of history, and, in individual cases, it at once informs the reader of the chronological relationship between a given title and other relevant works.

[Buhl:] *Hegel's Lehre vom Staat und seine Philosophie der Geschichte in ihren Hauptresultaten*. Berlin 1837. 99 pp.

Chalybäus, Heinrich Moritz: 'Philosophie der Geschichte und Geschichte der Philosophie. In Bezug auf Hegels Vorlesungen über die Philosophie der Geschichte [etc.]'. In: *Zeitschrift für Philosophie und spekulative Theologie*, 1 (1837), pp. 301–8.

Mager, Karl W. E.: *Brief an eine Dame über die Hegelsche Philosophie*. Berlin 1837. pp. 52–8.

Michelet, Carl Ludwig: *Geschichte der letzten Systeme der Philosophie in Deutschland von Kant bis Hegel*, Pt 2. Berlin 1838. pp. 791–801.

Binder: [Review:] 'Hegels Vorlesungen über die Philosophie der Geschichte'. In: *Jahrbücher für wissenschaftliche Kritik*. Jg. 1839. pp. 801–24.

Rosenkranz, Karl: 'Hegel's Vorlesungen über die Philosophie der Geschichte'. In: *Hallische Jahrbücher für deutsche Wissenschaft und Kunst*, 1 (1838), pp. 132–56. See also: Rosenkranz: *Kritische Erläuterungen des Hegel'schen Systems*. Königsberg 1840. Reprinted Hildersheim 1963. pp. 149–77: 'Hegel's Philosophie der Geschichte'.

Weiße, Christian Hermann: [Review:] 'Hegels Vorlesungen über die Philosophie der Geschichte'. In: *Blätter für literarische Unterhaltung*, Jg. 1840, No. 69–72.

Ulrici, Hermann: *Ueber Princip und Methode der Hegelschen Philosophie. Ein Beitrag zur Kritik derselben*. Halle 1841. pp. 195–208.

Rosenkranz, Karl: *Georg Wilhelm Friedrich Hegel's Leben*. Berlin 1844. Reprinted Darmstadt 1963. pp. 373–9: 'Die Philosophie der Geschichte und der Orient'.

Staudenmaier, Franz Anton: *Darstellung und Kritik des Hegelschen Systems. Aus dem Standpunkte der christlichen Philosophie*. Mainz 1844. Reprinted Frankfurt a. M. 1966. pp. 563–640: 'Die Philosophie der Geschichte'.

Springer, Anton H.: *Die Hegel'sche Geschichtsanschauung. Eine historische Denkschrift*. Tübingen 1848. VI, 93 pp.

Haym, Rudolf: *Hegel und seine Zeit. Vorlesungen über Entstehung und Entwickelung, Wesen und Werth der Hegel'schen Philosophie*. Berlin 1857. Second edition 1927. Reprint [of the first edition] Hildesheim 1962. pp. 443–53: 'Geschichtsphilosophie'.

Rosenkranz, Karl: *Hegel als deutscher Nationalphilosoph*. Leipzig 1870. Reprinted Darmstadt 1966. pp. 163–74: 'Die Philosophie der Geschichte'.

Bahnsen, Julius: *Zur Philosophie der Geschichte. Eine kritische Besprechung des Hegel-Hartmann'schen Evolutionismus aus Schopenhauer'schen Principien*. Berlin 1872. IV, 86 pp.

Dieterich, K.: 'Buckle und Hegel. Ein Beitrag zur Charakteristik englischer und deutscher Geschichtsphilosophie'. In: *Preußische Jahrbücher*, 32 (1873), pp. 257–302 and 463–81.

Stieglitz, Theodor: *Paralogismen in Hegel's Philosophie der Geschichte*. (Prachatitz:) Verlag des Realgymnasiums (1878), pp. 1–16. Prachatitz, k. k. Staats-Realgym., Progr. 1878.

Levi, Giuseppe: *La dottrina dello stato di Giorgio F. G. Hegel*. [Vol.] 2. Trieste 1881. pp. 240–57.

Morris, G. S.: *Hegel's Philosophy of the State and of History*. Chicago 1887; London 1888. 306 pp.

Barth, Paul: *Die Geschichtsphilosophie Hegel's und der Hegelianer bis auf Marx und Hartmann. Ein kritischer Versuch.* Leipzig 1890. 148 pp.

Tönnies, Ferdinand: 'Neuere Philosophie der Geschichte: Hegel, Marx, Comte'. In: *Archiv für Geschichte der Philosophie*, 7 (1894), pp. 486–515.

Barth, Paul: 'Zu Hegels und Marx' Geschichtsphilosophie'. In: *Archiv für Geschichte der Philosophie*, 8 (1895), pp. 241–55 and 315–35.

Fischer, Kuno: *Hegels Leben, Werke und Lehre*, vol. 2. Heidelberg 1901. Second edition 1911. Reprinted Darmstadt 1963. pp. 740–813: 'Philosophie der Geschichte'.

Rubinstein, Moses: *Die logischen Grundlagen des Hegelschen Systems und das Ende der Geschichte.* Halle 1906. 73 pp. Freiburg i. B., Phil. Diss. 1906.

Brunstäd, Friedrich: 'Vorrede'. In: G. W. F. Hegel: *Vorlesungen über die Philosophie der Geschichte.* Leipzig 1907. pp. 3–26.
Completely revised in the second edition, Leipzig 1924. This version is reprinted in: Brunstäd: *Gesammelte Aufsätze und kleinere Schriften.* Berlin 1957. pp. 48–68.

Croce, Benedetto: *Ciò che è vivo e ciò che è morto della filosofia di Hegel. Studio critico seguito da un saggio di bibliografia Hegeliana.* Bari 1907. pp. 129–43: 'La storia (Idea di una filosofia della storia)'.
German version: *Lebendiges und Totes in Hegels Philosophie.* Heidelberg 1909. pp. 109–21: 'Die Geschichte (Idee einer Philosophie der Geschichte)'.
French version: *Ce qui est vivant et ce qui est mort de la philosophie de Hegel.* Paris 1910. pp. 109–21: 'L'histoire (Idée d'une philosophie de l'histoire)'.

Kaulfuß, Otto: *Die Grundprobleme der Geschichtsphilosophie mit besonderer Berücksichtigung der Hegelschen Anschauungen.* Bromberg 1907. 78 pp.

Brunstäd, Friedrich: *Untersuchungen zu Hegels Geschichtstheorie* 1. 46 pp. [printed in part]. Berlin, Phil. Diss. 1909.

Dittmann, Friedrich: *Der Begriff des Volksgeistes bei Hegel. Zugleich ein Beitrag zur Geschichte des Begriffs der Entwicklung im 19. Jahrhundert.* Leipzig 1909. 109 pp. Leipzig, Phil. Diss. 1908.

Mayer-Moreau, Karl: *Hegels Socialphilosophie.* Tübingen 1910. pp. 77–83: 'Philosophie der Geschichte'.

Lasson, Georg: 'Zur Staats- und Geschichtsphilosophie Hegels'. In: *Zeitschrift für Politik*, 4 (1911), pp. 581–7.

Roques, Paul: *Hegel. Sa vie et ses œuvres.* Paris 1912. pp. 269–83: 'Philosophie de l'histoire'.

Dittmann, Friedrich: 'Die Geschichtsphilosophie Comtes und Hegels. Ein Vergleich'. In: *Vierteljahrsschrift für wissenschaftliche Philosophie und Soziologie*, 38 (1914), pp. 281–312; 39 (1915), pp. 38–81.

Cunow, Heinrich: *Die Marxsche Geschichts-, Gesellschafts- und Staatstheorie*, Vol. 1. Munich 1920. pp. 224–44: 'Hegels Geschichts- und Staatsphilosophie'.

Lasson, Georg: *Hegel als Geschichtsphilosoph.* Leipzig 1920. VI, 180 pp. (Phil. Bibl. 171 e.)

Rosenzweig, Franz: *Hegel und der Staat*, Vol. 2: *Weltepochen*. Munich and Berlin 1920. Reprinted Aalen 1962. pp. 174–84.

Brunswig, Alfred: *Hegel*. Munich 1922. (Philosophische Reihe, Vol. 54) pp. 200–12: 'Die Philosophie der Weltgeschichte'.

Leese, Kurt: *Die Geschichtsphilosophie Hegels auf Grund der neu erschlossenen Quellen untersucht und dargestellt*. Berlin 1922. 313 pp.

Dannenberg, Friedrich: *Der Geist der Hegelschen Geschichtsphilosophie*. Langensalza 1923. 48 pp. (Fr. Manns Pädagog. Magazin, H. 919)

Koeper, Otto: *Lotzes geschichtsphilosophische Auseinandersetzung mit Hegel*. VI, 77 pp. [MS]. Münster, Phil. Diss. 1923.

Blaschke, Friedrich: *Hegels System und seine Geschichtsphilosophie*. Crimmitschau 1924. 35 pp.

'Einführung in Hegels Geschichtsphilosophie'. In: *Württembergsche Lehrerzeitung*, 83 (1924).

Meinecke, Friedrich: *Die Idee der Staatsraison in der neueren Geschichte*. Munich and Berlin 1924. pp. 427–60: 'Hegel'.

Simon, Ernst: *Rankes Verhältnis zu Hegel*. VII, 171 pp. [MS]. Heidelberg, Phil. Diss. 1924. [printed 1928, see below].

Mehlis, Georg: 'Die Geschichtsphilosophie Hegels und Comtes'. In: *Jahrbuch für Soziologie*, 3 (1927), pp. 91–110.

Breysig, Kurt: *Vom geschichtlichen Werden. Umrisse einer zukünftigen Geschichtslehre*, vol. 2: *Die Macht des Gedankens in der Geschichte in Auseinandersetzung mit Marx und mit Hegel*. Stuttgart and Berlin 1926. pp. 166–420.

Breysig, Kurt: 'Zeit und Begriff als Ordnungsformen des geschichtlichen Geschehens'. In: *Philosophischer Anzeiger*, 1 (1926), pp. 427–77; see esp. pp. 431–45: 'Zeit und Geschichte bei Hegel'.

Also in: Breysig: *Gesellschaftslehre. Geschichtslehre*. 1958. pp. 127–39.

Herrmann, Wilhelm von: *Gott in der Geschichte. Eine Untersuchung des Hegelschen Gottesbegriffes auf Grund seiner Geschichtsphilosophie*. Berlin, Theol. Diss. 1926.

Kronenberg, M.: [Review of] Hegel: *Die Vernunft in der Geschichte*. In: *Kantstudien*, 33 (1928), pp. 265–8.

Kupfer, Johannes: *Die Auffassung des Sokrates in Hegels Geschichtsphilosophie*, III, 46 pp. Leipzig, Phil. Diss. 1927.

Löwith, Karl: 'Burckhardts Stellung zu Hegels Geschichtsphilosophie'. In: *Deutsche Vierteljahresschrift für Literaturwissenschaft und Geistesgeschichte*, 6 (1928), pp. 702–41.

Simon, Ernst: *Ranke und Hegel*. Munich and Berlin 1928. (Historische Zeitschrift. Beiheft 15) [= revised version of the dissertation of 1924, above]. Particularly pp. 121–94: 'Rankes Ideenlehre und Hegels Philosophie der Geschichte'.

Hartmann, Nicolai: *Die Philosophie des deutschen Idealismus*, Part 2: *Hegel*. Berlin and Leipzig 1929. pp. 350–65: 'Philosophie der Geschichte'. Second edition Berlin 1960. pp. 539–52.

Kayser, Ulrich: *Das Problem der Zeit in der Geschichtsphilosophie Hegels*. 88 pp. Berlin, Phil. Diss. 1930.

Moog, Willy: *Hegel und die Hegelsche Schule*. Munich 1930. (Geschichte der Philosophie in Einzeldarstellungen. 32/33) pp. 345–54: 'Weltgeschichte'.

Plenge, Johann: *Hegel und die Weltgeschichte. Ein Vortrag*. Münster/W. 1931, 72 pp. (Published by the Forschungsinstitut für Organisationslehre und Soziologie bei der Universität Münster. Kleine Schriften 3)

van den Bergh van Eysinga, G. A.: *Hegel*. 's Gravenhage 1931. Second impression Den Haag 1960. pp. 131–58. 'Hegel als historisch denker'.

Wittfogel, K. A.: 'Hegel über China'. In: *Unter dem Banner des Marxismus*, 5 (1931), pp. 346–62.

Lenin, V. I.: *Aus dem philosophischen Nachlaß*. Edited by V. Adoratski, German edition by M. Furschtschik. Vienna and Berlin 1932. Reprinted Berlin 1949 and in subsequent years. pp. 165–77: 'Zur Kritik der Vorlesungen Hegels über die Philosophie der Geschichte'.

Mell, Josef: *Die Geschichtsphilosophie Deutingers und Hegels. Ein Vergleich*. 80 pp. Bonn, Phil. Diss. 1933.

Plachte, Kurt. 'Die Schicksalsidee in Hegels Philosophie der Geschichte'. In: *Logos*, 22 (1933), pp. 273–94.

Günzel, Karl: *Der Begriff der Freiheit bei Hegel und Lorenz von Stein*. Leipzig, Phil. Diss. 1934. pp. 23–50: 'Das Werden der Freiheit des Geistes'.

Heimsoeth, Heinz: 'Politik und Moral in Hegels Geschichtsphilosophie'. In: *Blätter für Deutsche Philosophie*, 8 (1934–5), pp. 127–48.
Also in: Heimsoeth: *Studien zur Philosophiegeschichte*. Cologne 1961. (Kantstudien. Ergänzungshefte 82) pp. 22–42.
Spanish version: 'Politica y moral en la filosofia de la historia de Hegel'. In: *Revista de Occidente*, 46 (1934), pp. 113–49.

Flöter, Hans H. F.: *Die Begründung der Geschichtlichkeit der Geschichte in der Philosophie des deutschen Idealismus (von Herder bis Hegel)*. Halle/S. 1936. 152 pp. Halle, Phil. Diss. 1936.

Stich, Herta: *Von Herders 'Ideen zur Philosophie des Geschichte der Menschheit' über Kant, Fichte, Schelling, bis zu Hegels 'Vorlesungen über die Philosophie der Geschichte'. Ein Beitrag zur Philosophie der Geschichte*. [MS]. Vienna, Phil. Diss. 1936.

Thyssen, Johannes: *Geschichte der Geschichtsphilosophie*. Berlin 1936. pp. 69–86: 'Hegel'. Third edition Bonn 1960. pp. 69–86.

Bülow, Friedrich: 'Hegels Staats- und Geschichtsphilosophie als Gärstoff der abendländischen Geistesentwicklung'. In: *Zeitschrift für die Gesamten Staatswissenschaften*, 100 (1940), pp. 457–76.

Müller, Gustav Emil: *Hegel über Sittlichkeit und Geschichte*. Munich 1940. pp. 85–100: 'Die Geschichte'.

Löwith, Karl: *Von Hegel bis Nietzsche*. Zürich/New York 1941. pp. 283–312: 'Hegels Philosophie der Geschichte und Goethes Anschauung des Geschehens der Welt'.

From the second edition, under the title: *Von Hegel zu Nietzche. Der revolutionäre Bruch im Denken des neunzehnten Jahrhunderts. Marx und Kierkegaard.* Stuttgart [simultaneously in Zurich] 1953 etc. pp. 232–51. Also in English, Italian and Japanese translation.

Marcuse, Herbert: *Reason and Revolution. Hegel and the Rise of Social Theory.* London and New York 1941. Second edition 1954. pp. 224–48: 'The philosophy of history'.

German version: *Vernunft und Revolution.* Neuwied and Berlin 1962. (Soziologische Texte, 13) pp. 200–20: 'Die Philosophie der Geschichte'.

Vanni Rovighi, Sofia: *La concezione hegeliana della storia.* Milan 1942. VIII, 228 pp. (Pubblicazioni dell'Università Cattolica del S. Cuore. Ser. 1,35)

Hoffman, Rudolf: *Die Weltgeschichte und der deutsche Geist.* Munich and Berlin 1943. pp. 97–120: 'Hegel'.

Sistig, Peter: *Die geschichtsphilosophischen Beziehungen von Görres zu Hegel. Ein Beitrag zur Geschichtsphilosophie der Romantik.* 123 pp. [MS]. Bonn, Phil. Diss. 1943.

Collingwood, R. G.: *The Idea of History.* Oxford 1946. pp. 113–22: 'Hegel'; pp. 122–6: 'Hegel and Marx'.

German version: *Philosophie der Geschichte.* Stuttgart 1955. pp. 122–31: 'Hegel'; pp. 131–5: 'Hegel und Marx'.

Hyppolite, Jean: *Introduction à la philosophie de l'histoire de Hegel.* Paris 1948. 98 pp. (Bibliothèque philosophique)

Steinbüchel, Theodor: 'Ranke und Hegel'. In: *Große Geschichtsdenker.* Tübingen and Stuttgart 1949. pp. 173–215.

Kaufmann, Walter: 'The Hegel Myth and its Method'. In: *The Philosophical Review,* 60 (1951), pp. 459–86.

German version: 'Hegel – Legende und Wirklichkeit'. In: *Zeitschrift für philosophische Forschung,* 10 (1956), pp. 191–226; see esp. pp. 206–14: 'Geschichte. Große Männer und Gleichheit'.

Plebe, Armando: *Hegel. Filosofo della storia.* Turin [1951]. VII, 148 pp. (Studi e ricerche di storia della filosofia, 7)

Schmitz, Gert: *Die List der Vernunft,* 135 pp. Zurich, Phil. Diss. 1951.

Bloch, Ernst: *Subjekt – Objekt. Erläuterungen zu Hegel.* Berlin 1952. pp. 212–29: 'Hegels Philosophie der Geschichte'. Second enlarged edition Frankfurt 1962. pp. 226–44.

Litt, Theodor: *Hegel. Versuch einer kritischen Erneuerung.* Heidelberg 1953. Second impression 1961. pp. 95–159: 'Der objektive Geist'.

Löwith, Karl: *Weltgeschichte und Heilsgeschehen. Die theologischen Voraussetzungen der Geschichtsphilosophie.* Stuttgart 1953. Fourth edition 1961. (Urban-Bücher, 2) pp. 55–61: 'Hegel'. [The book first appeared in English under the title: *Meaning in History.* Chicago 1949.]

Liebrucks, Bruno: 'Zur Theorie des Weltgeistes in Theodor Litts Hegelbuch'. In: *Kant-Studien,* 46 (1954–5), pp. 230–67.

Ritter, Joachim: *Hegel und die französische Revolution*. Cologne and Opladen 1957. (Arbeitsgemeinschaft für Forschung des Landes Nordrhein-Westfalen. Geisteswissenschaften. No. 63) pp. 19–22. Reprinted Frankfurt a. M. 1965. (edition Suhrkamp, 114) pp. 24–30.
French version: 'Hegel et la révolution française'. In: *Archives de philosophie*, 26 (1963), pp. 323–56; 516–42.

Schultz, Werner: 'Der Sinn der Geschichte bei Hegel und Goethe'. In: *Archiv für Kulturgeschichte*, 39 (1957), pp. 209–27.
Also in: Schultz: *Theologie und Wirklichkeit*. Kiel 1969. pp. 128–46.

Wein, Hermann: *Realdialektik. Von hegelscher Dialektik zu dialektischer Anthropologie*. Munich 1957. pp. 23–38: 'Hegels Metaphysik der Geschichte'.

Adams, Alfons: *Transzendenz der Erkenntnis und Eschatologie der Geschichte*. Münster 1958. pp. 68–102: 'Die idealistische Geschichtsmetaphysik Hegels'.

Cornelius, Alfred: *Die Geschichtslehre Victor Cousins. Unter besonderer Berücksichtigung des Hegelschen Einflusses*. 79 pp. Cologne, Phil. Diss. 1958.
Reprinted Geneva, Paris 1958. (Kölner romanistische Arbeiten. New Series, No. 14)

de Ruggiero, Guido: *Storia della Filosofia*. Pt. 8: *Hegel*. Bari 1958. pp. 220–40: 'La storia'.

Findley, John N.: *Hegel. A Re-Examination*. London/New York 1958. pp. 328–33: 'Philosophy of history'.

Schulin, Ernst: *Die weltgeschichtliche Erfassung des Orients bei Hegel und Ranke*. Göttingen 1958. x, 325 pp. (Veröffentlichungen des Max-Planck-Instituts für Geschichte, 2) Göttingen, Phil. Diss. 1958.

Beerling, R. F.: *De list der Rede in de Geschiedenisfilosofie van Hegel*. Arnhem 1959. 180 pp.

Massolo, Arturo: 'Per una lettura della "Filosofia della storia" di Hegel'. In: *Studi Urbinati*. Urbino. Nuova Serie B. 33 (1959), pp. 5–26.
Also in: Massolo: *La storia della filosofia come problema*. Florence 1967. pp. 171–92.

Glasenapp, Helmuth von: *Das Indienbild deutscher Denker*. Stuttgart 1960. pp. 39–60: 'Hegel'.

Kroner, Richard: 'Vom Sinn der Geschichte'. In: *Erkenntnis und Verantwortung. Festschrift für Theodor Litt*. Düsseldorf 1960. pp. 194–206.

Löwith, Karl: 'Mensch und Geschichte'. In: Löwith: *Gesammelte Abhandlungen. Zur Kritik der geschichtlichen Existenz*. Stuttgart 1960. pp. 152–78.

Walentik, Leonhard: *Der Begriff des Endzweckes der Weltgeschichte bei Hegel*. 102 pp. [MS]. Vienna, Phil. Diss. 1960.

Nitsche, Roland: 'Von Hegel bis Droysen. Wandlungen der deutschen Geschichtsauffassung'. In: *Der Monat*, 13 (1960–1), No. 145, pp. 59–68.

Fessard, Gaston: 'Attitude ambivalente de Hegel en face de l'histoire'. In: *Archives de philosophie*, 24 (1961), pp. 207–41.
Also in: *Hegel-Jahrbuch*. Edited by W. R. Beyer. 1961, first half-volume, pp. 25–60.

Gulian, C. Jonescu: 'Les idées de Hegel sur le sens de l'histoire et ses lois'. In: *Hegel-Jahrbuch*. 1961, first half-volume, pp. 61–72.

Litt, Theodor: 'Hegels Geschichtsphilosophie'. In: G. W. F. Hegel: *Vorlesungen über die Philosophie der Geschichte*. Stuttgart 1961. pp. 3–34.

Mann, Golo: 'Die Grundprobleme der Geschichtsphilosophie von Plato bis Hegel'. In: *Der Sinn der Geschichte*. Edited by L. Reinisch. Munich 1961. pp. 11–30.

Seeberger, Wilhelm: *Hegel oder die Entwicklung des Geistes zur Freiheit*. Stuttgart 1961. pp. 561–8. 'Die Weltgeschichte und der Weltgeist'.

Avineri, Shlomo: 'Die Endlichkeit der Geschichte nach Hegel'. [Hebr.] In: *Jubiläumsbuch des hebräischen Gymnasiums*. Jerusalem 1962. pp. 109–14.

Goldstein, L. J.: 'The meaning of "State" in Hegel's "Philosophy of history"'. In: *Philosophical Quarterly*, 12 (1962), pp. 60–72.

Schweitzer, Carl G.: 'Hat die Weltgeschichte einen Sinn?'. In: *Aus Politik und Zeitgeschichte*. Supplement to *Das Parlament*. Bonn 1962. pp. 285–90.

Sichirollo, Livio: 'Hegel und die griechische Welt. Nachleben der Antike und Entstehung der "Philosophie der Weltgeschichte"'. In: *Heidelberger Hegel-Tage* 1962. (*Hegel-Studien*. Beiheft 1) pp. 263–83.
Also in: Sichirollo: Διαλέγεσθαι – *Dialektik*. Hildesheim 1966. pp. 185–206. Italian version: 'Note su Hegel e il mondo greco'. In: Sichirollo: *Storicità della dialettica antica*. Vincenza 1965. pp. 285–310.

Kimpel, Ben: *Hegel's Philosophy of History*. Boston 1963. v, 131 pp.

Chi-Lu-Chung, A.: 'A Critique of Hegel's Philosophy of History'. In: *Chinese Culture*. Yang Ming shan, 5 (1964), pp. 60–77.

Christensen, Darrel E.: 'Nelson and Hegel on the Philosophy of History'. In: *Journal of the History of Ideas*, 25 (1964), pp. 439–44.

Dumery, Henri: 'Logique et phénoménologie de l'histoire'. In: *Memorias del XIII Congreso Internacional de Filosofía. Comunicaciones libres*. Vol. 6, Mexico 1964. pp. 221–31.

Fleischmann, Eugène: *La philosophie politique de Hegel. Sous forme d'un commentaire des Fondements de la philosophie du droit*. Paris 1964. pp. 355–72: 'L'histoire mondiale'.

Gollwitzer, Heinz: *Europabild und Europagedanke*. (First edition 1951) Second revised edition, Munich 1964. pp. 212–27: 'Hegel und Ranke'.

Kudrna, Jaroslav: Studien zu Hegels Geschichtsauffassung. [Czech] Prague 1964. 169 pp.

Schmidt, Hans: *Verheißung und Schrecken der Freiheit. Von der Krise des antik-abendländischen Weltverständnisses dargestellt im Blick auf Hegels Erfahrung der Geschichte*. Stuttgart, Berlin 1964. 350 pp.

Costa, E.: 'Hegel y Jaspers ante la historia universal'. In: *Universidad. Argentinia*, 66 (Oct.–Dec. 1965), pp. 119–29.

Kaufmann, Walter: *Hegel. Reinterpretation, Texts, and Commentary*. New York 1965. pp. 254–96: 'Hegel on History'.

Papaioannou, Kostas: 'Hegel et la philosophie de l'histoire'. In: G. W. F.

Hegel: *La raison dans l'Histoire. Traduction nouvelle...* par K. Papaioannou. Paris 1965. (Le monde en 10/18. No. 235–36) pp. 5–40.

Beerling, R. F.: 'Kleine overdenking over geschiedenis, zin en vrijheid'. In: *Vrijheid. Horizon der geschiedenis* (Festschrift für H. J. de Vos) Nijkerk 1966. pp. 60–77.

Flechtheim, Ossip K.: *History and Futurology.* Meisenheim/Glan 1966. pp. 3–13: 'Hegel'.

d'Hondt, Jacques: *Hegel, philosophe de l'histoire vivante.* Paris 1966. 486 pp. (Epiméthée. Essais philosophiques. Collection dirigée par Jean Hyppolite)

Löwith, Karl: 'Geschichte und historisches Bewußtsein'. In: Löwith: *Vorträge und Abhandlungen. Zur Kritik der christlichen Überlieferung.* Stuttgart 1966. pp. 119–38.

Heftrich, Eckhard: *Hegel und Jacob Burckhardt. Zur Krisis des geschichtlichen Bewußtseins.* Frankfurt a. M. 1967. 42 pp.

Wilkins, B. T.: *Hegel's Philosophy of History.* Cornell University Press. 1974.

INDEX OF NAMES

INDEX OF SUBJECTS

INDEX

DAT

LaVergne, TN USA
26 August 2009
155942LV00002B/8/A

9 780521 281454